PISTOLS & PETTICOATS

13 FEMALE TRAILBLAZERS OF THE OLD WEST

by

Bob L'Aloge

Social Profiles by
Virginia C. Nelson-L'Aloge, M.A.

Flying Eagle-Thunderhawk Enterprises
P. O. Box 820
Los Lunas, New Mexico 87031

1995

First Edition
First Printing: September 1995

Edited by: Virginia C. Nelson-L'Aloge

Cover Design by: Bob and Virginia C. Nelson-L'Aloge
Front cover silhouettes by: Judith Housel; Box 1015; Leakey, TX, 78873

Picture credits: Frank Garo--pgs. 22, 93; Frank Leslie's Illustrated--pgs. 140, 143, 164; Jeni Burke--pgs. 4, 10, 29, 42, 51, 61, 80, 107, 126, 148-149, 158, 184, 188, 203, 236; National Police Gazette--pgs. 223, 226; National Police News--pgs. 17

Maps courtesy of Frontier Times, Old West & True West magazines. Also documents & pictures on pgs. 25, 26, 28, 85, 91, 92, 133, 138, 194, 225

L'Aloge, Bob 1948-
L'Aloge, Virginia C. Nelson

Pistols & Petticoats: 13 Female Trailblazers of the Old West

1. Old West History--1840-1900 Biography   2. Women's History--1840-
1930 Biography   3. American Pioneers 1840-1900   4. Psychology on Women
I. Bob L'Aloge   II. Virginia C. Nelson-L'Aloge   III. Title
     IV. Burke, Jeni--artist

Library of Congress Catalog Card Number: 95-90642

ISBN: 0-938147-99-4

Manufactured in the United States of America

This book is dedicated to:

My first love	and	my last love...
Carolyn June Dover		Virginia Constance Nelson
Washington, Oklahoma		Los Lunas, New Mexico

Special thanks to: Ms. Jeanine Jenkins of the Jackson County [OR] Court; Ms. Victoria Jones and the staff from Special Collections at the University of Oregon; Ms. Carol A. Harbison of the Southern Oregon Historical Society; Ms. Linda Blazer of the Archival Dept. at New Mexico State University; and the staff members from various other libraries who have helped me along the way. Additional thanks are extended to: my great-grandmother--Carrie Davis McCormack; my two grandmothers--Ester Bullard and Viola I. McCormack Weeks; my mother--Louise Weeks Laloge; my sister--Deborah Elaine Laloge Bryant; my first girlfriend--Ms. Patricia A. Witt [62-66] of Springfield, MO; and a host of other females in my life including (but not limited to): Roberta A. Thorstenberg [69--OK]; 14-year-old Windy Wyatt [71--MO]; Connie Frost [71--MO]; Susan [71--England]; Susan D. Crites [72-76--MO]; Laurel Letterman [75--MO]; Teresa Jackson [76-77--MO]; Sue [77--MO]; K. [77--Joplin]; Devery L. Maples [79-82--AZ]; Peggy [79--MO]; Angela Davis [79--MO]; Rene Carlton [80--AZ]; Lou Ann Thomas [81--MO]; Sue [82--AZ]; Jan [82--AZ]; Blanche J. Hiser [84--MO]; Mary Buser [85--MO]; Sue Shuffitt [86--MO]; Linda S. Covey [86--MO]; Cathy Prestridge [86--AL]; Marilyn Morriss [88--MO]; P. Hawk [89--NM]; Elizabeth K. Stephens [89--NM]; Celia Anchondo [91--NM] and Sally L. Burns [92--WA]. Each of you taught me something different about women!

In addition to all of these,

I want to thank you,

readers,

those who have been with me and those who are now joining me in this newest book.

I trust you will enjoy what you are about to read!

Table of Contents...   Page

"THEY WRESTLED WITH FROST AND BLIZZARD, FLOOD AND FIRE, TOUGH SOIL AND INSECT PEST, UNTIL THEY DEVELOPED STUBBORNNESS, ANGULARITY, AND REFLECTIVE SELF-RELIANCE."

Allan Nevins [1]

[1]   Ordeal of the Union: A House Dividing 1852-1857 by Allan Nevins, p. 160; Charles Scribner's Sons, 1947

Introduction by Historical Journalist Bob L'Aloge

For most of us, the lives of Old West women consisted of those television or movie episodes where men dominated the period, and females were confined to such roles as dutiful wives and genteel mothers, misguided yet submissive girlfriends, half-naked saloon girls or domineering women who 'wore the pants.' Worse, except for a few, most suffered from an Olive Oil complex--always finding themselves in trouble and crying out to Popeye for help. They were seldom portrayed as they really lived.

Despite this, there remains within many of us an adoration which still blossoms at these portrayals. Their reenactments of the Old West are like the early summer roses whose fragrant memories remain with us long after their representations upon the celluloid have faded. Their names are the legends within the film archives of Old West women. Names like the spitfire Maureen O'Hara in *McClintock;* predominant Barbara Stanwyck in *The Furies;* faithful Jean Arthur in *Shane;* inveigling Angie Dickinson in *Rio Bravo;* virtuous Jane Fonda in *Cat Ballou;* allegiant Amanda Blake as Miss Kitty of *Gunsmoke;* and wholesome Dale Evans who supported the King of the Cowboys--Roy Rogers; plus a host of others.

Though these vibrant thoughts and remembrances sit about the campfire of our minds, they were *not* the women of the Old West. Nor are their portrayals close to those women who endured the nineteenth-century. A deeper observation reveals women of that period were different. Books are being authored by knowledgeable 'professionals' probing the early day pioneering woman's psyche and proving differences between them and today's 'liberated' woman.

One of the better of these works is <u>The Women's West</u>. "The diversity of western experiences requires us to understand the different circumstances of western women's lives before we can arrive at large generalizations about what the West has been for women," the editors of this book write. [2] They add "...we believe that the first step, and probably the hardest, is to free ourselves from the all-pervasive masculinity of the popular image of the American West. Until that basic re-vision occurs, we cannot see women in their own right. Authors who write about western women without confronting this most

---

[2]   The Women's West edited by Susan Armitage & Elizabeth Jameson, p. 4-5; Univ. of Okla., 1987

basic reconceptualization fail, in our opinion, to meet the challenge posed by western women's history."

History will judge if this book has succeeded in presenting these women in this light. These thirteen women, along with others whose minor roles I've touched upon, represent an over-view of women who lived in the Old West. They were suffragettes, pioneers, spies, gamblers, firefighters, prostitutes, doctors, actresses, slaves, miners, politicians, warriors, victims, murderers, wives and mothers. Though at times their actions may be judged too heavily in the light of "good and bad;" it is, nonetheless, their own trail of deeds left behind. This work offers something other than what Susan Armitage brands "unconscious racism" in the history of the Old West by deliberately choosing from Anglo-Americans, Black-Americans and Indian-Americans. For not all the White women were 'virtuous', nor all the Black women 'trollops', nor all the Red women 'squaws', as so often heralded by our racist thinking and Hollywood mentality.

"Unless we can see women as they really were, we cannot understand their lives and feelings, or their perspective on the West," Susan Armitage writes in her essay titled *Through Women's Eyes: A New View of the West.* [3] Thus let us go beyond the stereotype and find the Old West women herein, the "lives and feelings" of these particular women, "as they really were."

So what exactly were they? They were more than "the typical Victorian gush," the *National Intelligencer* quoted. They were more than "the angel of man's home, the wife of his heart, the mother of his children, the sharer of his joys, and the soother of his sorrows." [4] They were as the river's fingers whose embracing course drifted freely through the prairies, plains, deserts and mountains of the Old West. They came bestowing and taking life; enduring, nourishing and confirming life. They pointed the way where the communities could be erected and others came along and built them into what they are today. They *were* the Old West. Absorbing both the intellect and creative emotion of pioneer life itself.

Where to begin? There were women like Alice Kirk Grierson, whose endearing letters to her military husband give us a most perceptive view of the way women tackled everyday life in the Old West; and Montana's Jeannette Rankin, the first Anglo woman elected to a national political office--that of the House of Representatives in 1917; or May Arkwright Hutton, who wrote *The Coeur d'Alenes: A Tale of the Modern Inquisition in*

---

[3]   Armitage & Jameson, p. 12

[4]   Ordeal of the Union: Fruits of Manifest Destiny 1847-1852 by Allan Nevins, p. 136;
Charles Schribners Son's, 1947

Idaho (Denver, 1900); or Bertha Ethel Knight who, born October 19, 1868, in Massachusetts, came west and was later elected mayor of Seattle, Washington. These and hundreds of other women experienced and changed the Old West.

Just think! If it weren't for these four women, and hundreds like them, there would be no Red Cloud, Nebraska; Steamboat Canyon, Arizona; Diablo, California; Hungry Horse, Montana; Horseshoe Bend, Idaho; Aztec, New Mexico; Castle Rock, Colorado; Lampasas, Texas; Indian Springs, Nevada; or Cody, Wyoming. Nor a hundred, yea, ten hundred other towns in today's illustrious West. It was these pioneering women, and the scores like them, that molded the West of today in all it's opulent glory and noble splendor. Today's West with all it's razzle, dazzling sunrises and sunsets amid vast, illuminated skies and unlimited future potential.

So why these particular women? First, because these were exemplary women whose lives were then, and still are, uniquely interesting. In addition, these Old West women are much like you--the women of today! They detail all you are and all you've been. Their presence, like yours, has certainly been a piquant education and an exalted adventure. "The women of the Old West are history!" [5] They followed, walked beside and sometimes led men into situations that the cowboys, gunfighters, farmers, cattlemen, gamblers, sheepherders, cavalrymen and others would not have encountered if the women had not been there. For certainly their presence, like today, shaped and *altered* the outcome of every event wherein they participated. They were an important part of the history of the Old West.

Hope you enjoy it!

Respectfully,

Bob L'Aloge

Happy Trails from the Pale Rider

Bob

---

[5]   Westward the Women by Nancy Wilson Ross, p. 5; Alfred A. Knoff, 1944. Miss Ross quotes Spengler.

Introduction by Virginia C. Nelson-L'Aloge, M. A.

The goal/purpose of the social profiles presented are two fold: first, to present to the readers how it was socially for women in the 1800's; second, to realistically present how it is for men and women at the end of the 1900's. The social messages for men and women during the 1800's were different from today. We have made great strides forward in society that governed the behavior and dress for men and women alike. The fact that women have gone into the work force enabling them to earn money is definite improvement. True education is now open to women. Education paves the way for women to earn higher salaries and to be eligible for better positions.

The singular change for the better, since getting the rights to vote and own property, is the financial possibilities for women today. Restrict people economically and you restrict their lifestyle and choices. This was done to women and minority groups for centuries. We need to know that it is happening to *all* middle Americans <u>at this time</u>! We are currently programmed into surrendering our freedoms while accepting the *untruth* that it is 'good for us.' The cost of living and taxes force couples into serfdom to merely stay afloat and have the essentials. The price of an economy car today is as much as a two-bedroom house in the 1950's. The present Federal government has more power, usurped illegally, than ever before in this country. Hard-working, honest citizens are harassed by government appointed departments with no regard for the citizen's Constitutional rights. These crimes are occurring. Let's do something about it NOW!

In talking to people across this beautiful land of ours we are *amazed* at how some are totally unaware. Some don't care provided they have three square meals a day, a home and get out on Saturday night. Yet, we find a majority extremely concerned by what is going on in this nation but do not know what they can do about it. All people have greater opportunity to contribute intelligently now than ever before. Apathy is our fiercest enemy whose bite is as deadly as the Tarantulas. Let's shake off the cobwebs of apathy! Let's follow these positive examples of female trailblazers who risk all. Let's take a stance and reclaim our rights as individuals. Let's enter into a life where we, women and men, still have the free choice to live as we choose. Let these social profiles within this book awaken those who need awakening, stir those that need stirring and cause *all* to think! Let's take appropriate action each in her and his own way--NOW!

Abigail Scott Duniway:
Social Profile on Chapter One
by
Virginia C. Nelson-L'Aloge, M. A.

Most of the women of the era 1850-1900 were placed by society in an inflexible tight social-economic box. They gave in to the "rules and accepted behavior" for a *lady* and women in general. These rules were forced upon them by not only men, who acted out of fear of displacement, but by themselves. The women stuck to the dictates of the *shoulds* and *oughts* of the time in order to be safe. Women were kept in their place by not being allowed to vote or hold property--thus no access to finances.

The belief was that women were not capable of decisions in politics or business. They were too emotional. The belief was that emotions were a weakness. Men denied their emotions. So, the men thought, they were strong and more able to make decisions in business and politics. Many of the bold women of the Old West were fore-runners of their sex in not taking *no* for an acceptable answer. They refused to accept limitations.

When Sister Blandina showed courage in facing the Apaches, or tending the needs of the wounded outlaw, she outlined the courage for all women to initiate change. Esther McQuigg Morris showed faith in herself and her abilities as she continued forward--even while she was the receiver of cruel jokes. They did not give in. They did not go weeping away as expected and as many would have done. Instead, they boldly strode forward to influence thinking men to recognize women's rights. While the help of such far-thinking men as John B. Henderson helped all men to expand their own thinking, the state of Wyoming led the country with the passing of women's right to vote.

The women who dared to break into "men's professions," whether physician or newspaper owner/writer, such as Dr. Mary P. Sawtelle and Abigail J. S. Duniway, experienced harassment and ridicule. Their intelligence would not be denied. Most of all they had faith in their own abilities, so no matter what was said or done, they prevailed.

These women used good decision making abilities, perseverance, and by combining their faith in their abilities and a very good sense of humor, they were victorious. Women of today continue to expand their natural capabilities of mind and body as they recognize within themselves their natural talents. Fortunately, men are also expanding as they recognize and accept, in a positive manner, the emotional side of themselves. Men and women are balancing as individuals. Even now they are continuing to break down barriers that society has placed around them for generations. However, it was those brave souls, like the ones in this chapter, and book, that truly set this needed change in motion.

Most people take themselves, and what other people think of them, too seriously. Abigail S. Duniway, however, had the true self-confidence to laugh and turn any situation to her advantage. The egg incident was but one instance and more follow. Through ridicule and insult she marched; ever forward, knowing, believing in herself and all women, she conquered inch by inch. Undaunted, she finally spoke at the Oregon State Legislature. Men refused to chaperon her as per requisite. But an equal, another trailblazing woman, consented. Women of today, can you imagine what you would feel, do or say if you were required to have a *chaperon* before you might speak up?

Women have assisted and stood behind many great men throughout history. Many a man would not have achieved their greatness without the aid of his wife, mother, sister or mistress. Abigail stood behind no one. She stood for herself and all women. Abigail's victorious crown was the presidency of the Pacific States Voting Alliance. But Abigail's shining star in her golden crown was when she jointly signed, with the Oregon governor, the bill granting women the right to vote. Here is a woman, one to whom all of today's women need to be grateful, who achieved her glorious victory! The fact she was in the West really did allow her more freedom. The thinking and social norms were much more tolerant there than in the East. But those working in the East for women's right to vote had the support of more females fed up with being treated as brainless creatures.

Often women breaking into *men's roles* or careers mistakenly thought they had to give up their femininity to do so. This was a disservice to themselves, other women and even to men. We females are not men. We are different and *viva la difference!* There are things we do that, because of our makeup of being, helps us approach life differently as is also true for men. Because of that difference we make invaluable contributions to any and all situations. Being a thinking woman in Abigail's time was not easy. Life often was literally on the line. It took great courage to stand up for what she believed. But she did so while still retaining her femininity.

Today we boldly continue as women to expand our future horizons. Let us faithfully remember as we do so the courageous women whom we follow. Those who gallantly trailblazed before us--so we are free to continue onward from where they left off. Let us females always remember we are women--proud, courageous, intelligent, witty and persevering. But let us also retain our femininity in the process. We are not better than men. Nor are we less. We are simply different and that is okay. We are partners with men. Each must be true to herself or himself in the process.

All people--you are invited to salute these women, these thirteen female trailblazers of the Old West who helped us be what we are today. Balance within each human being is happening inch by inch today just as it happened for Abigail S. Duniway. Thank you, Abigail! Thank you--all women trailblazers of yesterday and today! Thank you, men who are competent enough within themselves not to be threatened by these women and women of the future.

LIBERTY, EMANCIPATION
&
PROGRESSION

Women and devotion were synonymous in the Old West. Women's over-burdened hearts sought out worthwhile incentives or crusades for re-measuring their role in life. Telescoping these lives led me to conclude that "a woman's place is *NOT* always in the home." Though this episode weighs the suffrage movement, others seek to balance the scales of heavier burdens. From religion, to medicine, to family, to politics--their souls gave measure for measure--liberty, emancipation and progression.

For example, Rosa Maria Segale--an Italian emigrant to the United States when she was but a four-year-old little girl. Rosa was the fifth of eight children in the Segale family. Her family moved to Cincinnati and there, with the others, Rosa lived in subservient poverty. In 1872, Rosa took her vows and was christened Sister Blandina.

That year, age of 22-years-old, Sister Blandina journeyed West to the mining boom-town known as Trinidad, Colorado. The passionate district was still an unbroken, turbulent frontier underwritten by murder, lynchings and robbery. It was Sister Blandina, "a tough, compassionate, congenial woman, never at a loss for words or actions," [1] God ordained to the task of operating Trinidad's Catholic school. Her compassionate courage in bearing pain or trouble was often rewarded. In urgency of the new schoolhouse, uniformed Sister Blandina, armed with but an iron crowbar, made her way up to the roof-

---

[1]   Saints & Sinners Alike Touched by Sister Blandina by Lucie Mayeux; New Mexico Magazine, October 1992, p. 84-89. Mayeux speaks of "a journal" Sister Blandina kept which was published under the title At the End of the Santa Fe Trail in 1932.

top. She chopped and plunged the metal tool with such intensity the old bricks crumbled apart and were lopped to the ground below.

"Por amor de Dios, Hermana, que esta usted haciendo?" Exclaimed a fellow Sister. [2]

Sister Blandina, angelically-polite with Godly-determination, vocalized the earthly need of the educational structure and affirmed this was the way to get the job done. Her inspirational words brought several men to join and the new school house was underway. Two months later it was completed and opened. This sole inducement was not her only one to which she was enthusiastically lured. Rosa untiringly sought funds for New Mexico's first hospital by trudging the mining camps begging for money from the workers. Sister Blandina even dared climb over the fence of local Archbishop Lamy's garden, appropriating vegetables for the hungry patients at the hospital.

Four years after her arrival, an outlaw was shot down during a blazing gunfight near Trinidad. The wounded and bleeding gunman was left to die in an abandoned adobe hut. None of the local doctors would tend his wounds because of his brutish character. But not Sister Blandina. No! Believing a Christian should wear out their shoe leather just as fast as their knee pants, she went immediately and nursed the outlaw back to health. He promised her that if she ever needed his help or any of his gangs help, just asked and she would be given the most gracious assistance. Sometime later, while traveling on a stagecoach, outlaws held up the coach. It was that bandit she had previously helped. When he saw her on board the coach he ordered his gang to turn around and leave.

In December 1876, Sister Blandina was transferred from Trinidad, Colorado, to Santa Fe, New Mexico, performing both as a nurse and the treasurer of St. Vincent Hospital. She was instrumental in laboring for the rights of the Indians during this time.

One of the workman for the AT&SF railroad killed an Apache near the San Bernardino Mountains. The Indians threatened revenge and would have obtained it, too, had it not been for Sister Blandina. While the twenty-two men in the mining camp did nothing to stop the pending disaster, Sister Blandina walked alone to where angry Apaches sat atop their horses and spoke with the Indians. They told her to surrender the man who murdered their Red brother and they would not attack the railroad camp. She went back and informed the workers to do precisely that and, not seeking to anger the

---

[2]   "For the love of God, Sister, what are you doing?"

righteous finger of God being pointed at them from her shaking fist, they did. Thus, all but one was spared death and mutilation.

Sister Blandina returned to Ohio in 1894 and died there peacefully in 1941. Her testimonial life of "prayer and action" epitomizes women's dedication in the Old West.

Other causes were important to the women of the Old West, also.

"I present this petition without any apology," John Brooks Henderson told the United States Senate on Wednesday, February 21, 1866. "Indeed, I present it with pleasure."

Just what was that petition?

"Praying that the right of suffrage be granted to women!" Henderson demanded. "As we are proposing to enfranchise four million emancipated slaves, equal and impartial justice alike demands the suffrage of fifteen million women...the social position of woman in the United States is such that no civil right can be denied. To have free men we must have free women!" [3]

It was an United States Senator beseeching the law-making body of our government to grant women the right to vote. It was not to be the last. Many great orators would stand before that governmental body, imploring emancipation be freely given to the women of the United States, before that right would finally be granted. Most were prompted by their strong belief in the idea and, no doubt, the well-meaning support of their wives. For it was the unsurrendering woman, probably more than the men, who eventually brought to all women the right to vote within the states.

No one can say for sure where the idea started or where it will eventually end. But a dignified lady of fifty-five-years-old held a tea party in South Pass City, Wyoming, and that "set in motion the machinery that brought women the right to vote for the first time anywhere on earth." [4] The lady was a nurse named Esther McQuigg Morris. She was "a self-reliant lady of great charm...[with] an air of quiet reserve and a strong personality." Before long, Esther became the first woman to hold the office of justice of the peace "anywhere in the world." That was also in South Pass City. [5] During the latter half of the 1860's, the boom-town boasted of its "row of miners' shacks stretching along the ledge of the Wind River Mountains, with a population of three thousand, mostly males seeking

---

[3]   Emancipation & Henderson: The Man Behind the Reality by Bob L'Aloge, p. 102-103; Freedom Press, 1990

[4]   The Gentle Tamers by Dee Brown, p. 13; Univ. of Nebraska, 1968

[5]   Brown, p. 238-243

gold." As justice of the peace, Esther tried forty cases, "administering justice with a vigorous and impartial hand." She was even written up in such publications as *Police Gazette* and another called *Day's Doings.* The latter drew various cartoon caricatures of her that "barely amused" her.

On September 2, 1869, two and a half years after Senator Henderson's proposal, she invited twenty leading citizens to her house. The guests numbered such local honorables as Colonel William H. Bright, Democrat for the legislature and Captain Herman G. Nickerson, Republican for the same office. On the slumbering eve of Wyoming's first territorial election is when she threw the wildest party--later branded the "Esther Morris Tea Party." During the evening, Esther asked each man point blank if he would "introduce a bill in the new legislature that would give the women of Wyoming the right to vote." Colonel Bright agreed to do just that. Of course, being a typically "good politician," Captain Nickerson was obligated to agree also. Colonel Bright won the election the next day. Esther went directly to see Mrs. Betty Bright. Mrs. Bright went directly to her newly elected husband. Colonel Bright went to Cheyenne.

On November 9, 1869, he presented his bill to the legislature as "an Act to Grant to the Women of Wyoming Territory the Right of Suffrage and to Hold Office." It stated "every woman of the age of eighteen years, residing in this Territory, may, at every election to be held under the laws thereof, cast her vote. And her rights to the elective franchise and to hold office shall be the same under the elective laws of the territory, as those of electors." The vote taken, it passed--six to two with one absent. Finally, after several attempts to destroy the bill in the House, it passed six to four with one absent.

On December 10, 1869, nearly three years after Senator Henderson had introduced his United States Senate proposal, Wyoming Governor John Campbell signed the suffrage act. Dignified women all over the states and territories now worked harder for their right to vote. This episode is about one dignified woman--Abigail Jane Scott Duniway. [6]

Abigail, born October 22, 1834, the third of fourteen children, inhaled her first breath of life and joined her new family--Illinois pioneer John Tucker Scott, and his wife, Ann. [7] Abigail had only a few months of formal education in those days and, yet, she learned "to

---

6   Best of the Old Northwest by Marge Davenport, p. 61; Paddlewheel Press, 1980

7   Abigail Scott Duniway: Pioneer Woman by Patricia Riley Dunlap, Old West, Winter 1991

read by the age of three or four." [8] Their last winter in Illinois was a difficult one causing Abigail special hardship. Her mother was now an invalid requiring special care. The Scott family left Tazewell County, Illinois in 1852, traveling west by covered wagon. [9] She was seventeen-years-old at the time and had eight brothers and sisters. [10] Abigail, in addition to the burdensome chores along the six month journey, also kept "an overland diary in which she faithfully recorded events."

Along the way, "not far from Ft. Laramie, Wyoming, three months after leaving home," [11] Ann contracted cholera. It was a common disease due to the misunderstanding by the people for clean water. The disease, at the time, demanded an eighty percent death rate and the chance for Ann looked slim. For a while it appeared she might recover. But no such luck. The disease overwhelmed her body. Thus, while her husband and children stood helplessly by, Ann Scott writhed in an ocean of nausea, diarrhea and chills.

On June 20, Abigail wrote in her journal: "Her wearied spirit took its flight and then we realized that we were bereaved indeed." [12]

She became the first wagon train fatality. Her remains were lowered into a long-since desolate grave somewhere along the Platte River and a mournful family moved on west. Barely over two months later, on the 28th of August, Abigail recorded another death in the family. It was her three-year-old brother, Willie.

"The ruthless monster death, not yet content, has once more entered our fold and taken in his icy grip the treasure of our hearts." [13]

These physical manifestations altered, even molded her perception of how to conduct yourself in the game of life. Abigail's perception confirmed the adage a person must

---

[8]   Of Women's Rights and Freedom: Abigail Scott Duniway by Ruth Barnes Moynihan, p. 9-24; Women In the Pacific Northwest: An Anthology edited by Karen J. Blair; Univ. of Washington, 1988

[9]   Davenport, p. 61. The book is by Davenport, however, the author of the article quoted is Jean Ward. The article is titled N. W. Women: Half Dolls, Half Drudges and All Fools" p. 60-65

[10]   Jean Ward states that Abigail's mother gave birth to "12 children" but three died along the journey. p. 61. Moynihan also states there were twelve children born to these "Kentucky-born parents." p. 11.

[11]   Moynihan, p. 12

[12]   Davenport, p. 62

[13]   Davenport, p. 62

"trust in God and keep your powder dry." Likewise, she was convinced "self-preservation was the primary law of existence." [14]

Abigail S. Duniway

Eventually the Scotts, and the wagon train wherein they traveled, reached the country-side of Lafayette, Oregon. They settled on a small farm and, as time would have it, regrouped their lives. The older children took various types of work. Abigail's given position took flight with the Eola District as a school teacher. This was in spite of the fact that she had less than twelve months of formal education to her credit. Men, in those bleak years, outnumbered women nearly eight to one in the Northwest and a man need get his bid in quickly or lose out on any young maidens' swirling, fluttering, flirtatious affections.

The youthful, charming Miss Scott did not have to wait long before Benjamin Charles Duniway, a nearby young rancher from Clackamas County, came calling in courtship. He possessed an outgoing personality and the superb ability to make friends quickly and easily. This admirable characteristic prompted her to marry him in 1853, consummating their matrimonial agreement. But not without having at first convinced him that the word "obey" in the marriage vows was to be deleted. [15]

---

14   Moynihan, p. 12-13
15   Davenport, p. 62

10

Sometime later the happy newly weds moved to a farm in Yamhill County, Oregon. They lived there for the next five years, surviving "a destructive tornado, a disastrous fire, and near-fatal hemorrhaging during her second child's birth." [16]

The move from this farm was prompted because Ben signed three bank notes to help a friend in financial distress. The notes came due all at once and there was no money to pay them off. So he and Abigail sold the farm to pay the loan the friend had failed to pay. They moved from the Yamhill County farm to another, even smaller, farm near Lafayette, Oregon. Times were arduous and there was nothing else to do. Abigail simply had to return to teaching. She opened a private school of her own in Lafayette dubbing it the Oregon Union School. While the War for Southern Independence ravaged the Eastern United States, Abigail taught school and, by 1864, she was the principal.

Abigail apparently regretted little about her life during this time though it was difficult and demanding. She would get up every summer morning at three o'clock to begin her daily activities. In winter's worst blistering cold, she would get up an hour earlier so her chores could be done in time to make it to school on time. At midday, she would leave school a little before the lunch hour, hurry home to prepare the meal and serve her family, including six children, their lunch. Then, she would return to the school and teach until four. She would then conclude her daily domestic chores.

"Notwithstanding all this effort," she wrote, "I led an easier life than I had known on a pioneer farm."

Abigail's desire burned to create words upon paper. Despite her responsibility with family and school, she nevertheless found time to put down on paper meaningful passages--her first publications being poetry. Much of this poetry was sent unsigned to the Oregon City *Argus*. Likewise, in the *Oregon Farmer*, Abigail merely signed it "a farmer's wife." [17] Later, she turned her pen to novelettes. Some of the titles were *Edna and John: A Romance of Idaho Flat* and *Madge Morrison: Mollala Maid and Matron*. The year of 1859, Abigail wrote *Captain Gray's Company: Crossing the Plains and Living In Oregon*, published by S. J. McCormick. [18] The theme was "of western

---

16   Moynihan, p. 13
17   Davenport, p. 62
18   General History of Oregon by Charles H. Carey, p. 488; Binfords and Mort, 1971

migration." [19] Reviewers quickly critisized. They "objected to its fool love stories and even claimed her husband must be henpecked." Abigail was shattered but didn't stop. [20]

Before the end of the War for Southern Independence, Abigail sold the school and the family moved to Albany, Oregon. There she opened another school but, it was said, "the raging Civil War distracted her students and made teaching difficult."

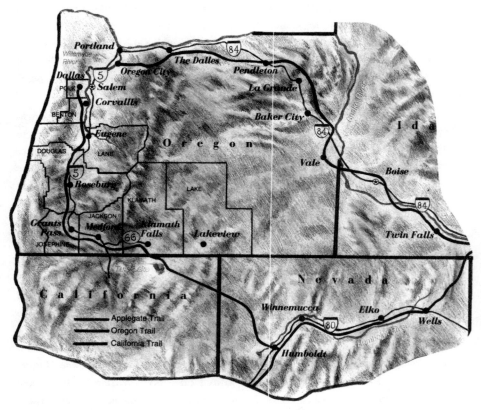

Difficulty challenged the enterprising woman. Armed with hammer, nails, a pencil or another nail for a marker and lumber; she measured, cut, joined, nailed and constructed wooden shelves, counters and showcases within the school; transforming it into a

---

19   Davenport, p. 62

20   Moynihan, p. 13

millinery, notions store. Frequent stories of women in trouble came to her. Many of them, whose husbands had lost savings on such vices as gambling, beseeched Abigail for part-time work. Abigail's consciousness focused on the women's communal needs. At thirty-six, in the spirit of Sister Blandina's holy-dedication, she became a suffragette.

The war years brought great changes even in Oregon. Drastic changes manifested beginning in 1862. Worse, Ben was injured later that year in a runaway horse accident. [21] Stampeding horses, pulling a heavy wagon, plunged against him, knocking him to the ground and dragging the wagon across his back. "Though he lived for many years thereafter," wrote Abigail in her autobiography, the accident "incapacitated him for physical labor on the farm, and threw the financial, as well as domestic, responsibility of our family upon my almost unaided self."

Nine years before the Oregon Legislature approved the Married Woman's Property Bill of 1874, Abigail sought out Jacob Mayer, a wealthy Portland businessman. They opened a millinery in Albany, Oregon. [22] Day after day and into the petite hours of night, Abigail noticed how other women fared in the men's world. Few actually overcame their fear of surviving. Even less manifested financial independence. This disturbed her soul to no end and gave birth to her noted comment: "Half of us are dolls, half of us are drudges, and all of us are fools." [23]

By May 5, 1871, living Portland, Oregon, she bought a printing press, type, moved it upstairs and founded a newspaper called the *New Northwest*--a weekly dedicated to *Free Speech, Free Press, Free People.* The first issue made the following statement up front:

"In coming before the reading public in the capacity of editor and proprietor of a newspaper, and presuming to occupy ground which has heretofore been *monopolized by gentlemen,* we feel the responsibility of our position, and realize the necessity of making our work come up practically to the high standard which alone should satisfy the gleaner after truth...We have served a regular apprenticeship at working--washing, scrubbing, patching, darning, ironing, plain sewing, raising babies, milking, churning and poultry raising. We have kept boarders, taught school, taught music, written for newspapers, made speeches and carried on an extensive millinery and dressmaking business...having reached the age of 36, and having brought up a family of boys to set type, and a daughter

---

21   Davenport, p. 63
22   Davenport, p. 63
23   Davenport, p. 63

to run the millinery store, we proposed to edit and publish a newspaper; and we intend to establish it as one of the permanent institutions of the country...to elevate woman, that thereby herself and son and brother man may be benefitted and the world made better, purer, and happier, is the aim of this publication...we shall prove to you if you will sustain our paper that we are not only in earnest, but that we know just what we are about." [24]

In each issue, Abigail made her views known to her reading public. Though the topic of today's *gay-rights* was not as much concern in 1871, she nonetheless tackled it in an article titled: *Feminine Men and Masculine Women.*

"There is nothing more detestable to be seen or endured upon the earth than a feminine man," the article started out, "unless it be a masculine woman. Both are monstrosities; hybrids between the two harmonial extremes of humanity, and both are stumbling blocks in the highway of human progress."

In her next paragraph, she described that while penning the article, lo and behold, "a specimen of feminine masculinity is seen passing down the street. He parts his hair in the middle--the darling--and he twirls a cane and sports a mustache--a very incipient mustache it is too, but it is the best he can produce, dear fellow, and we must be charitable. He doesn't believe in the equality of the sexes! Not he! 'Women are born to be protected,' he loves to say, with an air of importance that can only be equalled by a bantam rooster." She described several other features about him, concluding she "must call the reader's attention to yonder masculine woman."

Abigail explained this masculine woman's "voice is loud and course, her dress untidy and her general appearance repellent. She roughly demands her rights in a hard bargain...she doesn't believe in equal rights; not she...No wonder that gentlemen dislike such specimens of feminine monstrosity; and we only ask that they give us equal liberty to dislike apologies of manhood who are quite as numerous as masculine women." [25]

---

24   The New Northwest, May 5, 1871
25   The New Northwest, May 5, 1871

In an article titled *Presumption,* Abigail displayed her beautiful witticisms. She recently encountered a young man of merely twenty years who was "willing to give women all other rights except the privilege to vote." She asked how it was he came to possess the right to withhold such from women. The young man couldn't answer her but displayed "his presuming arrogance." Abigail went on to castigate him for being "a simple-minded, inexperienced, pert young stripling...who owes his very existence to the life and devotion of a mother who has more wisdom than he will be able to realize for the next twenty years." In concluding, her wit came to the forefront. "If we could purchase such striplings at their real value and dispose of them at their own appraisement, we'd be content to quit the newspaper business and turn our attention to making money." [26]

So it was every week, for sixteen years, Abigail published her newspaper filled with news, stories and her poems. [27] One poem was titled *Campaign Song.*

> *Hail to the brightly dawning day*
> *When the glorious Ship of State,*
> *With men and women all embarked*
> *To meet their coming fate,*
> *Shall navigate the ship, my friends,*
> *Where politicians play,*
> *For they've taken a trip in the Government ship*
> *And sadly gone astray.*
> *[Chorus]*
> Then blow ye winds a-ho--a voting we will go;
> We'll stay no more on the barren shore,
> But hand in hand with brothers bland
> We'll guide the Ship of State
> Across the raging main
> Of Governmental seas, my friends,

---

[26]   The New Northwest, May 5, 1871

[27]   Of Women's Rights and Freedom: Abigail Scott Duniway by Ruth Barnes Moynihan, p. 9-24; Women In the Pacific Northwest: An Anthology edited by Karen J. Blair; Univ. of Washington, 1988

To meet our coming fate.

Good-bye, good-bye to whiskey rings

Good-bye to Government broils

No more shall men with vote and pen

Appropriate the spoils;

For we'll navigate the Ship of State

Beside our brothers dear,

And when the breakers round us dash

We'll shun 'em--never fear.

[Repeat chorus]

Good-bye, good-bye to servile work

Where wages are not known;

John Chinaman is here to wash

And sew your buttons on.

He'll cook your breakfast too, my boys,

And darn your stockings well,

While we, like you, will legislate

And trade and buy and sell.

[Repeat chorus]

We'll keep the fire-side, too, my boys,

And read your musty tomes;

We'll use the money that we earn

To beautify your homes;

We'll use the wisdom we acquire

To legislate for good;

We know that with our cause you'll stand

When we are understood.

[Repeat chorus] [28]

---

[28] The New Northwest, Sept. 8, 1871

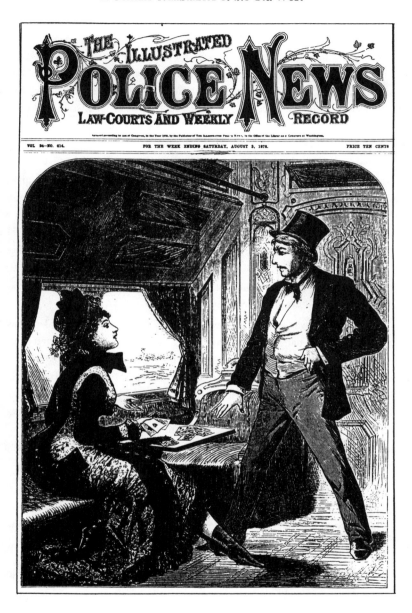

Later Abigail was speaking at eloquent engagements, traveling thousands of miles in all seasons of weather, helping to raise money for the woman's suffragette movement in Oregon. [29] In 1872, she journeyed by train to San Francisco, speaking boldly in theaters and private meeting halls as most churches refused the women's suffragettes to meet within their 'holy walls.' She vocally proclaimed such topics as: "Constitutional Liberty," "The Temperance Problem and How to Solve It," "Courtship, Marriage and Divorce," "Why Women Are Sick," and "Cooperative Housekeeping." [30]

One Portland newspaper best judged her speeches as "logical, sarcastic, witty, poetic and often truly eloquent. As a critic she is merciless, as an enemy forgiving; and after having her 'say,' conciliatory. As a writer she is forceful, argumentative and sometimes voluminous, but it's hardly necessary to add, never dull." [31] Not everyone was so kind toward her, however. There were times when she was harassed, harangued, ridiculed and even lied about. Most, nevertheless, provided her with the opportunity to display her wonderful gift of wit. One incident, in 1879, caused her to be egged.

"Only one egg hit us," she confessed, "and that was fresh and sweet, and it took us square on the scalp and saved a shampooing bill." [32]

A second incident was reported by the *Democratic Times* newspaper of Jacksonville, Oregon. "A young woman of the town had successfully subdued three boisterous young men with dexterous wielding of a bottle." This action, according to editor Charlie Nickell, was "attributed...to the recent appearance of Mrs. Abigail Scott Duniway, who had lectured on women's rights. He intimated that such conduct was the result of following the example of Mrs. Duniway." [33] A third incident involved a Valentine sent to Abigail. [34] The front cover showed a "trembling henpecked husband to whom squalling children were clinging, while an ugly witch of a woman brandished a broom." The inscription simply stated:

Fiend, devil's imp, or what you will

---

[29]   Ms. Ward, in Davenport's book, states "it was Ben who convinced her that conditions would never improve for women until they had the right to vote." p. 63

[30]   Davenport, p. 64

[31]   Davenport, p. 64

[32]   Editorial Correspondence, New Northwest newspaper, July 17, 1879

[33]   Jacksonville: Biography of a Gold Camp by Francis D. Haines Jr, p. 110-111; Gandee Printing Center, Inc., 1967

[34]   Westward the Women by Nancy Wilson Ross, p. 142; Alfred A. Knopf, 1944

You surely your poor man will kill,

With luckless days and sleepless nights,

Haranguing him with Women's Rights.

In 1872, Abigail helped establish the Oregon Equal Suffragette Association. The Oregon legislature entertained her before any other woman. State house procedures required her to have a chaperon. She made several contacts before locating someone--Dr. Mary P. Sawtelle. Despite the objections, Abigail was allowed to speak before the legislature and speak she did. The flamboyant spokeswoman voiced her approval of prohibition, women's rights, women's property ownership and was most beneficial in getting laws passed which gradually gave women more rights in Oregon.

In 1884, Abigail toured more extensively including Ashland, Oregon where she arrived on Sunday morning, November 23, 1884--three days after the murder of Lewis McDaniel. She was even nominated for governor of Washington Territory. [35] Oliver P. Mason bought Abigail's newspaper in 1886. He gave his word to continue running her columns. Yet, within two months, it went out of business. This placed her in the background of the movement and invitations became fewer and fewer. Probably the most damaging thing was that she was snubbed by the National American Woman Suffrage Association for her stand concerning the suffrage movement and the temperance movement. But the seventy-one-year-old Abigail was not to be outdone. She walked up to the platform, gained control of the floor and offered them all a piece of her mind.

Still voters refused to approve the women's suffragette bill. In 1899, Abigail, realizing the importance of organizing women, established the Pacific States Voting Alliance--uniting the women of Oregon, Washington, California, Utah and Idaho. The newly founded organization elected her president. The 1905 Lewis and Clark Exposition in Portland, Oregon held many fascinations. One was when Dr. Henry Waldo, a Portland physician, donated 20-tons of Oregon cooper for *Sacajawea, the Bird Woman*--a statue made by Alice Cooper. "When it was unveiled, two of the principal speakers were women suffragists Susan B. Anthony and Abigail Scott Duniway." [36]

Abigail praised Sacajawea in this verse from her *Centennial Ode:*

---

[35]   Moynihan, p. 9

[36]   Davenport, p. 92-93. This article within Davenport's book is by a different author. I've not been able to locate the book since and have been unable to record the author's name. My apologies to whoever wrote it.

And then, to make the prophecy complete,

An Indian mother led the devious way,

Foreshadowing woman's place, which man shall greet

Without a protest, in a hastening day,

When womanhood, benignant, wise and free,

Shall lead him to yet greater heights of strength and victory. [37]

During the Lewis and Clark Exposition in Portland, October 6th was set aside as Abigail Scott Duniway Day all over Oregon. Despite this, her true desire was not a reality until November 30, 1912, when she and Governor Oswald West jointly signed the bill granting women the right to vote. She became the first woman to register. The life of this emancipator, however, ended three short years later in 1915, when, at the age of eighty-one, she died of diabetes. The woman who fought so hard for the rights of women solemnly claimed that she owed, with "undying gratitude," everything to her husband "whose sterling character as a man [she] could not have" done without.

A year before her death, Abigail published *Path Breaking: An Autobiographical History of the Equal Suffrage Movement in Pacific Coast States.* Her closing remarks are most noteworthy.

"Women of today, free to study, to speak, to write, to choose their occupation, should remember that every inch of this freedom was bought for them at a great price. It is for them to show their gratitude by helping onward the reforms of their own time, by spreading the light of freedom and truth still wider. The debt that each generation owes to the past it must pay to the future." [38]

---

37   Westward the Women by Nancy Wilson Ross, p. 109; Alfred Knopf, 1944

38   Davenport, p. 65. See also Path Breaking: An Autobiographical History of the Equal Suffrage Movement in Pacific Coast States by Abigail Scott Duniway, p. 297; Schocken Books, 1971.

AN INDIAN WOMAN
MAY HAVE KILLED CUSTER

The women, whether White, Black, Yellow or Red skinned, have been the brunt of men's vulgar, chauvinistic sexual frauds. You have been lied to, cheated, deceived and degraded. You have been used and abused. You have been seduced by words of charm and raped by passions of anger and hatred. All too common are the instances of White slave owners in the South having sexual relations with one or more Black slave women in the history of this country. Likewise, it was not at all uncommon for White men upon the frontier to become involved with Red [Indian] women. [39]

Dee Brown writes when the "first white males ventured into the West, they left their women behind in the East or in border settlements. For female companionship they turned naturally to women of Indian tribes, buying or bartering" to satisfy lusty needs. Brown cites the logical reason "for uniting with Indian women" was convenience. [40] But buying or bartering was not the only way they obtained sexual favors. Nor were these men the unknowns to Old West history. Some names ring bells of familiarity when spoken such as Jim Bridger, Kit Carson, Joe Meek and Peter Skene Ogden.

---

[39] I might as well make it clear here and now. I refuse to surrender to the racially prejudiced terminology purported to be correct grammer these days. The words 'Native Americans,' used in reference to Indians only, are prejudicial. Anyone and everyone born within the territorial boundaries of the United States is a 'Native American.' No matter what nationality or color of skin!

[40] The Gentle Tamers: Women of the Wild Old West by Dee Brown, p. 212-213; Univ. of Nebraska, 1958

George Armstrong Custer

To ever dream among these 'White men' having sexual relations with 'Red women' was the celebrated George Armstrong Custer is practically unimaginable. Yet, such appears for after Custer's senseless attack upon Black Kettle and the Cheyenne at the Washita, Custer demanded all surviving women rounded up like wild cattle and 'herded' to Camp Supply. One Cheyenne woman was the teenage princess--Monahseetah.

"Custer, who never failed to sweeten Plains austerity with as much pleasure as possible, reputedly picked another victory plum--the nightly warmth of comely young Monahseetah, daughter of a chief, Little Rock, killed in the battle," writes historian John E. Weems.

"Custer certainly never admitted this, but contemporary army gossips rejoiced in passing on the rumor. Frederick Benteen said it was true; and many Cheyenne's, *who would have known,* asserted it was fact and that *the girl later bore Custer's child."* [41] "The evidence is pretty conclusive that Monahseetah was occupying Custer's tent with him...There's no question in my mind that there was a liaison with Monahseetah," stated historian/author Robert M. Utley. [42]

Elizabeth 'Libby' Custer, the Indian fighters devoted wife, later met Monahseetah at Fort Hayes. She described her as "young and attractive...acknowledged belle among all the other Indian maidens." Libby also met the child describing the baby as "a cunning little bundle of brown velvet with bright beadlike eyes." Though Libby dared not mention it, she knew of Custer's "only serious extramarital adventure." The half-breed, yellow-haired and fair-skinned Cheyenne was called Yellow Swallow. Custer learned Monahseetah was in attendance at the Cheyenne village near the Little Big Horn on June

[41]   Death Song: The Last of the Indian Wars by John Edward Weems, p. 69; Indian Head Books, 1976

[42]   The Real West: Famous Women--Elizabeth Custer, hosted by Kenny Rogers and shown on A&E Network.

25, 1876. [43] He made no attempt to conceal his belligerent attitude toward Indian women. During the early morning hours, he told one of his scouts "when we get to that village [Little Big Horn] I'm going to find the Sioux girl with the most elk teeth on her dress and take her along with me." [44]

It is highly probable our heroine, Buffalo Calf Road, knew Monahseetah and about the birth of Custer's *half-breed child.* To the Whites, Buffalo Calf Road was nothing more than "a squaw, a trouble-maker, a renegade Indian." Yet, could her story be the vindication of a woman upon a man for women of all time? Could the bizarre truth of the Old West be that Buffalo Calf Road *may* have been the person who killed Lt. Col. George Armstrong Custer at the Battle of the Little Big Horn?

"If there is one man living who can speak with authority about those last tragic minutes there on the knoll, in the heat and dust and smoke and terror of the battle's closing moments, it is James T. Gatchell." So what does historian Gatchell of Buffalo, Wyoming have to say? "I do not know whether Two Moons and Harshay Wolf were the Indians who actually killed Custer, or *whether he went down in a last mad, swirling charge.*" [45] No one really knows whose bullet brought the wretched Indian fighter down that hot, bloody Sunday. History simply records Custer and his men were killed at the Little Big Horn by Indians. [46] History also chronicles that Buffalo Calf Road was present on Sunday, June 25, 1876, when Custer and his men were slaughtered. There is further proof she was directly involved in the battle. [47] In June of 1879, Buffalo Calf Road (also called Brave Woman) died tragically of diphtheria despite the medicine of the "white eye's doctor" at Fort Keogh. Black Coyote, her husband, hung himself from his jail cell rafters on news of her death at the fort. The Cheyenne Indians, also hearing, "mourned

---

[43]   Brown, p. 72 See also: Conquest of the Southern Plains by Charles J. Brill, p. 45-46; Oklahoma City, 1938 and Following the Guidon by Elizabeth B. Custer, p. 90; New York, 1890.

[44]   Cheyenne Memories by John Stands In Timber and Margot Liberty, p. 199; Univ. of Nebraska, 1967. This author has a different spelling for the Indian who bore Custer's illegitimate child--"Monaseta."

[45]   I Fought With Custer: The Story of Sergeant Windolph, Last Survivor of the Battle of the Little Bighorn as told to Frazier & Robert Hunt, p. 223; Univ. of Nebraska, 1947

[46]   The Battle of the Little Bighorn by Mari Sandoz; Univ. of NE, 1966

[47]   Agonito, p. 40-41. All information about Buffalo Calf Road is from this article unless otherwise noted.

the death...keening their laments to the heavens as they buried her in the rocks above the Yellowstone River." [48]   This is her heart-rending story, that battle and its aftermath.

The Treaty of Medicine Lodge, Kansas defined the Sioux and Cheyenne as "agency Indians." Government demanded they live on the Great Sioux Reservation, obtaining "rations at agencies on the Missouri River or in Northwestern Nebraska." [49]   Many Indians, however, chose to remain in the Powder River country to the west. This angered the Indians who raided along the Platte and the Yellowstone. White's clamored about Indians breaking the treaty. Within six years, the domino affect had tumbled out of proportion. Custer journeyed amid the Black Hills through the Great Sioux Reservation discovering gold. As with California in '49 and Nevada in the '60's, confirmed word of the precious metal spread. Whites by the thousands, like vultures to a dying carcass, flocked in search of the precious mineral. Thus, the Whites were breaking the treaty.

Tension soared. By 1875, both reproached the other. The Bureau of Indian Affairs ordered "all Indians in the unceded territory to report at the agencies by January 31, 1876, or be regarded as hostile." The vast majority refused. The War Department's power-hungry warmongers launched a plan of Indian genocide selecting three ranking officers to lead the attack. Colonel John Gibbon would come from the West. The second assault, including Custer, coming from the East, was headed by General Alfred H. Terry. The third and final blow was headed by General George Crook from the South. Plans were resolved. The goal simple--conquest! The means--total extermination!

But the plans of mice and men do change. On March 17, 1876, General Crook and his men suffered heavy casualties at the Reynolds Battle on the Powder River. He found the renegade Indians, but; unfortunately for him, they knew of his presence before he arrived. In mid-June, him and his men left Ft. Fetterman. On June 17, eighteen miles south of the Little Big Horn, near the headwaters of the Rosebud River, "Crook and over 1,000 troopers were being given a sound lacing by the Sioux and Cheyenne." [50]   Nine soldiers were killed and twenty-one wounded, although losses among the Crow and

---

[48]   She Fought to Save Cheyenne Way of Life by Rosemary & Joseph Agonito; True West, November 1983; p. 40-43

[49]   Stands In Timber, p. 181-182 footnote

[50]   Hunt, p. 65

Shoshoni brought the figure to the fifty-seven killed and wounded reported by Captain Bourke. Only one Cheyenne, named Scabby, would be killed. [51]

Several brave acts were committed during that battle--one concerning Buffalo Calf Road. The slender-built, dark-haired, 25-year old female sat upon her mount atop a rocky bluff alongside the river. She stared upon the merciless battle taking place. She had spent the entire day fighting "with the warriors against the blue coat soldiers." At one point during the unrelenting struggle, as Comes in Sight rode through a gap, his horse crashed to the ground. Fortunately for Comes in Sight, he landed on his feet and rushed forward in a zigzag run to escape flying bullets cutting the air in every direction.

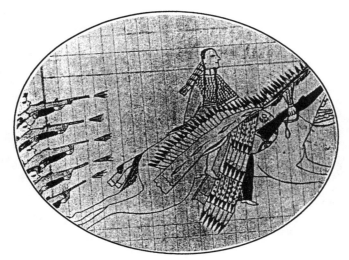

Above: Buffalo Calf Road saving her brother, Comes-in-Sight, as sketched by Spotted Wolf.

Buffalo Calf Road slapped her horse with the reins, riding out of the trees and swooping down the rocky slope to the gap below. Shots originated from every direction

---

[51]   Stands In Timber, p. 187. Scabby was wounded and didn't die until "two or three days later."

amid the chaotic disarray. Bullets buzzed past her head and supple body, failing to intimidate this determined woman of unflinching courage. She turned her horse and reined in. Comes in Sight, his rifle hanging from his arm, clutched madly at the animal and leapt aboard. With summers wind blowing, the two sped away to safety. Even Crazy Horse "watched in admiration at the brave woman's deed." [52]

Gathered around burning campfires after the battle, women and children listened intently to tales of heroic deeds performed that day. None surpassed how Buffalo Calf Road had saved her brother's life. As a matter of fact, the story was retold by the Cheyenne. She proudly stood alongside the other warriors and in her honor, the Cheyenne called it the *Battle Where the Girl Saved Her Brother.* [53]

Below: Buffalo Calf Road and her brother riding into battle, as sketched by Amos Bad Heart Bull.

The following day, Brave Woman, formerly Buffalo Calf Road, returned to her teepee, husband, daughter and the daily routines of a Cheyenne wife and mother. [54] The daily chores such as tearing down their teepee and moving to the area known as the Little

---

[52]   Stands In Timber, p. 188-189. See also: Fighting Cheyenne by John Grinnell, p. 336; Univ. of Okla., 1956

[53]   Agonito, p. 40

[54]   Name changes were common place among many Indian nations when someone exemplified bravery. See the chapter titled How Weasel Woman Changed Her Name.

Big Horn. There the Cheyenne, joining forces with the Sioux, pitched their lodges "along the stream for a distance of three miles." Another day passed and another until a week passed. Then word came Custer was going to attack. All of the warriors went out to turn Custer back in defeat. Of all the women, however, "only Buffalo Calf Road fought at the Battle of the Little Bighorn. With her six-shooter at her side, she rode into battle, joining Gall's Sioux forces attacking Custer." [55]

Custer's trail to the battle started sometime near May 10, 1876, when he "showed up" at Fort Lincoln. [56] Seven days later, on a foggy, dull Wednesday morning, him and his men pulled out of Ft. Lincoln and headed for the Little Big Horn country.

"Nobody was in a very good humor when the bugles sounded reveille at 4 o'clock. Soon as the men breakfasted and formed up, the heavy wagons led off in a column of fours. There were more than one hundred and fourteen...each drawn by six mules...the wheels of the heavy outfits making big ruts in the rain-soaked ground. General Terry suggested that Custer parade to the fort so that the worried women and children could see for themselves what a strong fighting force it was. The band on white horses led off and we paraded around the inner area. Then the married men and officers were allowed to leave their troops and say good-by to their families...Then the regiment, its guidons snapping in the morning breeze, marched off, while the band played over and over again, 'The Girl I Left Behind Me.'

"We struck bad going almost from the time we left Ft. Lincoln...From the start of the expedition the same general plan was followed in making camp. Whenever possible a camp site would be located along a stream...After we'd been out just about two weeks, we hit the valley of the Little Missouri...There was talk of Indians...It took us two or three days of hard travel before we marched over the divide into the valley of the Powder River...we stayed around our camp there at the mouth of the Powder for five or six days...It was around 8 o'clock in the morning when we broke camp at the mouth of the Tongue and marched up the Yellowstone and joined Reno.

"It was noon on June 22 when we broke camp, and started our march up the Rosebud...we rode some fourteen miles, and then made camp on the west bank of the Rosebud...We hit the trail at 5 o'clock sharp that [next] morning. Around noon we began to pass signs of big Indian camps...we made around thirty-three miles that day...But here

---

[55]   Stands In Timber, p. 191 footnote

[56]   Hunt, p. 50

it was Sunday morning, June 25. We were still more than twelve miles from the Little Horn and the Indian village, but the Indians knew where we were and all about us." [57]

Cavalry at the Little Bighorn as sketched by Red Horse.

During the heat of the day's battle, Buffalo Calf Road again exhibited heroism. A young Cheyenne brave, with the courage of a hundred men, charged the soldiers. A White soldier shot the galloping stead from under the warrior. He looked about to see where he could run and, no doubt, spotted Buffalo Calf Road riding straight toward him-- just as she'd done for her brother. She scooted forward, reined the animal to a stop and the Indian warrior hopped aboard the horse's back. The two sped off "for the river where the women had caught some of the soldiers' horses...Calf fought in the battle *until the last* of Custer's men lay dead." [58] After the battle ceased, the Indians moved their camp and Buffalo Calf "settled into the domestic routine of winter camp, hidden in the foothills of the Bighorn Mountains on a swift stream far up the Powder River." She was pregnant with her second child and daily stories were heard of the army's movements.

---

[57]   Hunt. These few paragraphs are various excerpts from Windolph's memoirs that describe the events of Custer and his men.

[58]   Agonito, p. 41

Was the mighty George A. Custer struck down by a bullet from Buffalo Calf Road's pistol?

Five months later, on November 25, Colonel Ranald Mackenzie's soldiers attacked the Indian village where Buffalo Calf Road slept. Indian men were slaughtered that day; but, in true Col. Chivington-style, over forty women and children were massacred as the village was burned to the ground. During the first night's flight, eleven Indian babies froze. Buffalo Calf Road protected her small daughter and unborn child. But she and her family lost all their belongings due to the unmerciful attack upon their village. Frantic, hungry, badgered by an army bent on revenge, the Indians sought help. [59]

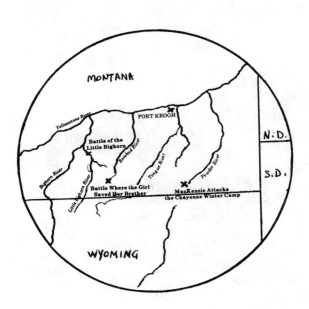

Should they just give up and go back to the reservation? Buffalo Calf Road, Black Coyote and many of the others felt 'No!' However, this belief was in the minority, and by the spring of 1877, all but a small band surrendered. Only 34 of them, including Buffalo Calf Road, her husband and child, refused to move to the Red Cloud reservation. She soon birthed a son. Times were hard. Food and shelter on the run were nearly impossible. By the beginning of summer, Buffalo Calf Road and the others surrendered at Fort Robinson.

As before, so again. Indians surrendered to government promises only to find out they'd been lied to and were being herded south to Indian Territory.

A year later, on September 9, 1878, Buffalo Calf Road, 92-warriors and 285-Cheyenne women and children, disgusted with government lies, left the reservation and

---

[59]   Col. Ranald Mackenzie later went insane was was confined to the Bloomingdale Asylum in New York. His insanity was attributed to "the rigors of Indian fighting." Weems, p. 254

headed North. Little Wolf and Dull Knife lead. [60] The relentless army gave chase. Buffalo Calf Road was forced into violence defending her family and herself. Violence against the merciless blue uniformed White savages whose only code of honor was 'just following orders.' The Cheyenne made it to Punished Woman Creek in western Kansas. There, trapped in a canyon, the Indians desperately fought against the Army.

"I'll not die trapped in a hole," Black Coyote hollered, jumping to his feet. He clutched his rifle and ran forward. Buffalo Calf Road leapt to her feet. She ran to a woman behind a rock safely holding Calf's infant child. The baby was tied to Calf's back and she ran forward to be with her husband. The two stood together--Coyote holding his rifle, Calf toting the child and clinching her six-shooter. Four Cheyenne joined them.

"Do not waste yourselves," one of them shouted. "We must keep fighting." Both were convinced, after a heated discussion, to withdraw into the trenches and resume the fight. But the Cheyenne who witnessed their bravery was proud of their fellow warriors. The soldiers withdrew and the Cheyenne escaped, traveling on to Nebraska.

Sometime in October, a full-fledged disagreement broke out among the Indians. One group, headed by Dull Knife, felt they could return to Red Cloud's reservation, especially since they had made their point. But Buffalo Calf Road was opposed. Her last year on the reservation proved over and over again you cannot 'trust the White' government. So her family and she went with Little Wolf's group. This latter outfit spent a cold winter hiding out in the sand hills of Nebraska, a few miles south of the Dakota border. This should have settled the problems. But it didn't. During those long, cold months, Black Coyote grew more disgusted with the Whites, making small raids against any he could locate. Several felt his actions would get them all caught if he didn't stop. He didn't. Shortly before crossing from South Dakota into Montana, Coyote and the old peacemaker, Black Crane, got into an argument. Coyote struck out and killed him in a fit of rage. Little Wolf declared Black Coyote exiled. Buffalo Calf Road subscribed to the philosophy 'whither Thou goest I will go, whither Thou lodgest I will lodge, thy teepee shall be my teepee and thy people my people.' Many of the other Indian women warned her of the inevitable doom. But she gave them no heed. No sooner had Black Coyote left, along with his wife and children, than Little Wolf and his band were captured between the Montana-South Dakota border and the Powder River.

---

[60] Amos Chapman: Scout Extraordinary by Glenn Shirley; True West magazine, July 1993, p. 27.

Cheyenne Escape From Indian Territory

Around the middle of April 1879, Buffalo Calf Road, Black Coyote, their two children and four other Indians were captured and taken to Ft. Keogh. Within a few days, she fell ill and died. It was the end of an Indian legend. "The last of the free Cheyenne."

So did Buffalo Calf Road kill Custer?

Serious-minded 'academic' historians may, no doubt, scoff at such an 'outlandish hypothesis' that the infamous Indian fighter would die at the hands of a *woman*. They would not even consider such a possibility that their heroic 'madman' could fall prey to such. But they cannot deny the fact Custer died at the Little Big Horn; nor the fact Buffalo Calf Road was there amidst the fighting with her weapon--blazing away at any White savage whom she felt threatened her security. Nearly all historians agree Custer and his men were so overwhelmed during the battle that confusion reigned supreme. Some claim it was so bad that day many of Custer's men committed suicide rather than await the fate rightfully and justifiably theirs. [61]

"Too many people were shooting," states John Stands In Timber--a Cheyenne whose dead grandfather's [Lame White Man] body was recovered from off the battlefield that day. "Nobody could tell whose bullet killed a certain man. There were rumors some knew but would not say anything for fear of trouble...Anyway they are all gone now, and if anyone did know it is too late to find out." [62] "If we could have seen where each bullet landed we might have known," stated Spotted Blackbird, one of the many thousand warriors who fought against Custer. "But hundreds of bullets were flying that day." [63]

Thus, with these facts in mind, the possibility *does* exist that a bullet from her six-shooter, at some point during the heat of the battle, may have been the one that penetrated the body of George Armstrong Custer. Perhaps, and this is only speculation, she smiled when she saw the great White warrior go down from the bullet. Perhaps within her heart she whispered every abused woman's prayer of revenge. 'This is for Monahseetah and the other women who've been mistreated by you and those like you.' [64]

But, then, who *really* knows!

---

[61]   Sandoz, p. 128-129

[62]   Stands In Timber, p. 203

[63]   Stands In Timber, p. 203

[64]   See also: She Watched Custer's Last Battle by Thomas Marquis, p. 1; Hardin, 1933

Buffalo Calf Road:
Social Profile on Chapter Two
by
Virginia C. Nelson-L'Aloge, M. A.

When, Oh, when will we wake up?

The victorious men, the strong men have often shown their "strength" by molesting the women of the vanquished. It is a way to further demoralize the enemy.

Three thousand years ago we on the earth lived with the Earth. Women were leaders, spiritually and politically, along with men. The Mother, the feminine, was honored. Some men feared Her strength and position and so sought to put her in her place. The great battle was on between the sexes.

Many of the invaders of this continent brought this consciousness with them. Over centuries of time woman had become desecrated by them. Their own wives and daughters were treated like brainless lackey's for the most part. Men sold their own daughters or sisters to others for gold or for power down through time. One instance of this is found in the files of the Arizona Daily Star where Mr. J. D. Patton traded his wife, Josephine, to Mr. John M. Hamilton for the Mountain Bell silver mine in Leadville, Colorado. [65] Women began teaching their daughters this is how it should be--religions formed by men, were written to prove it so. Any reference to a feminine aspect of being within a god was conveniently erased! So women accepted this as their lot in life. In some countries they walked behind the man or he rode and she walked. Only a very brave woman saw herself as more--as did only the brave men admit she was his partner-- equal in every way. Each acknowledged their own unique talents and capabilities but neither was less than the other.

---

[65]   Arizona Daily Star, May 14, 1880

So you will find Native Americans, Anglos, Hispanics, Blacks and Asian men who believe/believed in the supremacy of men over women and those brave souls who believe/believed in the equality of men and women.

The feminine aspect of the earth was honored by all American Indians. She was cared for and taken care of. Her name was/is Mother Earth. In many American Indian tribes the women of the tribe were honored. Women were recognized when they did deeds of bravery. The invaders of this land did not have this consciousness. The earth and all she presented: trees, buffalo, oil, gold, silver and so forth were raped and pillaged from the time of their landing upon her beautiful face until present time.

The Indians were generous people and, for the most part, they were willing to share all things. Sex for them was a natural part of life. They knew its necessity and even shared in this. But the people they shared so much with were greedy. Treaty after treaty was broken by the "white eyes."

The people who had been care-takers for Turtle Island [North America] witnessed the desecration from coast to coast and became fierce defenders of the lands honor. No one can own the land. Their way of life was true freedom. The American Indian believed it was right to take only what was needed--always giving something in return. No deer or other game was shot without asking permission of it first and leaving something-- honoring it and its ancestors. For each herb gathered a gift was left. For the rain, seasons, sun and moon--a prayer, dance and song. The way of life was free. They flowed with all about them.

The "civilized" ones came with their control mentality. Their conquering of the earth and taking 'dominion over her' attitude was the same already done to Europe and the female human being. Their attitude was that they had all the answers and only they were right. Only their god was true, only the way they worshipped was right. Now let's save the heathen! No time was given by most to listen or experience the fact that the American Indian view had any validity. There was only the thought of conquering. The thought of rightness measured on an unbalanced scale.

The invaders believed their way was the only way, they thought. 'The only good Indian was a dead Indian,' was the saying. In their incredible ignorance they came. They came running, with spiked shoe and tongue, over the sacred, the innocent, the trusting. They came--the mighty "white eyes." They won by sheer numbers and advanced technology. They drove back and mutilated. Gone from this earth was a way of life unsurpassed in its balance and beauty.

Who was the hero--Custer or Buffalo Calf Road? Who honored a life above their own to risk loosing it to save another? How would you feel if someone were to land now, in mass, upon these shores or from the sky? If they were to take over the way the "white eyes" did? Suppose it was someone who said: "You worshiped all wrong, you were savage because you believed differently!" Suppose it was someone who made a treaty with you that said: "If you give up your home, move to another not so nice we will feed you." Instead they send you rotten food or not enough or perhaps none at all. How would you feel if they took your mothers, wives, daughters, sisters--fathers, husbands, sons and brothers? What would you do when you saw loved ones starving or freezing to death? Would you stay there doing nothing? Who is the hero? Who broke the treaty of the sacred Black Hills?

It is all an issue of control based upon fear. When a person, male or female, is secure within himself or herself and honors the Self they then honor another. What does honoring mean? It means to respect. If I honor someone or something I respect its uniqueness. I do not obstruct its right to be different. A mutual honoring is to observe this between two beings. If I honor you I respect your right to be different, to be unique. If you honor me then you do the same. The main thing it has taken the invaders of this land so long to understand is the concept of honoring. The honoring of one's Self, the other beings around us, human and otherwise, the Earth herself!

We can also honor someone by recognizing something they have done or accomplished. On two occasions Buffalo Calf Road was honored with the warriors. She was esteemed by her people. She fought for her freedom and that of her family and tribe. Whether her bullet shot Custer or not, she put herself on the line. She did not hide but stood tall for her beliefs. Her reward was to know she did all she could do. Finally the white man's disease killed her.

There was no plague, typhoid or small pox, in the American Indian tribes before the invaders came. The Indians were taught by the English, French, Spanish and so forth how to torture, scalp, and mutilate. Counting coup was to touch the enemy not kill the enemy. But the bloody story has come full circle because we all must now do what the Indian was doing when the invaders got here. We must honor.

We must listen to the Earth's needs and honor her. We must listen to each other and honor each other. We must go back to that 'before time' and live in harmony with the seasons, the creatures of the earth and sea.

It is all an issue of control--the rape, the murder, the thievery, the I am better than you Custer mentality. We must finally acknowledge who the true heroes were.

Who are the true heroes of today? Are they the ones forcing what they believe to "be in our best interest" down our throats? How long are we going to allow the forcing control from without because we are too senseless to have Self-control? When will we say: "NO MORE! ENOUGH!"

When, Oh, when will we wake up?

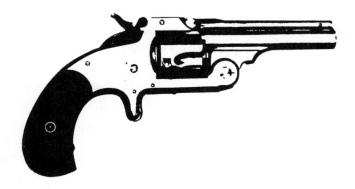

Smith & Wesson .32 New Model No. 1 1/2 Single Action, almost 98,000 of which were manufactured between 1878 and 1892. It is almost identical to the .38 caliber version, of which 108,000 were produced (1877- 1891). Source: Firearms of the American West 1866-1894 by Louis A. Garavaglia & Charles G. Worman; Univ. of New Mexico Press, 1985

Anna McIntire Morrow:
Social Profile on Chapter Three
by
Virginia C. Nelson-L'Aloge, M. A.

The subject of female prostitution has been debated down through time--sometimes even gaining favor and acceptance. Other times, it has been a crime with heinous punishments for the prostitute and historically fewer ramifications for the men buying the *favors*. The women of the last half of the 1800's were limited in resources, education among them, as to how to support themselves. So many women believed there was no choice but to *sell* themselves. They believed, and in some cases it was true, there was no other way to provide basic needs such as food, shelter and clothing. Some prostitutes were victims of sexual, verbal or physical abuse as a child or grown woman. So they did not think better for themselves.

There were women, mere girls, that rebelled against the society holding their natural needs confined as securely as the corset stays bound their bodies. They followed natural physical urges and became *loose* with their sexual favors. Males practicing the same *loose* sexual behavior were said to be *sowing their wild oats* or just being *boys*. Women, however, were condemned and banished from *respectable* society for these acts. This inequality led to the life of prostitution for many women while their male partners in 'crime' went on to be politicians, doctors, lawyers, merchants, businessmen and so forth. Some prostitutes were victims of rape thus considered *soiled*. Some had a child without marriage. Others such as Anna McIntire Morrow were merely orphans.

The stigma in being a prostitute back East in the "civilized" states was to be on the lowest level a woman could sink. The West, however, welcomed the *soiled doves* with open arms. Few women had the courage or desire to leave the familiar comforts to be had east of the Mississippi River. Women who had the ill-fortune to not marry, or the male protectors being so inconsiderate as to die leaving her without funds or home, were desperate. A great majority of these women often turned to prostitution for a living.

Those prostitutes who went West found a different reception than in the East. So the gold rush for the men was accompanied by a bodily gold rush in the form of women practicing the "oldest profession." The prostitute was, for the most part, honored as a necessary element and found herself often treated with higher regard than her *respectable* sisters back East. Her shrewdness and before unused, unacknowledged business sense came into play. A few managed to save their earnings. They launched into their own houses or clubs or invested wisely. Likewise, a few became as rich or richer than many a gold digger who found a strike. At times some earned the right to be respectable by their own money. Therefore, they became, in many instances, marriageable. To the female-hungry male of the West it was not necessary for the female to be White, pretty, trim or even likable. Many women who were outcast in traditional society went West to sell the one thing that would elevate them to a place of favor.

The story of Annie McIntire Morrow is one of tragedy, love, courage and devotion. Why would two women set out alone facing the hardships of a winter storm in order to be in town on Saturday night? The first thing coming to mind is that it was how they earned their living. Saturday was the *big night* for their customers. It was the night when the money or gold dust earned all week by the men was spent on liquor, gambling and women. Annie and Emma were concerned about missing out on the best earning night of the week. Perhaps they also looked forward to the excitement and the attention. It was a night to *howl,* so to speak. Further is the fear that if they were not there someone else might move into their turf. Of course, there could have also been someone special to see.

Once they had rested they believed the storm was over. Snows often hit swiftly in the mountains. Snows that are thick and blowing cause white-outs and anyone can get caught in one--even today. What occurred next and what proved to test the courage of both women was Anna's love for her friend. Anna's love and courage were at the highest degree when she unselfishly gave some of the clothes she desperately needed herself to her dear friend. The fact the Tate brothers and Elliott were concerned for the safety of these two women shows how the men felt about them. The *descent* people could not and would not help her because she was a prostitute. But others saw her as the caring human being she was--so they helped.

All over the West the *descent* people, mostly women, gawked down their stiff Victorian holier-than-thou noses at these *soiled doves.* Yet, stories abound of prostitutes who helped in times of disaster--often when others would not. Many of the women of the Old West performed great feats of love and heroism. Many of those women were prostitutes, outcasts of society. These prostitutes proved they had hearts bigger than the closed attitudes of society, men and women alike. These prostitutes nursed, unselfishly, miners and cowboys who were injured or ill even with contagious diseases. Many of these women were contributors of money when needed. Sadly, however, many were barred from such simple decencies as being buried in the same local cemetery as the customers they so faithfully served day in and day out.

People often judge another based on how they earn a living. They do not take time to learn or understand why a person is doing what she or he is doing. These hypocrites of such Pharisical piety judge on what others do--not who they are. Such is the case of Annie. The fact the town's people in Annie's instance had a change of heart was unusual and commendable. It reveals the spirit of what strengthens this country even today. Oh, there were scoundrels then as there are today. People who take advantage of another's love, good nature and trust. Such was the case of the Italian lover. What was truly admirable is Annie never complained and never lost her optimistic outlook about all people. She always saw the best of everyone and remained optimistic. We can all learn from Annie's story!

PROSTITUTE PEG-LEG ANNIE

Prostitution has been around probably since the beginning of time. Least, it was a strong influence in the Old West. "It is mere absurdity to assert that prostitution ever can be eradicated," wrote Dr. W. W. Sanger in *The History of Prostitution.* "Strenuous and well-directed efforts have been made [and] absolute monarchs have bent all their energies of will, and brought all the aids of power to crush it out...The guilty women have been banished, scourged, branded, executed; their partners have been subjected to the same punishment; held up to public opinion as immoral; denuded of their civil rights; have seen their offenses visited upon their families; have been led to the stake, the gibbet and the block, and still prostitution exists [because] prostitution is coeval with society." [66]

So what makes women turned to prostitution? Historian Allan Nevins writes: "Prostitutes might be held to indicate the general purity of American womanhood. A double standard of morals was taken for granted. Nearly all well-reared women were virtuous, many well-reared men were not. Moreover, the very rigidity of the moral code imposed on women , when accepted by harsh parents, thrust not a few seduced girls into the streets. The unhappy facts were that...underpayment in domestic service, the needle trades, and other occupations for women helped to furnish recruits." [67]

Though prostitutes shared commonalties they also competed. Dress and style were but one of these. Josephine Marie Micaud, for example, was a 16-year old prostitute with long Shirley Temple curls hanging down to her waist. Montana's infamous "Bertie" Miller, on the other hand, wore her hair trimmed neatly close to the ears. Her picture, dressed in a man's three-piece suit, reveals her youthful, comely features similar to a

---

[66]   Shady Ladies of the West by Ronald D. Miller, p. 208; Westernlore Press, 1985

[67]   Nevins, p. 63

young boy. Miller was eventually arrested as "Montana's only highway-woman" for stage robbery with her accomplice named Clark. There were other women who competed in other ways like the fat, masculine featured "beautiful Alice Abbott" (who was anything but beautiful) and Etta Clark (whose features were beautiful). Etta got into "a personal dispute" with Alice and the former wounded the latter in El Paso. [68]

Prostitutes offered the cowboy what he couldn't get elsewhere-- female companionship!

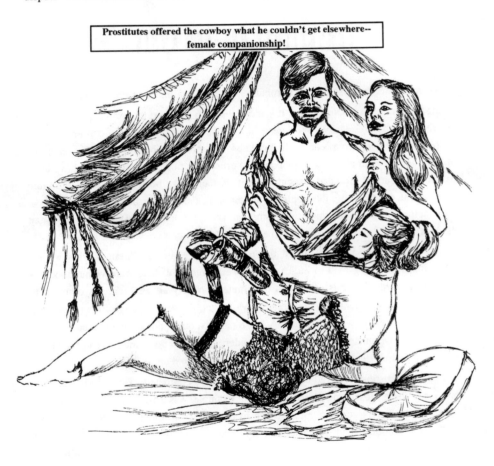

---

68   Painted Ladies & Bordellos of the Old West 1993; Published by Frontier Calendars, Missoula, Montana, 1992

Not all female prostitutes were White. Many impecunious women's ethnic group status was Black, Mexican, Indian or Irish and they were "relegated to social and economic inferiority within the mainstream of society [becoming] excellent candidates for prostitution." [69] These prostitutes were often the brunt of various legal squabbles. Worse, judicial altercations brought "disgrace" to so-called reputable families in the Old West. One such instance involved the post chaplain's daughter--Lizzie Simpson.

At Fort Union, New Mexico, in November 1877, Lt. Colonel N. A. M. Dudley was being court-martialed "on charges that he mismanaged the fort." Feeling this was not enough, the prosecutors tossed in the charge of "conduct to the prejudice of good order and military discipline." This involved a "titillating sexual scandal." Vast testimony given at the court-martial centered on Dudley's intervention "in the private affairs of Doctor Tipton, a young physician who resided in nearby Tiptonville." [70] Dudley learned from fellow officers that Miss Lizzie Simpson, daughter of the fort chaplain, was accusing Tipton "of seducing her on an occasion when the two were out riding in his carriage." Lizzie swore an affidavit, even possessed "three innocuous letters from Tipton...supposedly proving Tipton tried repeatedly to lure [her] to a private meeting."

So while enjoying a drink in the company of three officers, they discussed this incident's affect upon the preacher--a fellow military man in uniform. The soldiers concluded to kidnap Tipton and return him to the fort. They set out, promising Tipton after he'd done the "honorable thing of marriage toward Miss Simpson," the Simpson family would leave the fort within four days. They failed, however, to mention young Lizzie was pregnant. Tipton declined whole-heartedly to be "hog-swallowed."

"I have proof that the girl has been on it before, that she has made solicitations of the soldiers at the garrison," he instructed them. Tipton emphatically refused to return and, a day or two later, filed civil suit against the four soldiers. Lizzie's soiled reputation came under legal scrutiny. It wasn't difficult for the prosecution "to establish that Miss Simpson enjoyed a notorious reputation at the fort...as over and over witnesses agreed that Miss Simpson was...promiscuous and had been intimate with more than a few of the males at the post." It was clearly established "the character of the lady whose reputation he [Dudley] assumed so zealously to protect was bad." Fanfare, being what it is, did

---

69   Daughters of Joy, Sisters of Misery: Prostitutes in the American West 1865-1890 by Anne M. Butler, p. 142; Univ. of Illinois, 1985

70   Butler, p. 128-131

wonders for the young woman's career. The publicity for this *soiled dove* was such she graduated "from amateur promiscuity to [that] of professional peddler."

This young female prostitute, daughter to a man of the cloth, was "an embarrassing problem for her family." This could not be denied. Reverend Simpson, the fellow officer whose reputation Dudley and the others were trying to protect, "faced an awesome problem if he tried to keep her at his parsonage." Reverend Simpson's solution is not told by Anne M. Butler in her account of the incident. But it's most certain the father was shamed by the reputation of his daughter who practiced her trade among both the enlisted men and the officers of Fort Union, New Mexico in 1877.

No doubt family embarrassment is why many of these prostitutes assumed various nicknames. Such aliases included "Colored Susan," "Big Lil," "Madam Mustache," "Snuff Box Allie," "One Arm Annie," "Adobe Moll," "Sorrel Mike," "Cattle Kate" and "Squirrel Tooth Alice." [71] Ft. Laramie during the late 1870's claimed such fascinating prostitutes as "Big Dollie," "Dirty Emma," "Tit Bit," "Smooth Bore" and "Sizzling Kate." [72] These sobriquets were given to them by circumstances, by companions or themselves. This story is of one where life's hazardous affairs dubbed her with an alias.

On Independence Day 1864, 4-year old Anna McIntire's father carried her 53-miles in his back pack to the mining district of South Boise, Idaho stopping at the new mining camp of Rocky Bar. The death of his wife prompted her father, Steve McIntire, to forsake their homestead back in Ohio and head for the Idaho Territory. [73] Rocky Bar boasted a population nearing 2,500 before the end of the War for Southern Independence in 1865. The thriving mining community was the county seat of Alturas County. Many villages in the Feather River country looked to Rocky Bar as the center of action in south central Idaho. Hardships were a way of life. Hours of labor were long and often not too rewarding. But Steve McIntire did not quit. It wasn't long before he and his partner struck it rich. They called the mine the Golden Star Mine.

Steve was a good father, too. His first dollars went into building himself a cabin and hiring an Indian woman to nanny little Anna while he was working. Six years and three days later, however, Steve died in a street brawl. The fight was the culmination to a long,

---

71   Butler, p. 24, 173-179

72   They Called Him Wild Bill: The Life and Adventures of James Butler Hickok by Joseph G. Rosa, p. 286; Univ. of Okla. 1974

73   The Saga of Peg-Leg Annie by Hank Corless; Old West magazine, 1990

hard fought feud. Orphaned, 10-year old Annie's future depended upon fellow miners and friends of her father. Anna need not worry, however. She was an attractive girl, and by 16, had captured the affections of Michigan-born Bill Morrow--nearly twice her age. Anna's comeliness caught the affections of other men and, anyway, life in the mining community was tiring. So Morrow's next move came with no explanation. He packed his belongings, including his new woman, and left the mining camp. They traveled to Boise and married in August 1876. A year later, Anna mothered a child--having four more children before the end of this marriage union.

Still, tragedy hauntedly dogged her trail. Before the birth of her final child in 1889, the three earlier children had died and this, coupled with a failing marriage, brought great heartache to Anna. She turned alcoholic. Before long, though no divorce was recorded, Anna left William Thomas Morrow. It was said he eventually wound up in the county poor farm in later years. By the mid-1890's, Anna returned to Rocky Bar where memories of childhood and happier times were nestled deep within her mind. The town of Rocky Bar had changed little since she left nearly two decades earlier. Day after day gunfighters, gamblers, miners, prostitutes and other *unsavory characters* stalked the streets and alleys. But it was just not the same. Most of the earlier associates, friends and companions had relocated. Without a proper education, Anna became one of the well-known saloon girls, dancing her way into miners lives while picking pockets and sweet talking them into free drinks. Of course, she allowed them other favors. Sexual favors for the price of a little gold or silver. After all, a girl had to 'get by some way.'

"For many of these women," wrote Anne M. Butler, "the transition...to sexual labor involved little or no adjustment in their societal concepts. They brought with them the baggage of the past and became part of the frontier sexual marketplace. [74] Prohibited by society's censure from establishing a wide range of friendships, prostitutes circulated freely among their own colleagues," continues Butler. "Cast in the framework of a vague, uneasy truce, these friendships took on a strange hue." [75]

A short distance of only fourteen miles separated the two mining camps of Atlanta and Rocky Bar, Idaho. The road itself twisted and turned like a Texas sidewinder from Atlanta's infant mountain valley, journeying past the foot of the 9,000-feet Bald

---

[74]   Daughters of Joy, Sisters of Misery: Prostitutes in the American West 1865-1890 by Anne M. Butler, p. 11; Univ. of Illinios, 1987

[75]   Butler, p. 41

Mountain and then steeply dropping to the Feather River and on down into Rocky Bar. She quickly teamed up with Emma Von Losch in the nearby mining camp of Atlanta, Idaho. Emma, calling herself "Dutch Em," was a short Bavarian German woman and spoke seven languages. By 1896, the two were operating a brothel in the area lustily referred to as 'red light alley.' The two prostitutes, accompanied by a large Newfoundland dog Anna had coerced into friendship, made the rounds of nearby mining camps. For the right price, a miner could bed down with Anna or Em, perhaps both, and enjoy the finer pleasures of a worldly woman.

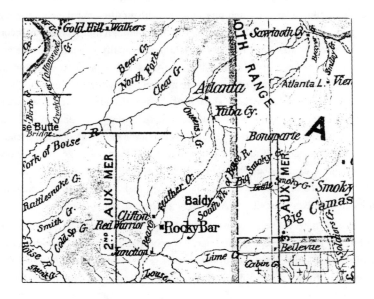

But Anna was soon to become "one of Idaho's most legendary characters." There were times during the ugly winter month's when the snow piled as deep as 12 to 14 feet and traffic along this bleak route often came to a complete halt. In the middle of May 1896, a late winter storm approached the area. Anna and Dutch Em were lured by a big payday weekend for the miners at Rocky Bar and it was just too great for them to pass up. Storm or no storm, Anna and Dutch Em made up their minds to be in on the good times.

The two women waited until late Friday night, knowing the cold winds and temperatures had hardened the snow, and set out for Rocky Bar.

"You better go back," Bill Tate advised the women, meeting them five miles south of Atlanta. "You can't make it." Tate was the Atlanta mail carrier and knew the dangers to travelers upon the 14-mile path during severe snow storms. Already two fellow workers and friends, Otto Meyer and Jimmy Hicks, had died trying to make it through the pass in inclement weather. A third, Rufus Lester, caught in an avalanche, had never returned. But Dutch Em and Anna had spent the entire night, exhausting themselves, to get as far as they had come. They would not go back now!

"We'll make it or die," one of them told Tate.

"I think you'll die," he repeated matter-of-factly.

Tate continued and soon reached Summit Cabin about lunch time. He met his brother John, the Rocky Bar mail carrier, and the two men converged and exchanged bags of mail. On this particular day, Bill spoke about passing the women and their determination to go on to Rocky Bar.

"You better tell them to turn back with you. We're in for a real storm," he warned Bill. Ninety minutes later, Bill headed back for Atlanta. He journeyed less than a mile when he came upon the two *soiled doves* still plodding along.

"Well, do you think you can make it?"

"I don't know, Bill," Anna remarked, her voice shaking amid the frigid cold winds. "Em is about to give out and I have been packing her for the last half a mile."

It was obvious Anna was frazzled and even plainer Dutch Em was exhausted as she leaned against Anna. Tate knew deep within his soul these women had traveled too far and were incapable of returning to Atlanta. He must do something, he knew. He escorted the women to the Summit Cabin. They would be safe, warm and have some-thing to eat until the storm passed. Completing his mercy mission, Bill gathered his mail sack, bid them farewell and traveled back toward Atlanta by himself. The women took advantage of the warmth and food within the cabin. All too soon, however, as the storm died out, they concluded they could make it to Rocky Bar before nightfall. Alas, they bundled themselves and headed out. They traveled barely an hour when the storm unleashed all its fury and wrath once more upon the vulnerable women. The cold wind sliced their faces as hardened flakes of icy snow BB'ed their eyes, nose, cheeks and mouth. Their earlier experience was mild compared to this blizzard savagery. Three feet of snow fell by the time they reached Bald Mountain. The snow-blinded women took the wrong turn in the fork--right instead of left. It was too late. Time was their worst enemy. Hope was lost. They were lost. What could they do? Dutch Em's exhaustion made it futile to try to reach the cabin.

"Go on," she pleaded with Anna. "You can make it and bring back help."

Anna refused to leave her friend to die alone in the glacial frozen wasteland. That night, while icy winds blistered the terrain, temperatures yielded and dropped far below zero. The women cuddled against the dog to maintain body heat, unable to sleep for fear of not waking up. By Sunday noon, with no food, they were hallucinating. Anna thought at one point she saw miners in a gorge at the canyon's head. But it was nothing more than a rock landslide. Later that day, Em grew excited over what she thought was a cabin. It turned out to be a large, black-faced boulder protruding above the snow line. That was when Dutch Em gave out. Despair became her lover. All will to live and go on forsook her. She slumped forward into the snow, determined that whatever the end, it would beat the hopelessness of going on in vain. Dutch Em mumbled all night long. By early morning, May 18, she was dead. Anna, with cold, frozen fingers of death drawing her into the frigid abyss, crawled to where she thought the trail lay covered with ice.

During all this, another story unfolded involving the folks in Atlanta. By Monday, Bill Tate and others were worried. He quickly hefted his mail sack and headed for Summit Cabin. Before long, he arrived to find no sign of the two women anywhere in the cabin. Only extinguished burnt ashes remained in the fireplace. Tate was really worried now. He left the cabin and headed toward Rocky Bar, praying he might meet his brother, and learn good news about Dutch Em and Anna. Before Tate located his brother, and while still on the Atlanta side of Bald Mountain, he heard someone yelling. It was Anna, down on all fours, hysterically crawling alongside her loyal dog, struggling through the snow. She was incoherent and "raving as if completely out of her mind."

"Hello, Tate. I've had a hell of a time since I saw you last," she barked out. Tate removed his heavy coat and placed it around her shoulders. He picked her up and carried her back to the road. There, the two met up with John Tate. Both took turns carrying Anna back to Summit Cabin. They built a fire. Then, Anna talked.

Complications set in as Anna's bodily limbs thawed. When the blood returned to her legs and arms, her body strongly reacted and she had convulsions. A doctor was needed fast. The closest one, however, was in Mountain Home--eighty miles away. There was nothing else to do but get her off that mountain. Yet, the two men were themselves too tired to carry her all the way back and Anna, now delirious, was no help. Bill Tate journeyed back to Atlanta. None believed the seriousness of Anna's condition. None of the 'descent people' cared for a fallen woman's condition. Such was not rare in the Old West. Men of the Old West were "to respect good decent women and protect their character...The old-time cowboy was most respectful of women as long as they kept their place. If they let down the bars, one of those boys would go the limit," Oliver Wallis, a rancher in the Medicine Bow, Wyoming area related. [76]

However, miner Winnie Elliott cared. Elliott grabbed his skies and headed back to Summit Cabin. Arriving, Elliott remained with Anna while the two Tate brothers headed for Rocky Bar. The people of Anna's home town responded more positively. They sent for a doctor and rounded up five miners to rescue the frozen Dutch Em. On Tuesday, however, the miners returned without the body of Anna's friend. Anna was taken to Atlanta. Her arrival proved the severity of her condition and several miners, embarrassed at their earlier decision, went in search of Em. But, like the group from Rocky Bar, they returned a couple of days later without her body. Finally, the townspeople focused their attention on John Tate and requested he go in search of Dutch Em's body. They would assist in whatever manner they could. Tate agreed. He asked Charley Gates and two other mines to go with him.

The four men set out in search of Em's body. Past the cabin and into the snowy, frozen wasteland they journeyed. Placing one foot in front of the one previously sunken into the never-ending Arctic white snowy depths. On and on they trudged. Before long, they reached the area. Sure enough! They beheld the frozen body of Emma Van Losch, a human chunk of ice, sitting against a pine tree--surrounded by an unexpected eeriness. Anna proved herself a heroine. For upon the stiff, cold remains of Em were Anna's clothes, unselfishly removed from her own freezing body and given to her dying friend. Without regard to her safety, Anna risked her own life in a vain attempt to save Em. The four men cried viewing the sight of unsurpassed devotion to a friend.

At Atlanta, where Anna desperately sought recovery from severe exposure, the miners pitched in and hired Effie Prey to care for the heroine. Still, as a nurse, Effie was not completely able to deal with the problem. Hour after hour elapsed and, with increasing pain, Anna, at times delirious, passed in and out of consciousness. Outside,

---

[76]   Cowboy Culture: A Saga of Five Centuries by David Dary, p. 279; Avon Books, 1981

unknown to her, word of her merciful sacrifice spread rapidly as the Tate expedition returned with the frozen body of Dutch Em. Suddenly, many who spoke against the *soiled dove* repented of their misjudgment. These changed feelings rallied the community as the prostitute nestled in death's bosom. Each gave freely for Anna's care. Even Ella, the proud haughty wife of Charley Gates, forsook her pious Christian attitudes and helped Effie Prey nurse Anna. Likewise Maggie Brown, the pretentious woman postmaster, came to her aid. Everywhere people learned of the heroic deeds and offered to help this suffering, gallant courtesan.

For 120-hours the pain of her frozen legs agonized Anna. That was the amount of time before Dr. M. J. Nieukirk made it into the mining camp of Atlanta. [77] He took one look. The diagnosis was clear--amputate both legs. They placed her upon a kitchen table. An anesthetic was administered. There and then, aided by Effie and a couple of others, Dr. Nieukirk truncated Anna's legs just below the knees. Anna recovered from surgery. She was forever grateful for how people helped her. After recuperating, Anna made a pair of woolen pads for her legs. She even learned to walk again. But her career as a 'soiled dove' was over--never again to earn her living in such manner. Nor feel the massive weight of a man's body pressed against hers. Nor smell his perspiration as he lustily spent long hours within her chambers. Nor hear those faint whispers passed during the height of passion. She moved back to Rocky Bar and became a laundress. Many miners were loyal supporters and customers. They dubbed her 'Peg-leg' Annie and paid her handsome sums of money to scrub their clothes.

The years passed and 'Peg-leg' Annie continued to live in Rocky Bar. She never voiced any bitterness about her plight in life. Her positive attitude remained intact and the stories about her heroism grew. By 1924, 'Peg-leg' Annie accumulated $12,000 from business adventures. She fell in love with an Italian saloon keeper, Henry Longheme. Henry wanted to return to Italy to visit family members. Annie put every bit of confidence in Henry and, when he agreed to deposit her money in a San Francisco bank, she willingly gave him the opportunity. She lovingly bid him farewell and Henry departed. Afterwards, Annie got a letter from Henry in New York City. He told her he would write again once he reached Italy. But she never heard from her true love again.

---

[77]   Nancy Wilson Ross (Westward the Women; Alfred A. Knopf, 1944; p. 126-127) states that "Idaho old-timers...will tell you, one and all, that a local amateur hacked them off with a meat saw and Annie had nothing to sustain her but a generous shot of whiskey."

Nor did she ever see any of her money. But Annie was loyal and the rest of her life felt he had met up with foul play--never once voicing anything to the contrary.

At the end of the Roaring Twenties, Rocky Bar and several surrounding camps turned into ghost towns. On September 13, 1934, 'Peg-leg' Annie Morrow died of face cancer in Boise, Idaho. She was a well-known and colorful celebrity of Idaho's past. Her reputation brought her the attention of politicians, businessmen, miners and a host of the curious. Through it all she was one of the nicest women anyone ever met as this former prostitute became a legend. [78]

Peg-Leg Annie

---

[78]   Shady Ladies of the West by Ronald D. Miller, p. 134; Westerlore Press, 1985

QUEEN OF THE DESPERADOES

Whether male or female, people in the Old West were in many ways no different from today. Men often were inclined to sacrifice themselves for the reputation of a woman. One example concerns a man who spent 10-years in prison for bank robbery. His reason was his devout love for Miss Alice Clapp. Alice's father, Milton B., was manager of Tombstone's Safford-Hudson Bank. He was a conscientious banker--always putting bank business first. This was proven during the summer fire of 1881. "The moment the alarm was given," reported the *Tombstone Epitaph,* he "rushed all money and valuables into the inner safe--the books being taken outside to a safe place--and proceeded to lock everything up." It was further added Milton barely escaped the blaze himself for "while locking the outer door the plastering began to fall around his head and he escaped...by the back door--the front being inaccessible from the flames." [79]

But our incident concerns Milton's fear of the bank closings during the 1880's and a devoted bank clerk. Recognizing the coming financial panic, Milton withdrew $30,000 in gold one night and hid it in his house. The following day, to his chagrin, the money was missing. But the money wasn't all that was missing. So was Wiley Clapp--Milton's wayward son and Alice's brother. Some felt Wiley stole the money and disappeared. Such was not the case. For to the surprise of the entire town, bank clerk George Meley, madly in love with Alice, claimed he stole the money.

---

[79]   Tombstone Epitaph: The Truth About the Town Too Tough To Die by Douglas D. Martin, p. 128; Univ. of New Mexico, 1951

The lawmen questioned George. But George wouldn't tell. He was placed on trial, convicted and sentenced to 10-years in prison. There's no known record if Alice ever visited him during those long years. Nor if she ever wrote him any letters. But his love for her remained steadfast. Ten years later, George was released from prison. When he got out, he moved to Tucson and, to his surprise, ran into Alice exiting a small cafe. Both knew the other. They talked. George learned Alice's father died and Wiley was murdered by renegade Apaches. She confided she never married because she was in love with him all these years. Further, Alice told George she inherited the family estate.

One thing led to another. George and Alice soon were married. From her inheritance, she bought a men's clothing store for George to operate. George, on the other hand, never stopped being amazed at how his luck had turned nor did he ever stop wondering why Alice loved him. After all, hadn't he confessed to robbing her father's bank? Yet her love for him never ceased. They lived a long, happy life together lasting 40-years. He never stopped loving her as when a bank clerk at her father's bank. Nor did she ever doubt his love. But life, like every fairy tale, has an ending. George realized he was dying. Alice held his hand, comforting him as he lay dying. But George felt a compelling urge before death's womb swallowed him. In his final breath, he confessed to Alice so he might clear his conscious.

"My dearest, I want to tell you that I did not rob your pa. I confessed that I did to protect Wiley. By doing that," he told her, his life's breath escaping him, "I was able to spare you and your pa from disgrace. I did it because I loved you so much and I didn't want you to know." Completing his confession, George sighed his last breath and passed through death's eternal birth canal.

"But I did know, George, my love," Alice said, as George stepped into eternity, unable to hear her finish the sentence. "I took the gold--not Wiley!" [80]

Not all women were as fond of their men folk. Occasionally, and sometimes justifiably, they were 'sinister' in their regards for their men. One example, reported by a New Mexico newspaper in January 1883, was the wife of Wakefield Starkey of Austin. Starkey was "a perfect tyrant of the deepest dye," known to beat his wife and lock her up in the wardrobe...without any provocation. One day, he rode across the tracks of the International and Great Northern Railroad. No reason was given why Starkey didn't see

---

[80]   Martyr by Intent by Ben T. Traywick, p. 63-64; Old West, Fall 1993

nor hear the approaching train. Nevertheless, he failed to get out of the way in time and was run over by the powerful vehicle. Needless to say, it killed him *and the mule.*

"When [Mrs. Starkey] heard of his death, it was not so much a case of heavy bereavement as it was mitigated affection," the reporter commented. There seemed no doubt "the engineer of the locomotive was clearly to blame [and] it was suggested to the widow she bring suit for damages." After giving it consideration, and realizing she was a widow without any substance, she decided to contact the railway company.

"Now, madam, we are willing to do what is fair in the matter," the railroad official told her. "There is really no occasion for going to law. It is a delicate subject to discuss, so I think, without going into the merits of it, I will tender you a check for $3,000, and you will sign a paper releasing the company from all further demands."

"How much?" She asked.

"I am authorized to pay you $3,000."

"I accept it," she agreed.

The signed check was handed her and she signed the necessary papers releasing the railroad from further claims. She left the office and went straight to the bank.

"I didn't expect to get more than $50," she said, standing, waiting for the cashier to transact her business. "Reckon that railroad fellow didn't know how old that mule was!" Nothing was said about "any loss in the death of her husband." [81]

Women of other nationalities were no different. One was the daughter of Chief Lobo Blanco (White Wolf). Unfortunately her name appears lost in the annals of history. Her story, however, has not. It began on August 16, 1849, when a group of U. S. troops attacked a band of Jicarilla Apaches outside Las Vegas, New Mexico. Out of the nearly forty Apaches in the camp, "eight or ten escaped [and] six prisoners and three bodies [were] brought in and many of the dead remain in the ravines where they were sabered." One of these prisoners was the chief's daughter. She was jailed with five prisoners. Shortly afterwards, she was removed from her imprisonment. Troops escorted her to Wagon Mound, New Mexico, a natural landmark along the Santa Fe Trail. They demanded she point out the Jicarilla Apache camp from atop the highest peak. New Mexico Indian Agent John Greiner added he thought she was to be exchanged for a White woman captured earlier by the Apaches. The following morning, soldiers tried to

---

[81]   Silver City Enterprise, January 25, 1883

load her into the wagon. She grabbed a knife and stabbed at one of them. She ran. They chased her. She got between the mules and the soldiers and, hoping to stop them, stabbed one of the mules hitched to the wagon. Sgt. Martinez pulled his weapon and shot her in the head. The following year, her father, Chief Lobo Blanco, sought revenge near where his daughter was murdered. Though the attack was successful, the Indian chief lost his own life, when shot and bludgeoned in the head with a large rock. [82]

Racial problems existed between the women in the days of the Old West. These were not resolved so easily. Another unnamed woman in Fulton, Callaway County, Missouri made the news. [83] The family left their house on Saturday evening, November 3, to attend a meeting. With the exception of their daughter, no "white person remained about the premises. When the family returned the young lady was found murdered. Her brains had been smashed and the house showed signs of a severe struggle." A female slave was immediately suspected, owing to known ill feelings on her part towards the murdered young girl. The slave girl was found in a nearby corn field where the family sent her to husk some corn before leaving the house. She was questioned and denied all knowledge of the murder. They noticed, however, she was wearing different clothing.

A thorough search revealed her earlier clothing in the corn field, badly torn with several blood stains on it. The slave girl was immediately arrested and brought before the local Justice of the Peace. She confessed and was shackled, loaded aboard a wagon and driven to Fulton, Missouri. A vigilante mob formed to discuss the murder as well as the Black murderess and decided to take care of the matter themselves. They mounted their horses and gave chase, overtaking the wagon about three miles outside Fulton. The girl was forcibly taken by the group of vigilantes and hanged from the nearest tree by the roadside where when our informant left Fulton, stated the *St. Louis Bulletin* on November 8, "she was still hanging." [84]

Family loyalty in the Old West contributed to make women outlaws. Two more women, Kate Kelly and her daughter, Kit, portray this truth best. Like our Black slave girl, the Kelly women were taken by vigilantes. The Kelly's lived in No-Man's Land, later called Oklahoma. It was reported the Kelly women, along with husband William and son Bill, "lived in a dwelling frequented by travelers journeying from Meade Center,

---

[82] Wildest of the Wild West by Harold Bryan, p. 29-34, 48; Clear Light Publishers, 1988
[83] Santa Fe Weekly Gazette, December 15, 1860
[84] Santa Fe Weekly Gazette, December 12, 1860

Kansas to Beaver City, Oklahoma." [85] Near the middle of December 1887, the Kelly's were no where to be found. A Chicago traveling drummer was reported missing and the trail led directly to the old Kelly place. A thorough search revealed the body of the missing man in the cellar "nearly eaten up by rats." Accompanying the dead drummer were five other decomposing bodies. A larger and more detailed search disclosed four more nude bodies buried beneath the stable--one of which had been a woman about thirty years old. Near the barn another man and woman were found in 3-feet graves. Their heads had been brutally crushed.

When news spread to Beaver City, it was remembered the Kelly family recently passed through the town on their way to Memphis. They were herding a group of horses and had plenty of money. A 20-men vigilante posse formed and followed. The trail led along the Palo Duro Creek, turned south and headed toward Wheeler, Texas. Then on Thursday, January 5, 1888, the vigilante posse learned they were within a few miles. Two hours the chase continued. Suddenly Katy's horse stumbled and fell, breaking the poor animal's neck and killing Katy. None of the family stopped. A few minutes later the posse neared close enough to shoot at Bill and Kit, the son and daughter. Several bullets flew through the air before the vigilantes shouted: "Halt!"

The brother and sister reined up their horses while the father sped on his way. The Kelly girl begged for mercy and claimed "she never killed anybody."

"Oh, shut up, it ain't any use, you've got to go with me anyway," her brother screamed at her.

The vigilantes pulled out their ropes. One climbed a nearby tree and tied the ropes to a limb. The nooses were made, slipped about the girl and her brother's neck and both were asked if they wanted to say a prayer or make a statement.

"Let her go," Bill said, "I've had my share of fun."

"Shall I tell?" Kit asked.

"No!" Shouted her brother.

"Then let them find out for themselves," she replied.

What exactly it was Kit might have told died with her for neither she nor her brother confessed or prayed. The horses were slapped away. The ropes quickly tightened. Their breath forsook them. Their brains screamed out. Their legs kicked for support. The blood

---

[85]   Las Vegas Daily Optic, January 9, 1888

in their head turned purplish-black. But there was no air. There was no scream from their throats. There was no place to stand. Strangulation swallowed the young people in death. The posse rode on after the father. He, too, was captured and, like his son and daughter, met his fate at the end of a hemp rope. Vigilante justice had struck. Whether right or wrong, one thing was certain, the Kelly's would never again murder another human! [86]

All these circumstances made these women outlaws. Yet none was more deserving to the title 'Queen of the Desperadoes' as the forthcoming one. She is described as about "the handsomest woman on the frontier." She was further depicted as "beautiful, accomplished, highly connected, well educated, [and] she might have chosen her place in the highest walks of life." During her life she was a "belle of society, an affianced bride, a spy, a hospital nurse, a lobbyist, a gambler's wife, a gambler, a confederate of robbers, a saloon keeper," a poet, an alcoholic and opium addict and an inmate of the San Francisco jail house. She was Belle Siddons, alias Monte Verde, alias Mrs. Cummings, alias Madam Vestal, alias Mrs. Hallet. This is her story! [87]

The *Las Vegas Daily Optic* failed to mention exactly where and when Belle Siddons was born and who her parents were. But sources do tell us she was closely related to Missouri Governor Claiborne F. Jackson who served immediately prior to the War for Southern Independence. They further added she made quite a sensation in Jefferson City when Belle made her debut on society. She arrived in Jefferson City directly from attending the Female University at Lexington, Missouri. [88] Her success was attributed to her accomplishments and "remarkable beauty, combined with her distinguished family connections." The beaus flocked about Belle like the Tarleton brothers around the fictional Scarlett O'Hara. Like Miss O'Hara, Belle was "intensely Southern at heart" in her political beliefs. Yet, despite the "homage of all the gay and hot-blooded youths hovering in and about the state capital," her affections were bestowed only upon a young journalist, Capt. Parrish of St. Louis. More surprising, he didn't seek her inclinations as he was engaged to a young lady from Louisiana, Missouri. But her beguiling spell overwhelmed the callow journalist. He became an orthodox suitor of the seductive, well-bred woman causing him to fight a duel with the brother of his jilted fiancée.

---

[86]   Las Vegas Daily Optic, January 9, 1888

[87]   Las Vegas Daily Optic, October 18, 1881

[88]   Bryan refers to the school in his book as the Missouri Female Seminary at Lexington. The Optic calls it as I have in this story. Further still, Bryan also adds that Gov. Jackson was Belle's uncle, p. 125-126

But the eminent rebellion altered the involved lives of all--even lovers. Governor Jackson and General Sterling Price left Jefferson City, Missouri, in early June 1861, for St. Louis and met with Federal officials. They wanted to stop the recruiting of troops in Missouri to fight against the South. They failed. A few days later, Governor Jackson and his Southern sympathizers fled Jefferson City. [89] With Jackson was Capt. Parrish. Before long, word came Capt. Parrish had been one of the first men slaughtered by Yankee forces in Missouri. Alas, Belle was widowed before wedded. She was not one for mourning, however. To the contrary, she became the gayest of the gay as the War for Southern Independence engrossed the country. The officers assigned to the invading Union forces of Gen. Halleck or Curtis quickly enlisted among her devoted admirers. Daily Miss Belle Siddons flirted with their lusty emotions, accompanied them upon daring buggy rides without chaperoning, wantonly danced with them and was often seen nightly in their company at the local De Bar's Opera House. With an alluring charm, this seductive enchantress coaxed revealing priority secrets concerning all the 'damn Yankees' were doing in Missouri. Then, loyal to the noble Cause, she related that most valuable information to the Army of the Confederacy headed by the illustrious General Sterling Price in Missouri.

This continued until December 1862, when it was learned Belle was a spy and an order was issued for her arrest. However, a Union officer, stationed under Union General Curtis, warned her. Belle attempted to escape south by means of the "grapevine railroad," known only to Southerners, but was captured outside St. Geneveive, Missouri. There was no doubt of her guilt, either. Positive evidence was found upon her at the time of her arrest and she was taken back to St. Louis. When brought before Union General Schofield, she admitted her guilt and proclaimed proudly she "informed of every movement made at the Union general headquarters." She further claimed the honor of having assisted Confederate General Gorrest's well-executed raid on the Memphis & Mobile Railroad, cutting off General Grant's supplies at Holly Springs and forcing the drunken Yankee general to take the river enroute to Vicksburg. Belle did everything but spit in the eye of General Schofield as she stood haughtily before the military tribunal.

Belle was sentenced to Gratiot Street prison in St. Louis. A few months later, because of "the influence of her remarkable beauty upon the provost marshal general," Belle was

---

[89]   The Maiden Waved A Snowy Scarf by Bob L'Aloge, p. 9-11; BJS Brand Books, 1993

released and allowed to go South. Nothing further is known until the end of the war. [90] Belle was back in Jefferson City, Missouri, shortly after General Lee surrendered his troops at Appomattox. She became active lobbying during the "corrupt regime of Governor Thomas C. Fletcher and Governor McClurg--the last radical governor of Missouri." Her subtle, persuasive powers and enticing influence upon certain members of the Missouri legislature inspired hundreds of "scandalous stories of carousals, wine suppers and mysterious excursions to St. Louis." [91]

Whether going to Kansas City or whether Doctor Newt Hallet came into her life at another location is not revealed. However, in 1868, Belle met the influential doctor and married him. The newly-weds left Missouri and went to Ft. Brown, Texas. Shortly afterwards, they journeyed to Houston, Texas. While living there, during a yellow fever epidemic in 1869, Hallet died. Belle worked as a tutor at the Red Cloud Indian Agency for a short time. But times were not exciting enough for the femme fatale. [92]

Belle quickly disposed of her married name and took the alias of Madam Vestal. She moved to New Orleans, dealing Monte and Black Jack in a local saloon. As her experience increased, so did her skills and before long she was one of the more popular dealers in town. But Belle possessed an insatiable appetite and the French quarters were unable to satisfy her opulent tastes for titillation. She moved from town to town. She set up gaming tables in such boom-towns as Wichita, Ellsworth, Cheyenne and Denver and Deadwood. Wherever money was to be made, men of the Old West could count on the fact Madam Vestal would show up and make her share and more.

"Thousands who visited such places," wrote the San Francisco editor, "will remember seeing this remarkable woman, attired in velvets, lace and diamonds, presiding over a faro table, or sometimes twirling the roulette wheel in the most popular gambling saloons in those cities. There she would sit, night after night, month after month, pale, stern and impassive. No matter how the game went, whether the bank lost or won, Madam Vestal never changed a muscle of her countenance. She was regarded as infallible by the sporting fraternity with whom she associated." [93]

---

[90]   Las Vegas Daily Optic, Oct. 18, 1881

[91]   Las Vegas Daily Optic, Oct. 18, 1881. See also Bryan's book p. 124-129

[92]   Shady Ladies of the West by Ronald D. Miller, p. 135; Westernlore Press, 1985

[93]   This author was unable to learn exactly what San Francisco newspaper is referred to here. Both Bryan and the Optic refer to the original article appearing first in the S. F. paper.

Yesterdays' prejudices often become todays hatreds that, in turn, create tomorrows wars. Perhaps the loss her beloved South had suffered. Perhaps the lifestyle she lived. Perhaps one might even attribute it to her early childhood, if we but knew more about that childhood. Perhaps it was her increased usage of opium and whiskey when not dealing cards. Quien sabe? But something within Belle changed. She grew colder, hardened in spirit, soul and heart. Belle's aura portrayed her apathy toward the men about her, not caring if they went to hell or not. Further, Belle despised all women. She seldom spoke and never quarreled or exchanged words of anger. Instead, her prompt argument was her six-shooter, which always lay beside her stacks and piles of winnings.

"Many a pistol has been taken from maddened disputants by her white bejeweled fingers, and many a boisterous bully sneaked, cowed and trembling, from her presence while she pointed her deadly revolver toward him and the door. Her will was law and no queen ever ruled her subjects with greater ease, or treated her worshippers with more supreme contempt. Belle laughed scornfully . . . of ruined, disparaging dupes, who nightly left her table only to go forth and kill themselves or rob others. She boasted she had never done a kind act, returned a dollar won, or asked a favor since she became a gambler...My luck was invariable, and I had a superstition that if I allowed the first thought of kindness to enter my soul it would break the spell. I hated every man who came to play against me. They came to break my bank. Why should I spare them! My husband never gave back money or spared either friend or foe in play. Why should I?" [94]

One can but imagine, if they will but close their eyes for a moment, this dark-haired, almond-eyed, ivory-skinned goddess as she sat nightly---sober, silent, her long, slender fingers flicking the cards from one player to another. Shuffling! Dealing! Taunting her victims. Raking in her gold dust and silver dollars. All the while, laughing with a charm making them think they had been the winners. Her favorite costumes were red or black velvet dresses with a low front exposing plenty of breast cleavage and ornamented with a profusion of gaudy jewelry, mostly diamonds and rubies. Her thick, luxuriant black hair hung carelessly looped over her milky shoulders, flaunting gold and diamond hair clasps. Belle's image was a part of her professional livelihood. "It excites curiosity and draws in the suckers," she said. [95]

---

[94]   Las Vegas Daily Optic, Oct. 18, 1881
[95]   Las Vegas Daily Optic, October 18, 1881

"It excites curiosity and draws the suckers,"
Belle was often heard to say.

When the Black Hills gold diggings and the town of Deadwood boomed in 1876, Belle bought a 4-horse omnibus wagon in Denver. She hired workers to overhaul it and turned it into a beautiful boudoir with a bedroom. She enlisted the service of several of her admiring "sporting men" and, with wagons loaded full of tents and gambling furniture, they traveled overland to Deadwood, Dakota Territory. She changed her alias to Lurline Monte Verde. Upon arriving in the wild-west town, her and her cohorts built a gambling establishment under the tent right on the main street. It was here Belle met the one man in her entire life she really loved. He was everything she had ever dreamed about and hoped for, all rolled into one masculine hunk of manhood. The ruffian's qualifications greatly endeared him to her cold, cold heart. He was Archie McLaughlin, alias Archie Cummings. [96] Archie was leader of a band of road agents or stagecoach robbers. But his most endearing quality was that, during the War for Southern Independence, he had ridden with William C. Quantrill. [97]

Though maligned with the butchery of Lawrence, Kansas by Union sympathizers, Quantrill was fondly spoken of by Missourian Cole Younger. "Quantrell," Younger wrote explaining the actions of his guerrilla boss, was simply out to "settle some old scores with the Jayhawkers." [98] These Red Legs, as the Kansas Yankees were called, massacred innocent Missourians simply because of political allegiance to the South. [99] Quantrill was a guerrilla fighter, his militia army riding back and forth between Kansas and Missouri to halt the Yankee robbing and pillaging of poor farmers along the border.

Aided by Archie, Belle quickly learned the member's names, becoming the adviser and confidante to the gang. No robbery was undertaken unless she sanctioned it and all which had her blessings were successful. Every night she'd sit in her gambling hall, listening to the conversations about her. Detectives were purposely lured by capers to learn the activities of the authorities. Belle permitted them to win to keep them interested

---

[96] See Old Deadwood Days by Estelline Bennett; Univ. of Nebraska, 1982. Ms. Bennett, who as a small child grew up in Deadwood during the 1870's, speaks of "the artistic sense of Judge McLaughlin." She doesn't say though whether the two men were related, p. 38, 240.

[97] In his autobiography, Cole Younger, who rode with Quantrell, states his name is Charles William Quantrell instead of as stated here. The Story of Cole Younger by Himself, p. 14; Triton Press, 1988 (reprint)

[98] Younger, p. 15

[99] The Called Him Wild Bill: The Life & Adventures of James Butler Hickok by Joseph G. Rosa, p. 67; Univ. of OK Press, 1974

in her table every night. The end always justifies the means, though a cold-hearted attitude, proved a major asset to Belle.

Disaster struck, however, on July 2, 1878, when armed guards, concealed in a decoy treasure coach between Deadwood and Rapid City, effectively struck back at the gang during a robbery. [100] Gang member Alexander Caswell was killed while Archie and another outlaw were seriously wounded. The lawbreakers fled to their hide-out in Wyoming Territory. Belle heard the tragic word, quickly shut down and journeyed into the nearby woods to give medical aid and comfort. Having done some nursing during the recent war, Belle was most familiar about dressing and caring for wounds. "Her cunning devises," it was reported, "baffled all efforts to discover the hiding place of her beloved stage robber and his companion and by her management they were even taken into Deadwood unseen by the detectives, and there treated successfully for their wounds." [101]

After this, Belle, described as the "Queen of the Desperadoes," met a handsome detective named Boone May. May was a "young and daring chief of detectives on the Sidney, Cheyenne & Black Hills Stageline." When he first met Belle he was little more than a driver. Since he was "cunning, reckless and brave to a degree almost incredible," May soon won Belle's affections with his gentlemanly charm. Perhaps Belle thought him a likely candidate for gang membership. Whatever her reason, however, May soon learned enough about the gang to locate them. He telegraphed the sheriff in Cheyenne. The authorities acted. Archie and the others were arrested boarding the train to Laramie City, on their way to San Francisco, where Belle had agreed to meet them.

The chained outlaws were taken to Cheyenne and on to Deadwood. After crossing the Platte River near Ft. Laramie, over twenty vigilantes approached. Armed with six-shooters and rifles, the community 'watch group' demanded authorities turn over the prisoners to them. They did. They pulled all three out of the wagon. One by one a hemp rope was placed about the necks of the three ruffians. One by one the outlaws were hoisted into the silent summer sky to dangle before their Creator in judgment. One after the other, as the last watched the two before him die, the three stagecoach robbers met death at the hands of vigilante justice--a sure and exact rectitude.

Before they strung Archie up by the neck, he requested a chance to pray and scribble a note to his mother. The vigilantes agreed that in exchange for names of the other

---

100   Bryan's book gives this date. The Optic says it was in 1877.

101   Las Vegas Daily Optic, Oct. 18, 1881

members and their confederate in town, they would grant him the opportunity. But Archie was no squealer. He declined. The vigilantes agreed to spare his life if he would talk and surrender the stolen treasure. Finally, at the last moment, as they readied to slap away his horse and send Archie into eternity, he agreed to reveal the location of the stolen money in exchange for his life. They agreed. He talked. Then, recognizing plea bargaining as the downfall of justice, the vigilantes hanged him until he was dead! An attached letter warned passer-bys to let the bodies swing. The date: November 2, 1878. This place: Cottonwood Creek on the Black Hills & Laramie Stagecoach road. [102]

One vigilante volunteered, for a portion of the hidden loot, to tell Belle the gory facts about the Cottonwood Creek lynching. She listened intently. When he finished, Belle contacted the local newspaper, gave a reporter her obituary, drank an undisclosed quantity of poison and lay down to die. Fortunately, some would say, Belle did not succumb to the poison. The "large dose of morphine" consumed failed her. Believing the lynchings the results by Boone May's activities, Belle let it be known she would kill Boone if, and when, she saw him again. The threat was never carried out. [103] She made other threats about the community, too. One involved the reporter who'd taken her obituary. She stated that "if he published the details of her confession she would make her men put his lights out." Apparently the confession was never published. From here, Belle moved to Cheyenne and on to Leadville, Colorado, in the fall of 1879. [104] She made herself quite prominent as the proprietress of the largest music hall and dance house on State Street. [105]

---

102   Miller, in his book, says the date was November 3, 1878.

103   After leaving Deadwood, May journeyed to Bolivia in South America--sometime after 1881. He wrote back to some friends of his in Deadwood that he "had aquired valuable mining interests there and was doing well." His next letter, however, talked about trouble in Bolivia "with a Brazilian officer over a dark-eyed South American beauty." Boone had shot the man and fled to Rio de Janeiro. His next, and last letter, told about the fact that "the yellow fever was bad in Rio." Apparently, he must have caught it and died for "no one ever heard from him again." Old Deadwood Days by Estelline Bennett, p. 88

104   There is an obvious error here in the dates. Belle had to be here sometime earlier as she arrived in Las Vegas, New Mexico in September of 1879.

105   Bennett speaks about a "Belle Haskell...the best known Madame in town" in her book about Deadwood. This may or may not be the same Belle. Not much is said about the "madame" which might be explained by the fact that Bennett was but a small child when Belle Siddons was in Deadwood during the late 1870's. Belle Haskell's house was called "the Four Hundred" and later burned to the ground, p. 276.

The "largest and best of the gambling halls, however, was Jeff Winney's California Concert Hall. Miners looking to take a chance could try their luck against the agreeable form of Kitty Crawhurst, lady gambler, who has become a professional woman to spare herself a worse fate." Perhaps this was merely another alias for Belle Siddons. [106] "Every night, Saturday and Sunday nights especially, pandemonium reigns almost from dark to dawn along State Street, a tumultuous half mile brightly lighted by the great kerosene flares blazing before dance houses, variety theaters, gambling hells, saloons, beer halls and brothels. As it descends from Pop Wyman's Great Saloon at the corner of Harrison, the street grows steadily more disreputable until it ends among the pines on the sand flat in two dark lines of 'cribs,' notorious Coon Row and still more notorious French Row, a dangerous neighborhood into which many men stray innocently to be seen no more."

Nothing satisfied her any longer. She turned to heavier drinking and habitual use of opium. Daily she declined as alcohol and drug's disease devoured her beauty. Finally, in despair, Belle moved to Las Vegas, New Mexico in September 1879, and assumed another alias--calling herself Monte Verde. The local press, however, referred to her as Monte Holman because of her association with Gene Holman, "her solid man." Belle utilized her talents at the Toe Jam Saloon on Center Street dealing faro and leading a life of dissipation.

Dora, the tattooed lady was a featured attraction in Las Vegas, New Mexico in Oct. 1888

---

106   The Gold Rush: The Search for Treasure in the American West by George F. Willison, p. 211-212, 218; Indian Head Books, 1992

In no time at all the 42-year old was a leading lady of variety, appearing live, performing banjo solos at the Globe Theater. [107] Later that winter, Belle visited El Paso for a few weeks. From there she journeyed to Tombstone and on to Tucson. She returned in early March 1880, and opened her own place on Sixth Street, calling it The Palace. The business was "a palace of pleasure," which meant a saloon/whore house. Belle's continued diversion of acting on stage at the local theater and her 'heavy girl' routine in a Railroad Avenue vaudeville act, was outstanding. She pleased audiences immensely and soon convinced a local male citizen to build the Center Street Theater. Unfortunately, it was among the businesses badly destroyed in the fire of September 1880.

While in Las Vegas, Belle was widely accepted and loved by many. Among these were the *Las Vegas Daily Optic* reporters with who she 'courted' favors. She wrote "several effusions of poetry to the *Optic*." Belle was still restless, however. In late September or early October 1880, she packed and returned to Colorado, never again to see New Mexico. Belle then moved to California--eventually winding up in San Francisco. During a police raid on a Chinese opium den on Grant Avenue, Belle, giving her name as Lurline Monte Verde, was arrested in October 1881. [108]

"There is a woman sitting there in that cell whose history is a very remarkable one," said the turnkey of the San Francisco city prison in October 1881. "But she has such an utter detestation for officers and newspaper men that I doubt whether you could get her to talk to you. She is too drunk now, and when she is sober, she won't talk."

The San Francisco reporter observed Belle, sitting with head bowed upon a rough wooden bench, in the corner of the barbaric female drunk tank. The reporter said she was "a complete picture of abject misery and despair." Her hat and shawl were torn in the struggle to arrest her. Her dress was dirty. Her long, black hair covered her face. [109] She stood and approached the bars. Her voice was course, hoarse and profane. Belle demanded a drink of water. She agreed to grant an interview the following day. It was published in the San Francisco newspaper and on October 18, 1881, reprinted in the Las Vegas *Daily Optic*. The reporter summed up his story best by saying "she might have chosen her place in the highest walks of life." No doubt the circumstances, the times, the

---

[107] Bryan, p. 124

[108] Notorious Ladies of the Frontier by Harry Sinclair Drago, p. 150; Dodd, Mead & Company, 1969

[109] Las Vegas Daily Optic, Oct. 18, 1881

addictions and the despair she felt when Archie McLaughlin was lynched played an important role in bringing her to her wretched end. So what became of Belle?

"Perhaps she died in a San Francisco jail, dreaming of her romantic past or of her tragic love-life...this is the last record of Belle." [110] Another report states "a police department doctor found her in the last stages of cancer [and] she was removed to the police ward of the general hospital, where she died, the minor charge of inhabiting a proscribed opium den having been dropped." [111]

But what about those "effusions of poetry" she wrote for the *Daily Optic*?

A thorough search of all the copies from the time she arrived in Las Vegas in late 1879 to the 1881 biographical article revealed no published poetry by anyone using the names she often employed. However, there were dozens, if not hundreds, of poems published which bore no credit to anyone. It was noticed the only poems with by-lines (names of the author) were those written by men. So, perhaps, one of those uncredited poems could have been written by Belle Siddons. The following two poems, I believe, may have come from the pen of Belle Siddons:

Stone the Woman

Yes, stone the woman, let the man go free
Draw back your skirts lest they perchance
May touch her garments as she passes
But to him put forth a willing hand
To clasp with his that ledger to destruction
And disgrace. Shut up from her the sacred
Ways of toil that she no more may win an
Honest meal, but open to him all honorable
Paths, where he may win distinction
Give him fair, pressed down measures of
Lifes sweetest love. Pass her, O, maiden
With a pure, proud face, if she puts out
A poor, polluted palm, but lay thy hand in

---

110   Miller, p. 136
111   Drago, p. 150

His on bridal day, and swear to cling to him
With wifely love and tender reverence
Trust him who led a sister woman
To a fearful fate.
Yes, stone the woman, let the man go free
Let one soul enter for they are of two
Is the doctrine of a married world
Two out of breath for nothing balances
Where nice distinctions and injustices
Are calmly weighted. But how will it be
On that strange day of trial (here and home) [112]
When men shall stand before the one true
Judge? Shall sex then make a difference to
Sin? Shall he, the measurer of the hidden
Heart, in his eternal and divine decree
Condemn the woman and forgive the man? [113]

Somebody's Mother

The woman was old, and ragged and gray,
And bent with the chill of a Winter's day;
The streets were white with a recent snow,
And the woman's feet with age were slow.
At the crowded crossing she waited long,
Justled aside by the careless throng
Of human beings who passed her by
Unheeding the glance of her anxious eye.
Down the street with laughter and shout
Glad in the freedom of 'school let out.'

---

[112] These three words are extremely weak in the original and I'm not certain they are correct

[113] Las Vegas Daily Optic, June 25, 1881

Come happy boys like a flock of sheep,
Hailing the snow piled white and deep,
Past the woman, so old and gray,
Hastened the children on their way.
None offered a helping hand to her,
So weak and timid, afraid to stir,
Lest the carriage wheels or horse's feet
Should trample her down in the slippery street.
At last, came out of the merry troop
The gayest boy of all the groups
He paused beside her, and whispered low
"I'll help you across if you wish to go!"
Her aged hand on his strong, young arm
She placed, and so, without hurt or harm,
He guided the trampling feet along,
Proud that his own were firm and strong;
Then back again to his friends he went,
His young heart happy and well content.
"She's somebody's mother, boys, you know
For all she's aged and poor and slow;
And someone some time may lend a hand
To help my mother--you understand
If ever she's poor and old and gray,
And her own dear boy is far away."
"Somebody's Mother" bowed low her head
In her home that night, and the prayer she said
Was-- "God be kind to that noble boy,
Who is somebody's son and pride and joy."
Faint was the voice, and worn and weak,

But heaven lists when its chosen speaks

Angels caught the faltering word

"Somebody's Mother's" prayer was heard. [114]

Kohl & Middleton's

PALACE MUSEUM

Week Beginning Monday, Jan. 20.

CALAMITY JANE !

The Famous Woman Scout of the Wild West! Heroine of a Thousand Thrilling Adventures! The Terror of Evildoers in the Black Hills! The Comrade of Buffalo Bill and Wild Bill! See this Famous Woman and Hear Her Graphic Description of Her Daring Exploits!

A HOST OF OTHER ATTRACTIONS

Two Big Stage Shows!

that's all | ONE DIME! | **that's all**

Martha 'Calamity' Jane Cannary was born in Princeton, Missouri on May 1, 1852. She was one of the many women able to do just about anything a man could do and, occasionally, better.

This ad appeared in the Minneapolis Journal on January 20, 1896. The drawing of Calamity Jane is made from a photo by H. R. Locke.

---

114   Las Vegas Daily Optic, August 17, 1881

Belle Siddons:
Social Profile on Chapter Four
by
Virginia C. Nelson-L'Aloge, M. A.

What caused a woman of the 1860's to turn outlaw? The questions answer is the same as for a man who is outlaw--rebellion and frustration for how things are or are perceived by him or her.

Many women of the South used the only weapons they had available to aid their beloved cause and way of life--themselves. They were taught the arts of coquettishness, coyness and flattery with men. They received hours of instruction in the effective use of the fan, walking and sitting gracefully, grooming, household management, the art of dining rather than just eating. The love of life's way in the South for Southern gentleman and lady was deep as was the fierce pride that kept them fighting long after the War for Southern Independence was lost.

The downfall of the South left many totally bereft, in a grief so deep all softness or love was encased in a bitter wall of resentment and seething anger, contempt so thick nothing could penetrate it. They could not and would not stay in their beloved South as it was devoured by the jackals who spat on its very soul. They went West, shells of living beings needing excitement to bury the pain, seeking ways to be better, to be superior to all other human beings. These people are no different from many today who, experiencing injustices all around them, build impenetrable walls around themselves.

Today we see our former way of life insidiously disappearing as freedoms and liberties are gradually being usurped and changed/destroyed by a government thinking itself too big to be challenged. We face the same cry and challenge for States rights today that was faced in the 1840's, 1850's and 1860's. The federal government threatens not only the rights of the State but each and every man, woman and child within this beloved country. We were to be *united* states, states each with their right to govern itself as its people choose for that state. We find ourselves now being told more and more by federal government how to live, worship, speak and be, taxed far beyond the point we broke from England for. The War for Southern Independence was an issue of States rights to rule themselves. Slavery was on its way out and would have gone naturally as mechanized industry took over.

The people of that former time often did the same things to escape emotional pain of loosing the only person they loved, they turned to alcohol and drugs to obliterate, for a time, reality that seemingly hurts too much to not stupefy the nagging thoughts and feelings of loss. The difference between then and now is that all but alcohol is illegal. Again we see Big Government making laws that increase crime. The people who are going to use drugs are going to use drugs. All that forced restriction does is put in underground smuggling and create crime rings. The Mafia got its hold because of and during Prohibition while generally law-abiding, hardworking citizens became outlaws by making 'bathtub gin,' 'cellar wine,' 'barrel beer,' etc. This author remembers her own father talking about this and speakeasy's. Many who would not have imbibed in alcohol use did because of the excitement involved in being "outlaw" and rebellious. The programs that involve self-knowledge and knowledge of alternatives do far more to eliminate the need of alcohol's use and other drugs than laws that make them illegal.

What would occur that a young Southern lady, educated, beautiful, charmingly cultured would eventually be named the Queen of the Desperadoes?

Although her first love was killed early on in the War for Southern Independence, Belle Siddons was undaunted and became a spy against the Union using the weapons she was so well trained for by Southern tradition.

Still undaunted she endured months in prison for her 'crime' and when released went home. She, at the end of the war, continued attempting to influence politics to aid her beloved South. The only option for a true 'lady of the South' was marriage and Belle took that option. But like so many people who live in war time, ordinary life is just not exciting enough and excitement can be an addiction.

Alone, at her husband's death, needing to earn money, she turned to gambling but in doing so gave up her former identity. At that point she died to her former life and closed off emotionally. Her way of life was gone in the South. Where was she to go or what was she to do? Her options were slim. She became a shell of her former self.

When emotional pain becomes deep one option is to become numb, to lock away in a place no one can get to--even ourselves. We then go through day to day as if a character in a play. This is what Belle did. Often to totally annihilate thought people also turn to drugs of all sorts. She could not afford any of her former self to surface or she would crack, like a struck alabaster statute. She had no support system either personal or in society. So when a man of Archie McLaughlin's strength appeared in her life she found her equal. Both had fought for their beloved South, both were rebels to rules imposed upon them. She could afford to love this man. She could again have the excitement of 'spying.' Her pain at Archie McLaughlin's death was so deep life entirely became worthless. She then rode the horse of self-destruction.

Belle did not have the aid of therapy groups, psychiatric hospitals, or drug programs. Society had taught her and she believed her value as a woman came from the man who loved her and whom she served. Without Archie she was empty, so she believed.

Today we know, or have the opportunity to know, our *worth* as a woman as a human being with or without a man in our lives. Belle did not know or believe this. When the opportunity for really living rather than existing presented itself in Las Vegas, New Mexico, she was so broken she was unwilling to accept it. The risk was too high. She continued her ride of self-destruction until she was relieved of living. Her life ended in tragedy a true victim of her time and belief system.

The true solution in society is found, not in outer control by government or Big Brother/Sister watching, but self-control and belief in the Self. It is in honoring and respecting each of us has the right to be different, to believe differently, and one's belief cannot nor must not infringe on the right of another that true democracy reigns. We are as individuals becoming more aware of this truth but our governments have not grown to this knowledge and still impose control and believe they know what is best for us. We must speak out for our individual rights before it is too late. We must be heard.

Women are accepting their worth as partners in this world. Men accept they are feeling human beings, in this we have made progress. However, individual freedom is currently threatened as never before. The people of Belle Siddons time did not have the advantage of therapy, chemical dependency programs or self-knowledge groups. So she did what she thought she had to do to survive. That's all any of us can do.

Fanny Wiggins Kelly:
Social Profile on Chapter Five
by
Virginia C. Nelson-L'Aloge, M. A.

During the time of 1850 to 1900, there were marriages where men asked their women if they wanted to move West. More often they simply told them they were moving. Some were given reasons. Some were not. Those women who chose to go often came from sheltered environments so they had no idea what they were getting into.

We need to understand the time, the threat of civil war, and then the actuality of war upon their very door steps. Following the War for Southern Independence there was a vast amount of renovation and forced changed. Many lost homes as well as all their possessions during the war and after. Fortunes were lost and made. Industry was birthing and putting people out of work. Folks would work all day for pittance. Many lived or existed in squalor. The American dream soared with the finding of gold prior to the war. Dreams of owning a farm or ranch were realized. Rather than trudging in monotony the chance to be free economically beckoned. The prospect of being rich dangled as the 'golden carrot' before men and women. This 'golden carrot' was the West.

For the women who didn't want to go the hardships on the trail seemed insurmountable. The tough ones with steel in their spines met obstacles with tenacity. The first challenge was how and what to pack. They had to have what was needed for all seasons for each person traveling with them. All household necessities had to go along. There were no convenience or discount department stores down the street. What would you pack if you had to live off the supplies for five or six months? What necessities of living would you include if all the room you had was the size of a van? How would you feel about leaving all your possessions you hold so dear? What is more important, how would you feel saying 'good-bye' to friends and family knowing you, very well, would not see them again? Such was the case of the female pioneer. Then what would you do if your spouse died along the way? Many a lonely grave marked the way West.

The land was rough. There were no expressways to ease the way. My husband and I have often looked at the unoccupied land of today, wherever we are, and say, "Can you imagine taking a covered wagon over that?" The answer is always no. Drinking water was a huge problem. Most were green-horns who knew only that water came from nicely dug wells. The shock when reality hit was great. The guides or wagon master had to be tough so the trip was often grueling. Many believed as they started out that it was an extended picnic they were going on.

Fanny Wiggins Kelly had the normal enthusiasm of a young woman for adventure. She was excited about the trip. She had homesteaded as a child so felt confident as they set out. She was apparently a hardy soul and had little difficulty adapting to such meager ways of living. She still noticed the true joys in life in the flowers and beauty around her.

The Indians were increasingly feeling threatened and rightly so because they knew that the balance of land was in grave danger. Their way of life was being wiped out and naturally they felt the need to stop the invasion. If we look at the events from both sides we see each had "rights." The wagon train merely wanted to pass through. They had no intention of stopping there. They were peaceful people unaccustomed to the Indian way of life and worship. The travelers were treated without mercy. After they offered overtures of friendship they received none. But the same had previously happened to the Indian at the hands of the Anglos.

Fanny maintained a cool head and showed great courage. This saved her life as well as that of the other woman and little girl, at least for a time. Her escape plan was a good one and it almost worked. Had she been hysterical it would have meant instant death. Someone who torments a physically weaker person often will not harm them if they show emotional courage. The captors admired Fanny's courage. Her fear, stated in her own words, was too powerful to allow her to "give way to emotion." This was her lifesaver. Even under these circumstances she noticed the beauty of life continuing all around her. Most would have been so centered on self they would not have even noticed. But in situations like Fanny's, focusing outside one's self will help in enduring the hardship. If beauty is recognized, be it a full-blooming flower, a field or meadow, a nurturing mother bird, a fluttering butterfly, and so forth, it relieves the stress and there is hope. This makes clear thinking more possible.

Because of Fanny's courage she was taken as mistress by the chief and was most likely unaware it was an honor to be selected by the chief. Yet, the honor is shallow when one is held against their will. Many white captives witnessed unspeakable horrors and death often appeared to be the only escape from the nightmare. They were in shock like a plant uprooted with its tender roots dangling in the cold wind! The name 'real woman' reveals the fact Fanny was admired. Her courage and adaptability were rewarded when Sitting Bull offered her release because she silently, uncomplainingly, was unhappy. He even provided an escort to insure her safety! This remarkable woman had the admiration of both Anglos and Indians alike. We can only imagine the astonishment of the soldiers when nearly a thousand warriors so honored her. The Indians rarely did that!

Gone now were the thoughts of adventure and the gold fields. She now craved the healing solace of the kind of love she could understand. We often must retreat to allow the emotional wounds to heal. It is to Josiah's credit that he accepted Fanny back after her being the mistress of an Indian. Many men and whole communities did not. They turned wives, former sweethearts, out because they were considered *soiled.* Many were condemned. Many a White woman, joyful at her return to *civilization* and her own kind, found they had been better treated by the tribe or Indian of which they were captives! Some of these women were forced into lives of prostitution because they felt low and degraded, outcasts among their own kind. Some even dared return to the tribe of which they were formerly the prisoner. Others committed suicide.

Fanny proceeded in courage after her beloved Josiah's death by taking in laundry. She was rewarded finally with a new love and lifestyle worthy of her. She received recognition of her hardships and how courageously she withstood them. Fanny Kelly is a heroine! She showed courage and faith rising above adversity during experiences we can only wonder about. Fanny is an example of positive perseverance for both men and women alike! Her story has been and is being repeated in the lives of women of all nationalities and ethnic groups from her time until now. We salute them!

THE WINTER WHEN
THE WHITE WOMAN WAS RESCUED

Life was such between the years of 1850-1900 that when the husband said 'we're going to move, get packed'--the wife usually started packing. Many a man chose to move his family for one reason or another. Such excuse as gold, silver, plagues, famine, boom-times, etc., was reason enough for a man to pack his family off to another part of the frontier, facing dangers they'd never faced before. So the women would go. Fortunately, most lived through it. Some didn't.

Perhaps the most haunting story of a woman who didn't is found in this account. Colonel James F. Meline, traveling along the Platte route in 1866, noticed in the distance a grave marker. There amid the gloomy shadows, some distance off the road upon a solitary hillside, he approached the grave. There was no doubting the origin of the marker had been torn from the portion an unneeded wagon. "The inscription was more remarkable than any I ever saw," he wrote. It was, in his words, "touching and beautiful in its simplicity." There was merely one word upon the tombstone: WOMAN [115]

Sometimes women refused to go with their husbands.

"Sometimes women grew desperate on the trail," wrote Nancy Wilson Ross. Often the women "set fire to their wagons, struck their children, threatened to kill themselves rather than endure another hour of heat, flies, dirt, dust, weariness, lack of water, lost cattle, sick babies and a receding horizon." [116] Ms. Ross doesn't footnote so we have no

---

[115]   Two Thousand Miles On Horseback by James F. Meline, p. 34; New York, 1867. See also: The Gentle Tamers by Dee Brown, p. 17; Univ. of Nebraska, 1958
[116]   Westward the Women by Nancy Wilson Ross, p. 7; Alfred A. Knopf, 1944

way of knowing to whom she was referring, but, one woman decided not to go. Ms. Ross quotes the woman's journal entry dated September 15th. No year is given.

"Laid by. This morning our company moves on," the pioneer wrote, "except for one family. The woman got mad and wouldn't budge or let the children go. He had the cattle hitched on for three hours and coaxed her to go, but she wouldn't stir. I told my husband the circumstances and he and Adam Polk and Mr. Kimball went and each one took a young one and crammed them in the wagon and the husband drove off and left her sitting. She got up, took the back track and traveled out of sight. Cut across and overtook her husband. Meanwhile, he sent his boy back to camp, after a horse he left, and when she came up her husband said, 'Did you meet John?' 'Yes,' was the reply, 'and I picked up a stone and knocked out his brains.' Her husband went back to ascertain the truth, and while he was gone she set fire to one of the wagons that was loaded with store goods. The cover burnt off with some valuable articles. He saw the flames and came running and put it out, and then mustered up spunk enough to give her a good flogging." [117]

Perhaps such instances were not that rare for "whatever her dress, she had endurance, she had courage, sometimes she was wilder than the land she tamed," wrote Dee Brown. Such women had to be tough. And, so often neglected in her portrayal, "the pioneer western female was certainly a woman of tenacity and quiet force." [118] Sometimes women persuaded husbands or lovers--not realizing they'd undergo unforgettable experiences. Often it was by mutual agreement they moved. But again, no one really knows what's in store at some future date. Eighteen-year-old Fanny Wiggins Kelly had no expectation she was to undergo such circumstances when she and her husband rolled out of Geneva, Kansas on May 17, 1864. [119] Rather, Fanny was filled "with high-wrought hopes and pleasant anticipation's of a romantic and delightful journey across the plains, and a confident expectation of future prosperity among the golden hills of Idaho." [120]

Fanny, born in 1845 at Orillia, Ontario Canada, was one of three children to New York native James Wiggins. [121] In 1856, her father joined a New York colony bound for Kansas. He settled in the area of Geneva, Allen County. After completing the necessi-

---

[117]   Ross, p. 7

[118]   Brown, p. 12, 17

[119]   Real Woman: The Fanny Kelly Story by Larry Underwood; Old West, Summer 1987

[120]   Narrative of My Captivity Among the Sioux Indians by Fanny Kelly, p. 12-13; Gassette & Loyd, 1880

[121]   Kelly, p. 11

ties, he returned to Canada to bring his family to their new home. The Wiggins family packed their belongings and set out for the flat Kansas prairies. James got as far as the Missouri River before contracting cholera and dying. Such was not uncommon. As a matter of fact, it was probably the second greatest fear of early day pioneers--Indian attacks being the first. "The first serious cholera epidemic in the West...was in 1849." The disease followed the emigrants like a faithful dog from the Atlantic seaboard up the Mississippi River. When ready to leave St. Joseph and Independence, the disease struck hard and pursued them clear to Ft. Laramie. An estimated 5,000 people died that year "before they knew what affected them." [122]

Fanny's mother, in obedience to her father's dying instructions, continued the family journey. "But, oh! with what saddened hearts we entered into its possession. It seemed as if the light of our life had gone out. He who had been before to prepare that home for us, was not there to share it with us, and, far away from all early associations, almost alone in a new and sparsely settled country, it seemed as though hope had died." [123] No doubt Fanny, being old enough, walked most of the way or maybe all. Such things were not infrequent when families moved across the frontier. One example follows:

"My own mother was thirteen and a half years old when she started across the plains with her parents in April 1847," writes Ms. Ross about another pioneer child. "She walked practically all the way from the Missouri River to the Willamette Valley [in western Oregon]. She was the oldest of six children, and as there were some loose horses and cattle every day that would not follow the trail unless made to do so, she was required to trail behind them and see that none was lost. To be sure, the distance made would average more than ten or twelve miles a day, but it necessitated walking in the dust caused by hundreds of tramping oxen and horses, besides the duty of keeping the stubborn or contrary or indifferent animals from lagging behind. And her duties were not deemed particularly hard when compared with those assigned to every other member of the train who was old enough to stand alone." [124]

---

[122]   Brown, p. 36

[123]   Kelly, p. 12

[124]   Ross, p. 7-8. Ms. Ross is not speaking about her own mother but the mother of an unnamed pioneer whom she quotes.

Fanny Kelly

Fanny was no different. Arriving in Kansas, they moved into their new home around Geneva, Allen County, situated in the extreme southeastern corner of Kansas near the Missouri border. The town of Geneva is about forty-five miles north of Chanute, Kansas. The area was already a hot bed in terror and turmoil when the War for Southern Independence officially broke out in 1861. Guerrilla warfare, mounted upon horses snorting fire and brimstone, road the countryside. Such avengers as Quantrill [125] and 'Bloody Bill' Anderson burned their brands across the settling plains by giving stripe for stripe, fist for fist and blood for blood. Theirs was a war of vindication against those Yankees in Kansas who had ridden into Missouri--looting, pillaging, raping, burning, maiming and murdering. Such items made the Kansas plains practically intolerable.

One woman, originally from Boston, spoke about other hardships. Her cabin of 'shakes' near Lawrence, Kansas, had newspapers plastered over the walls to protect her and her family from the fierce western winds, "which shook the frail edifice til it seemed about to fall." She was appalled by "the prevalent typhoid, malaria and digestive ills; by the rough fare of bread, milk, and small game. The want of good wells, the crowding of invalids in rooms half-freezing, half-roasting and the abundance of vermin." At night she listened to the terrible noises of the prairie. "Far off across the river," she wrote of her ordeal, "in my wakefulness, I hear the whoop of the Indian, or the echo of a rifle; or quite as often, the sound of hungry and quarreling wolves." [126]

In November 1863, young Josiah, a Union war veteran, was troubled. [127] Due to failing health, he resolved upon a change of climate. They packed their belongings and prepared to head for Idaho. Such a task as preparing to travel in those days was quite an undertaking. The man and woman had "to outfit a wagon with supplies that must last the average of five months required for a westward crossing." [128] Good-byes were said. Kisses were given and hugs received. Parting tears flowed down faces and dropped onto Kansas soil. Well wishes were freely distributed and the happy group departed on May 17, 1864. Accompanying them on that fateful pilgrimage were 5-year old Mary, the daughter of Fanny's sister; a long time friend, Gardner Wakefield; and two of Fanny's black slaves, Franklin and Andy. None were aware of what was ahead within their separate, and yet combined, futures.

---

[125] The Story of Cole Younger by Himself; Triton Press, 1988. Younger claims the last name was spelled Quantrell. As of this moment in my research, I've not located any other spelling for the base, stalwart guerrilla fighter.

[126] Ordeal of the Union: A House Dividing 1852-1857 by Allan Nevins, p. 383; Charles Scribners' Sons, 1947. See also: Six Months in Kansas by A Lady (H. A. R; 1856) p. 99.

[127] Surprisingly, in this author's opinion, Fanny failed to mentioned the date of her marriage to Josiah. Since most women put so much stock in this point, I thought it worth mention, p. 12

[128] Brown, p. 15

A few days outside Geneva, the travelers were met by Reverend Sharp, a Methodist minister. A few more days and the wagon train caught up with William J. Larimer, wife Sarah and their 8-year old son. The Larimer's were also from Allen County. Mr. Taylor joined up with the group about this time. That made eleven people and five wagons in the bantam wagon train. Mile after unsure mile the rickety-wagons bumped along. The hot burning days and the cool refreshing nights settled lazily upon the vast prairie expansion. The wagons tumbled deeper and deeper into the West. Beyond prairies, removed plains, roundabout hills and amid valleys. Rolling on and on like autumn clouds that aren't ever going to disappear. Young Josiah Kelly scouted and rode ahead each day to locate another camping sight. Franklin and Andy, the two black slaves, would set up the camp and break it down the following morning.

"The hours of noon and evening rest were spent in preparing our frugal meals, gathering flowers with our children, picking berries, hunting curiosities, or gazing in rapt wonder and admiration at the beauties of this strange, bewildering country. Our amusements were varied. Singing, reading, writing to friends at home, or pleasant conversation, occupied our leisure hours. So passed the first few happy days of our emigration to the land of sunshine and flowers." [129] Fanny remarked how the lovely yellow, purple, white and blue flowers made "the earth look like a rich carpet of variegated colors." Also, she witnessed the illuminating storms as "a gleam of lightning, like a forked tongue of flame, shot out of all the black clouds, blinding us." [130] "Cooking among emigrants to the far West is a very primitive operation," she wrote about preparing meals. "A frying-pan and perhaps a Dutch oven comprised the major part of the kitchen furniture. The scarcity of timber is a source of great inconvenience and discomfort, 'buffalo chips' being the substitute. At some of the stations, where opportunity offered, Mr. Kelly bought wood by the pound, as I had not yet been long enough inured to the plains privations to relish food cooked over a fire made with 'chips' of that kind." [131]

Four days were spent crossing the Platte River. From time to time, the travelers spotted Indians. All appeared friendly. No problem was too big to handle and they soon reached Ft. Laramie, Wyoming. Things at Laramie were not the same. These young people heralded to the Indian that "buffalo and other game and food supplies diminished.

---

[129]   Kelly, p. 13
[130]   Underwood, p.
[131]   Kelly, p. 16

The timber that served as firewood and the grass that furnished forage grew scarce along the White man's roads and vanished altogether around the White man's settlements." [132] Laramie offered something else to the early day traveler. Angling off to the Northwest, "along the eastern base of the Bighorn Mountains to Bozeman and Virginia City," wagon trains had the advantage of being on the "shortest route to the Montana gold fields." [133]

How did local authorities in Ft. Laramie feel about Indians? Just two years later, in 1866, feelings were portrayed as the area around Ft. Laramie was the edge of the zone hostilities, even though General Sherman had not yet recognized the full magnitude of the [Indian] war. The Teton Sioux Indians had no aim of withdrawing from the Bozeman trail to Montana and no intention of allowing the White traveler to use it. Nevertheless, in 1864, authorities assured the miniature wagon train all was well ahead and they should have no problems with Indians. So, after a short rest and resupplying the necessities, Fanny and the others were on the road again and underway.

Regarding the Sabbath, Fanny wrote, "the Eye that never sleeps watched over us in our lonely camp, and cared for the slumbering travelers...Every recurring Sabbath was gratefully hailed as a season of thought and repose; as a matter of conscience and duty we observed the day, and took pleasure in doing so. We had divine service performed, observing the ceremonies of prayer, preaching, and singing, which was fully appreciated in our absence from home and its religious privileges." [134]

Eighty miles west in the valley of the Little Box Elder, situated in the foothills of the Laramie Range in Wyoming, on Tuesday, July 12, 1864, destiny's hand slapped them across the face. It was "a warm and oppressive day. The burning sun poured forth its hottest rays upon the great Black Hills and the vast plains of Montana...We looked anxiously forward to the approach of evening, with a sense of relief, after the excessive heat of the day." [135] That inevitability consisted of about 250 Indians "painted and equipped for war." Command was given to circle the wagons and hold your fire. Fanny drew attention to the fact they were outnumbered nearly ten to one and if any one should fire his weapon it would certainly diagnose their fate. The Indians, she concluded, would

---

132   Frontier Regulars by Robert M. Utley, p. 2; Indiana Univ. Press, 1973
133   Utley, p. 95-98
134   Kelly, p. 14, 18
135   Kelly, p. 19

"at once massacre all of us." [136] Casually the Indians, led by Ogalalla Sioux chief, Ottawa, rode from atop the bluff towards the wagon train. Tension mounted within every White person's chest as fear and doubt took command. What would these Indians do? Were they friendly? Or were they out to destroy every White person they came upon? Josiah agreed to meet them as they had not offered to attack.

"Good Indian, me," Ottawa said. He lifted his hand and pointed to the others with him. "Heap good Indian, hunt buffalo and deer." Both men shook hands. Several braves admired Josiah's horse and wanted to trade.

"No," he told them. Eventually, however, "very much against his will, [Josiah] acceded to their request, and gave up to them the noble animal to which he was fondly attached." [137] He volunteered to give the Indians flour. They took it, opened the bag and dumped the flour in the dirt, wanting only the bag. Ottawa held his ground. Fanny noticed the Indian was "painted and equipped for war." She yelled to Josiah: "If you fire one shot, I feel sure you will seal our fate, as they seem to outnumber us ten to one, and will at once massacre all of us." [138] The Indians begged for clothing. One gave Fanny "a pair of beaded moccasins." His behavior grew "bolder and more insolent." One Indian combatant yanked at Kelly's weapon but the White man refused to surrender his gun. Ottawa approached Kelly informing him "they would not be bothered; they could go." This brought a dramatic lull and within the hour, the wagons were once more underway. But Kelly could not quench the apprehension. He feared ambush!

As they rolled "toward a rocky glen, the Sioux still in sight...Kelly ordered the five wagons halted." Each watched the majority of Indians proceed on their way. However, several warriors remained behind with the halted wagons. The two Black slaves were ordered to prepare food for those Indians who remained. William Larimer assisted Franklin with the fire building. Josiah and Andy went to collect fire wood. Gardner Wakefield started taking food out of the wagon. Only Reverend Sharp, busy handing out sugar to each of the tribesmen, was interested in visiting with the Indians. Then, with no warning, the Indians mood shifted. No survivor would remember the precise manner the events happened. But they happened and this much was certain. A leaden bullet tore into Taylor's head--splattering brain tissue in every direction. Someone killed Reverend

---

[136]   Underwood, p. 22
[137]   Kelly, p. 22-23
[138]   Underwood, p. 22

Sharp and he fell to the ground. Franklin, like a dark, lumbering porcupine, arrows piercing his dead body in thumping melon-like sounds, fell near the fire he'd been building. Gardner Wakefield, long-time friend of Fanny, was mortally wounded.

"Suddenly our terrible enemies threw off their masks and displayed their truly demonic natures...I recall the scene with a sickening horror. I could not see my husband anywhere, and did not know his fate, but feared and trembled...my senses seemed gone for a time, but I could only live and endure...what horrible sights met my view! Pen is powerless to portray the scenes occurring around me," Fanny wrote concerning her feelings during those few eternally suspended moments of time. [139] Several feral Sioux seized the wagons. Four calloused hands grabbed Fanny. She screamed. She fought. But their superior masculine arms enabled them to hold the struggling White woman, forcibly pulling her from the wagon and into the dirt. She clung to Mary.

"Mercy!" She begged them.

Warriors went on destroying wagons. Ripping canvas mingled among the screams and yells of conquest as the Indians celebrated. Rupturing. Severing. Wrenching. On

---

[139]   Kelly, p. 25-26

and on they destroyed. Ottawa placed his hand upon the six-shooter he'd recently picked up and shoved it "into his belt and signed for her to be quiet." Fanny lifted her eyes and, in the distance, spotted a wagon approaching. The Sioux saw it, also. Many quickly mounted and "charged off in a cloud of dust," killing the man in the wagon.

"The men have all escaped," Mrs. Larimer cried out, aware of the men's actions, "and left us here to the mercy of the savages."

"They would be killed and then all hope of rescue of us would be at an end," Fanny reprimanded Mrs. Larimer.

One Indian located Mrs. Larimer's camera and supplies and threw them upon the ground. She screamed. Fanny forbade her to resist. Several warriors terrorized the women. Ottawa planted a "feathered wreath" upon Fanny's head and walked away. The long, blistering July summer day was closing upon their lives. Would it be their last? Would the sun ever rise again from behind the shadowy, curtain-like eastern ridges? Only God knew, Fanny silently assured herself. Except for the guards, Fanny noticed the other murdering Redskins continued to pillage the wagons. One found women's clothing. He brought these to Fanny and Mrs. Larimer. Another followed bringing papers. Another brought books. Odds and ends were soon piled before their feet. From wagon to ground. So quickly. So suddenly...

Everything that had made the journey from Kansas, all of life's treasures, was piled in one giant heap by the yelping Indians and set afire. Fanny was placed upon a horse, along with Mary, and led out of Little Box Elder valley in Wyoming. It symbolized the birth of a new life. What lay ahead, beyond the valley's birth-canal, as the three women exited from the womb of the Little Box Elder, no one knew. Only the afterbirth of the past remained behind! Fanny entered a life as a prisoner of war. A captive held against her will--the will of her friends, her family and her loved ones.

What about those loved ones? Her loving Josiah, and faithful Andy, neither carrying his gun, was gathering firewood. The wounded, bleeding Larimer escaped into the woods when the fighting started. Young Josiah and Andy crept along the eastern slopes in hopes of locating someone to help. Sometime later, the men returned--alone, to the wagon train massacre. They walked among the mutilated, putrid smelling bodies of Reverend Sharp, Taylor and Franklin. Each survivor had lost someone. A friend, a lover, a wife, a child. One noticed "Franklin's legs were pinned together with an arrow [and] his head was bashed in." Gardner Wakefield's disfigured corpse lay nearly a quarter mile from the wagon with three piercing arrows, and droves of flies swarming about, hanging loosely from the body that had formerly housed his soul.

Strangely enough the Indians had stolen the horses but left the cattle. The men decided to go on to Deer Creek Station. No doubt, they agreed, help could be had there. After all, these were White women taken prisoners. White women held by Redskins! Unthinkable! It was a seemingly endless twelve mile trek to Deer Creek Station. [140] They could not hurry too fast as they trudged along. One foot in front of the one they'd just placed upon the ground previously. Faster and faster they moved along on their journey. Naked rocks sticking barely above the ground snagging at the toe of their shoes and causing them to stumble. They must have perceived the unkempt flowers, the whirring bees, the sinking sun and rising moon and the prehistoric, dusty dirt every foot of the way. Their memories, unable to escape to a time beyond, remembered screams of friends now held prisoners of the fierce Red Sioux. Recollections blustering over and over through their mind in hurricane proportion.

Reaching Deer Creek, Josiah sent a telegram to Fort Laramie. Colonel Collins, of the Eleventh Ohio Cavalry, ordered to Captains Marshall and Shuman and two companies of troops out of the fort and after the Sioux. For the next 72-hours, the military scoured a one hundred mile strip in search of the hostile renegades. Finally an Indian encampment was discovered. Brown ordered his men to attack. Realizing the attack futile, his fellow soldiers fled, leaving Brown and Josiah. Brown tried to reason with the Indians and one shot him with an arrow, "causing him to fall from his horse...the effects of which caused his death a few hours afterward." [141] Fanny eulogized him as a "brave young man! the ardent friend of Mr. Kelly, and the husband and father of an affectionate wife and child, stricken down in his early manhood."

Meanwhile, Fanny gathered her thoughts and feelings into something now more constructive. She had to survive. "I was constantly annoyed, worried and terrified by their strange conduct...I knew not how to get along with them. I always tried to please them, and was as cheerful as I could be under the circumstances, for my own sake." [142] Her captives headed north amid some bluffs. All along the trail, the Indians chanted. Songs, unusual songs Fanny thought, which neither she nor Mary understood. She

---

[140]   Kelly, p. 51

[141]   Kelly, p. 223

[142]   Underwood, p. 24

remembered that first night alone, with nothing but the starlit sky, and "the sounds of water rippling over rocks in the distance, night birds crying out in the cool night air, and insects chirping." And the Indians! [143] Clop! Clop! Clop! With every cadence of the horses hoof against the Earth, Fanny silently plotted their escape. Along the path, she dropped pages of letters the Indians brought her earlier that day, praying someone would discover and rescue them. Once Mary was free, Fanny concluded, she could follow. At one point she turned and spoke silently to the child. "Drop gently down, and lie on the ground for a little while, to avoid being seen; then retrace your steps, and may God in mercy go with you. If I can, I will follow you," she told the child. [144]

Mary did. Fanny fearfully held her breath. What if the Indians noticed the missing youngster? But they did not. A long moment passed and Fanny slid from her mount. She embraced the Earth, her body firmly against the ground. One by one the Sioux rode on. Then, they were gone. Fanny sighed. Could she safely retreat? Not hardly. Horses were coming toward her and they were close. Forty or fifty Sioux braves rode up. The horses, her presence alarming them, caught wind of her and reared up. Fanny stood. She explained "Mary must have dozed off and fallen from her horse. She was only looking for the little girl," she assured the Sioux. But Fanny was never to see Mary again. She later learned the poor child's fate. The innocent Mary had made it to the main road and hid herself awaiting assistance. Later, "three or four soldiers returning from Fort Laramie, where they had been to meet the paymaster," spotted her standing atop a ridge "holding out her little trembling hands." Each was aware the area was inhabited by hostiles and feared they might be using her as a decoy to lure them into killing range. Sure enough, they no sooner spotted her than they also could see several Indians. They left and went on to Deer Creek Station to report. Mr. Kelly arrived a short time later and, learning what they had seen, beseeched the "officer in command for a detail of soldiers to go with him to search for her, but all [was] in vain."

Two days later, Josiah obtained enough help to look for the girl. He found her with "three arrows [in her] body...the tomahawk and scalping-knife had done their work. When discovered, her body lay with its little hands outstretched as if she had received, while running, the fatal arrows." He buried her there in a lonely, deserted, forgotten grave. "The whizzing arrows," Fanny wrote, "were sent into the body of the helpless

---

[143]   Underwood, p. 23
[144]   Kelly, p. 46

88

child...The bright angel spirit went home to rest in the bosom of its Father." [145] She affectionately added "of all the strange and terrible fates, no one who had seen her gentle face in its loving sweetness, the joy and comfort of our hearts, would have predicted such a barbarous fate for her. But it was only the passage from death into life, from darkness into daylight, from doubt and fear into endless love and joy. Those little ones, whose spirits float upward from their downy pillows, amid the tears and prayers of broken-hearted friends, are blest to enter in at heaven's shining gate." [146]

The following morning, after Fanny's capture, the Indians crossed the North Platte River--still headed north. She wrote of the journey deeper and deeper into the mountains. Even as a captive, Fanny witnessed the beauty of the morning as the sun dawned upon a new day. After all, she was alive. And that was a lot to be said. "After crossing the river and issuing from the bluffs we came to a bright, cool stream of water in a lovely valley, which ran through its bosom, spreading a delicious freshness all around. Brilliant flowers opened their gorgeous cups to the coming sunshine, and delicate blossoms hid themselves among the rich shrubbery and at the mossy roots of grand old trees. The awakening birds soared upward with loud and joyful melodies, and nature rejoiced at approaching day. The beauty and loveliness of the scene mocked my sleepless eyes, and despair tugged at my heart-strings; still I made superhuman efforts to appear cheerful, for my only refuge was in being submissive and practicing conciliation. My fear of them was too powerful to allow me to give way to emotion for one moment...The scenery we passed was wildly grand; it now became serenely beautiful, and to a lover of nature, with a mind free from fear and anxiety, the whole picture would have been a dream of delight." [147]

Once on the other side, the Indians split up and went different directions. The group with Fanny headed north by northwest. They crossed Deer Fork, Rock Creek, Crazy Woman's Fork and Clear Creek and on to the Powder River where Fort Reno would someday be built. By July's end, Fanny states, the Indians arrived at the village near Tongue River in Montana Territory. It stretched for miles along the banks of the stream. She became the mistress of the "Ogalalla leader she called Ottawa. To the Sioux, he was known as Brings-Plenty." Fanny learned she was not alone. Other White captives were present. One, who was stolen 25-five years earlier, "was a girl from an Oregon-bound

---

145   Kelly, p. 218-221
146   Kelly, p. 221
147   Kelly, p. 51-52

wagon train." Among the other captives was a 14-year old boy, Charles Sylvester, from Quincy, Illinois. He'd spent half his life already among the Indians. Another, a girl of "refinement, despite her neglected covering...I was startled to behold a fair-faced, beautiful, young girl sitting there, dejected and worn, like myself," wrote Fanny. She spoke of feelings while gazing at the White girl. "Almost doubting my reason, for I had become unsettled in my self-reliance, and even sanity, I feared to address her, but stood spell-bound, gazing in her sad brown eyes and drooping, pallid face." The chief handed Fanny a book stolen earlier from her wagon. She accepted and moved closer to the girl.

"What book is that?" The girl asked.

Fanny said: "The sound of my own language, spoken by one of my own people, was too much for me, and I sank to the ground by the side of the stranger, and, endeavoring to clasp her in my arms, became insensible." [148]

"My name is Mary Boyeau," she told Fanny, sharing the story of her capture. "These people call me Madee. I have been among them since the massacre in Minnesota, and am now in my sixteenth year. My parents were of French descent, but we lived in the state of New York, until my father, in pursuance of his peculiar passion for the life of a naturalist and a man of science, sold our eastern home, and came to live on the shores of Spirit Lake, Minnesota. The Indians had watched about our place, and regarded what they had seen of my father's chemical apparatus with awe and fear. Perhaps they suspected him of working evil charms in his laboratory, or held his magnets, microscopes, and curiously shaped tubes in superstitious aversion. I cannot tell; I only know that we were among the first victims of the massacre, and that all my family were murdered except myself, and, I fear, one younger sister."

"You fear!" Fanny stated. "Do you not hope that she escaped?"

"From a life like mine death is an escape," the young girl commented, bitterly. Mary related she had been bought for the price of a horse by a young Yankton Sioux warrior who wanted her for his wife.

"Do you love your husband?" Fanny asked.

"Love a savage, who bought me to be a drudge and slave! No! I hate him as I hate all that belong to this fearful bondage. He has another wife and child. Thank God! I am not a mother!"

---

[148]   Kelly, p. 113

"Does he ill treat you?" Fanny inquired.

"His wife does. I am forced to do all manner of slavish work, and when my strength fails, I am urged on by blows...I do so fearfully dread the chilling winters, without proper food or clothing; and I long to lie down and die." [149] Fanny recorded Mary's memorable, grisly incident involving a woman and infant child. Indians snatched the crying protege and threw it in a burning oven. The mother, restrained by savages, observed the horror

---

[149]   Kelly, p. 114-116

for several minutes before they finally stabbed her to death. The Indians removed the living baby from the oven and "dashed out its brains against the walls of the house." [150]

Days and nights passed and no rescue party arrived. September came. Captain James L. Fisk, heading a 100-wagon escort, neared the Indian camp at one point. Through some trick of fate, a note was sent to Fisk telling about Fanny being a prisoner. No one believed the note, however. Thus, a second note was smuggled stating Fanny would

---

150   Kelly, p. 117

stand on a nearby hillside and soldiers could see her through their binoculars. But Fisk was still suspicious. Was it a trick? Other attempts were undertaken to rescue Fanny. Colonel Charles S. R. Dimon and his men rode forty miles out of Fort Rice in temperatures plunging to thirty-four degrees below zero that winter. Dimon's effort failed due to suffering "frozen feet, faces, and fingers." October came and went. So did November. December 1864, however, brought good news for Fanny. Real Woman, as Fanny was called by Brings-Plenty, was to return to her people. The Blackfeet Sioux leader, Crawler, rode into camp early one cold day. Several Blackfeet Sioux rode with him into "the Grand River valley...at Laughing Wood, where the Hunkpapa camp was, near Bullhead, near the mouth of Rock Creek." When Brings-Plenty learned Crawler came for a trade, he took Real Woman in his teepee. Crawler remained outside in the cold wind. Sitting Bull, the Hunkpapa Sioux medicine man, was present that day.

"Friends, this woman is out of our path," Sitting Bull told all within hearing. "Her path is different. You can see in her face that she is homesick and unhappy here. So I'm going to send her back."

The medicine man looked at Crawler. Crawler glared back at him.

"Go in and get her. And tell him [Brings-Plenty] I said so," Sitting Bull told Crawler.

Crawler entered Brings-Plenty's teepee. Brings-Plenty sat opposite the door directly behind the fire. Fanny, considered the property of Brings-Plenty, was to his left.

"I have come for this woman," Crawler told Brings-Plenty after warming his hands by the burning fire. Brings-Plenty did not raise his eyes from the burning flames.

Sitting Bull

"I have no use for your horses. I will keep the captive," Brings-Plenty said.

"My friend, I would advise you to exchange the captive for the horses."

"My friend, I have no desire to part with the captive."

Crawler moved closer to the fire. He again asked for Real Woman. Brings-Plenty refused. Crawler drew a six-shooter from his belt and aimed it directly into the face of

Brings-Plenty. With his other hand, he took Fanny's shoulder, pulled her past him and motioned her to stand behind him. Crawler kept the pistol aimed at Brings-Plenty's face. Then, Fanny and Crawler backed out of the teepee. "Care for her well," Sitting Bull told Crawler and the Blackfeet. "Choose good men to see that no harm comes to her." [151] For several extremely cold days they traveled toward Fort Sully. An ugly blue norther tugged desperately at her tattered, worn clothing, slapping her face, freezing her tears and blurring the soldiers silhouetted above the fort walls. [152] Beyond, flapping vigorously in the strong wind, the red, white and blue flag cracked and popped amid the blowing gale. Soldiers watched nearly a thousand warriors approaching the fort--escorting one White woman. The front gate opened. Major A. E. House, accompanied by several officers and an interpreter, marched out. The interpreter talked first. Fanny sat and listened. After several minutes, Captain John Logan, Company K, stepped over to where Fanny sat.

"Am I free, indeed free?" She asked him.

"Yes," he mumbled amid his tears.

It had been over one hundred-fifty lengthy, enduring days since her capture. Now she was safe, free and again among her own people. For the next few weeks, Fanny remained in the fort hospital due to poor health. Josiah got word and came by early February 1865. Afterwards, they returned to Geneva, Kansas. The Kelly's moved to Shawnee-town and then settled in Ellsworth, Kansas. They operated a hotel until Josiah died of cholera on July 28, 1867. [153]

"The voice that had ever been as low, sweet music to my ear was hushed forever; the eye that had always met mine with smiling fondness was closed to light and me, and the hand so often grasped in tender love was palsied in death! Mr. Kelly, the noble, true, and devoted husband, my loved companion, the father of my innocent child, was gone. Oh! how sad that word! My heart was overwhelmed with grief, and that did its work, for it prostrated me on a bed of illness nigh unto my death." [154]

---

[151] According to Underwood's article, the winter of 1864-1865 was referred to by the Hunkpapa's as "The Winter When the White Woman was Rescued." p. 30

[152] A Dictionary of the Old West by Peter Watts, p. 227; Promontory Press, 1977. Watts says a norther is "a cold wind blowing from the north...this could be a cold, wet wind...a bad one was [called] a blue norther."

[153] Kelly, p. 235

[154] Kelly, p. 235-236

Fanny sold the hotel in 1868, moving to Sherman, Wyoming, at the request of William and Sarah Larimer who, Fanny learned, escaped in the early days of captivity.

"Fanny was a pitiful person," one person later recalled who knew her in Sherman, "eking out a living...by taking in washings for the railroad crews."

The following year, Fanny traveled to Washington to see President U. S. Grant. She made "a claim against the United States Government for her losses in the Indian raid," appealing for recompense because the Indians had "treated her in a manner too horrible to mention." [155] Finally in April 1870, she was allotted $5,000 from the Congress "for her service in saving Captain James L. Fisk's wagon train and Fort Sully." [156] Two years later, a publishing company in Philadelphia published Fanny's autobiography: *Narrative of My Captivity Among the Sioux Indians.* [157] The book achieved success going "through four [editions] in nine years." [158] Eight years later, she married William F. Gordon, a Kansas journalist. They moved east to Washington until her death on November 15, 1904. She is buried in Glenwood Cemetery.

A soldier, described only by his initials [W. S. V. H.] penned a rather lengthy poem titled *Dedicated to Mrs. Fanny Kelly.* It was included in her autobiography and I take this opportunity to quote the beginning and ending of that poem.

In early youth, far in the distant west,
With gentle steps the fragrant fields you pressed;
Then joy rebounded in thy youthful heart,
Nor thought of care, or trouble, bore no part...

The great Jehovah reigns; His arm is strong,
He sets the captive free, though waiteth long,
And turns the darkest hours of midnight gloom,
Into the effulgent brightness of noon. [159]

---

[155] Women and Indians on the Frontier 1825-1915 by Glenda Riley, p. 20; Univ. of New Mexico, 1984

[156] Notable American Women 1607-1950 Vol. 2 by Howard H. Peckham; 1971. See also Ghost Towns of Wyoming by Mary Lou Pence & Lola M. Homsher, 1956.

[157] Westward the Women by Nancy Wilson Ross, p. 103; Alfred A. Knopf, 1944

[158] Brown, p. 19

[159] Kelly, 268-269. Other sources about Mrs. Kelly include: An Indian Captivity & Its Legal Aftermath by Alan W. Farley (Kansas Historical Quarterly, Winter 1954); Captured By Indians by Howard H. Peckham, 1954; and Sitting Bull: Champion of the Sioux by Stanley Vestal, 1932.

A WOMAN WHO LOVED
CHASING FIRE WAGONS

Equal rights concerning women in the work place and the home have been an important matter in many ways. Women felt they deserve equality in both and rightfully so. During the Old West, however, many were not permitted this right. Often, as you've already read, they were consigned to such mundane chores as cooking, sewing, gardening, cleaning, birthing and rearing children. Little opportunity was afforded to explore the professional work fields the majority of women enjoy in today's workplaces. Yet, one cannot dismiss that being a 'dutiful housewife' is a full-time profession. Merely ask any woman who has chosen this career and she'll tell you so. So credit is due within this tome to one of those 'dutiful housewives.' Such a woman was Mary Carter--loving wife to Lt. Robert Goldthwaite Carter. The happy couple were married on September 4, 1870, "after a rather long and lingering engagement of three years." [160] Afterwards, in late November 1870, Mary accompanied her husband of two and a half months into the vast, forsaken frontier to Fort Concho, Texas.

Along the way, in Humboldt, Tennessee, the groom exited "to get a pitcher of coffee. It was early morning. When he re-appeared the train with the nervous bride had disappeared." The distraught Lieutenant made several inquiries of workers at the train station, learning it merely pulled down the track about an eighth of a mile and was

---

[160]   On the Border With Mackenzie by Capt. Robert G. Carter, p. 3; Antiquarian Press Ltd.; 1961

backing up to be rejoined with another train. Their devotion was, though separated only a few moments, great at the joy of their reuniting. They traveled from Boston, Massachusetts, by way of San Antonio, Texas to be a part of Troop E of the 4th Cavalry. It was "a hard trip through Indian country [and]...neither the Lieutenant nor his wife possessed the background to take up frontier life without a pang of concern." [161]

Upon arrival, an icy norther pushed sand across the prairie like a giant broom. Mary affixed blankets to the tent's north side, aiding against the indiscriminate wind invading their living area. The wind was but one scourge tolerated as the wife of a military man on the Texas prairie. Scorpions, centipedes, rattlesnakes and tarantulas, plus the distracting night sounds, were a permanent presence and need for alert. The hullabaloo of dawdling soldiers across the nearby river in the local drinking and gambling halls was another. But these didn't bother Mary as much as those haunting, lonesome cries like "some faraway spirit world." Barking coyotes, awakening Mary's slumbering sleep, caused her husband to notice "she would jerk up in bed to a sitting position, then shrink back under covers." [162] If all this wasn't enough, there was always the fearful Indian menace to fret over. The Redskins raided a town "within sixteen miles of the post" and then, less than a month later, these fearsome warriors attacked another position across the river. Would they strike the fort next? She wondered. These nearby attacks provided a difficult situation. It forced Mary to watch her husband ride off into nearby mountains in search of marauders--never knowing if he'd return alive or dead or return at all.

Mary, six months pregnant, and Robert were ordered on March 25, 1871, to move their tent an 180-mile trek from Fort Concho to the "tumultuous frontier area around Jacksboro--to Fort Richardson," to relieve the 6th Cavalry for duty in Kansas. Mary found herself two days later bound for Fort Richardson, Texas. The caravan of troopers, covered ambulances and canvas-topped supply wagons waded across the Concho River, through the town of San Angelo (then called Over-the-River) heading for Texas' Colorado River--thirty miles away. A torrential downpour drenched them as they halted for the first night; yet, Mary located enough dry wood to make a campfire and cook her husband supper. Colonel Mackenzie, Lt. Carter's commanding officer, observed Mary's

---

161   Death Song: The Last of the Indian Wars by John Edward Weems, p. 99-101; Indian Head Books, 1976

162   Weems, p. 102-103

devotion and "reflected his bewilderment at observing women of sensible appearance who would give up eastern refinements to accompany their men." [163]

The next day, Mary and the others traveled northeast along the old Butterfield Mail route. That night they halted at Fort Chadbourne, a post containing two companies on Oak Creek. The following day, they journeyed, Mary viewing a herd of buffalo grazing contentedly on the western prairie and found another storm sweeping toward them. That night they camped along Bluff Creek. The next day, they traveled through Mountain Pass where renegade Indians often found amusement attacking mail stagecoaches, robbing them of their contents. They marched on the next day to Fort Phantom Hill and on to Fort Griffin, Fort Belknap and traversed across the Salt Creek Prairie.

During the last two days of the journey, Mary took ill and was in grave need of bed rest. Finally, after 13-days of plodding along, they arrived at their destination of Fort Richardson on April 8. It was quite a junket for the pregnant wife of the soldier. Her new home would not provide any comfort. She and her husband were assigned their quarters: "a one-room jacal walled with mesquite branches placed upright and chinked with red clay that had, in spots, broken and dropped to the ground. The cottage, unporched, had been roofed with material similar to that used in the walls, but the overhead had cracked, too, so that it allowed occupants to lie in the cots furnished and gaze at stars through the ceiling opening." The Lieutenant called it a place where "a New England farmer would hardly stable his animals." [164] Mary recovered from her travel sickness and, on the morning of June 21, 1871, aided by the post surgeon, gave birth to a daughter. Later, Mary gave birth to a second child--a boy named Robert D. Carter who also became a career military man. Mary died in November 1923, after a long life of devotion and dedication to her chosen career of a housewife and mother.

"Following a man to this frontier demanded [a] genuine devotion," John Edward Weems wrote. [165] Yet, even in the Old West, there were women who wanted more. Some, perhaps, even wanted to be men. This was probably true in the sense of Josephine Monaghan of Buffalo, New York. Miss Monaghan, a society girl in 1866, changed her identity to Little Jo Monaghan and, in the spring of 1875, taking up the rancher's life in

---

163   Weems, p. 115

164   Weems, p. 116-117. See also: On the Border With Mackenzie by Robert G. Carter; Washington, 1935

165   Weems, p. 118

Idaho, spent her remaining years disguised as a man. She, as a man, "could run faster, shoot straighter, and handle a lariat with the best." [166] Jo was 5-feet 2-inches tall and weighed 135-pounds, seldom had much to say, was quick in thought, speech and action and was a top-wrangler. She spent her first years as a male rancher supplying beef for the miners in the Owyhees mining area near Ruby City, Idaho. Afterwards, she worked on a sheep ranch near Payette, Idaho.

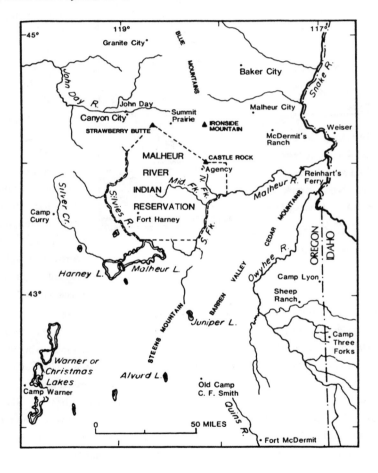

---

166   Little Jo by Roger Rickert; Frontier Times, July 1971, p. 39, 52-53

Along about the 1880's, Jo bought a small ranch in Malheur County, Oregon on the Succor Creek next to the Emery Ranch. As a man rancher, she was active in civic affairs, was on best terms with all 21-people living in the town of Rockville and voted in the elections and served on jury duty.

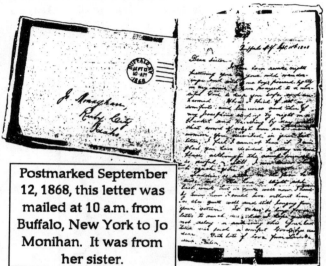

Postmarked September 12, 1868, this letter was mailed at 10 a.m. from Buffalo, New York to Jo Monihan. It was from her sister.

She even rode in the "Whaylen's Wild West Show" billed as the 'Greatest Show on Land or Sea' at Reinbeck, Iowa. Owner Andrew Whaylen offered $25 to anyone who could "bring in a horse that Jo could not ride." None did. Her secret of being a woman pretending to be a man remained until she died in 1903 when an embarrassed mortician loudly exclaimed, "Little Jo--he was a woman!"

Besides Little Jo there was Charlie D. Parkhurst, a woman disguised as a man "who drove a stagecoach during the gold rush in California." Born Charlotte Darkey Parkhurst in New Hampshire about 1812, Charlie developed an insatiable taste for chewing tobacco and smoking two-bit cigars and was "one of the best whips in the West." [167] Charlotte was orphaned in her early childhood and, at the age of fifteen, dressed herself in boys' clothes and ran away. She got her first job at the stables of Ebenezer Blach in Worchester, Massachusetts, developing a lifetime love for handling horses. She arrived in California during the early 1850's, quickly becoming known as Jehu. Dressed as a man, Charlotte cracked a whip with some of the finest including Hank Monk, Charlie

---

[167]   Women of the Sierra by Anne Seagraves, p. 117-121; Wesanne Publications, 1990

Crowell and Jared Crandall. [168] She was medium build and height with broad shoulders, dressed in expensive trousers, pleated blousy shirts, a buffalo skin coat, high-heeled boots, a hat the size of Texas and embroidered buckskin gloves. Her voice crooned like a "whiskey tenor." She'd been kicked by a horse and it damaged her eye, causing her to wear a black patch for the rest of her life. Thus, she earned the nickname of 'One-eyed Charley.' [169] She died in December of 1879 of throat and tongue cancer.

In addition, there was Loreta Janeta Velazquez, alias Harry T. Buford, a soldier and spy for the Confederacy during the War for Southern Independence. Loreta also bounty hunted, wrote and gold prospected during her life. [170] All these women, pretending to be men, strongly believed women were entitled to equal rights in the work place. Least wise, that is the way they lived their lives.

Lucy Hobbs Taylor also felt this way about equal employment rights. [171] Lucy was born approximately 1833, and at 26-years old, decided to enter the dentistry profession. At that time, most dentists were skilled through college or working as an apprentice. Lucy tried desperately to get a college to accept her but met with failure at every turn. All were shocked Lucy would "consider such foolishness." Finally, after several attempts of absolute, unrelenting determination, Lucy persuaded a male dentist to allow "her to clean his office and watch--if she promised not to tell anyone she was learning dentistry." Day after day for ten years, Lucy cleaned, watched and learned. Finally, a dentist professionally adopted her and she opened up her own practice. She worked at this until rewarded by admittance to the Ohio College of Dental Surgery. In 1865, among a class of 18 men to graduate, she was the "first woman to get a doctor of dental surgery degree."

Another 'medically minded career' woman was pioneer herb doctor Nancy Parker in Content, Texas. During the 1870's, Content peacefully rested among the mountains of Runnels County, south of Taylor and Abilene. It went by several different names including Blue Gap and Tokeen. But Content is what most folks wanted to call the place. "Although in the village itself there was an air of progress, in the postoak and wild ivy thickets of the mountains...here in a log cabin surrounded by hackberry thickets and cedar

---

[168]   Ibid, p. 117

[169]   Ibid., p. 118

[170]   Gender-Bending in the Wild West; Parade Magazine, Aug. 22, 1993

[171]   "History books slight accomplishments of women of the world" by Richard Maschal; Yakima [WA] Herald Republic, March 14, 1993.

brush...life was as primitive as in year's past." Nancy administered to the sick and needy "with her bag of herbs." Hardly a day passed her services weren't needed. Even at odd hours of the night sick folks summoned her. These Texans called this woman herbalist because they believed in her and her medicine. Or maybe because the only other doctor was clear over in Brownwood, Texas--a two day and one night ride by horseback. Nancy mixed various herbs and plants to form the hillside medicines. Such items as "tea from the balmony weed, which was very bitter," were administered for billiousness. The side affects were "quite weakening, and many a hardy frontiersman after drinking this tea, found himself unable to stand on his wobbly legs." She dispensed several other medicines during her life using "the redroot plant" to mix as a brew for diarrhea, a broomweed tea for coughs, and sassafras tea for "a general spring cleaning out." Adults suffering from asthma were to "smoke dried leaves of the mullein weed." If, on the other hand, Nancy was treating a child, the leaves would be brewed, sugar added for sweetener and a candy would be produced. This candy was given to the child. [172]

A third woman was Elizabeth E. 'Lizzie' Johnson, born in Missouri in 1843. Nine years later the family moved to Hays County, Texas where her father founded the Johnson Institute, the first school of higher learning west of the Colorado River, in 1852. [173] At 16-years old, Lizzie taught school at the Institute. Later, she taught in other Texas towns--Manor, Lockhart, and Austin. In addition, this enterprising young lady wrote stories for Frank Leslie's Magazine and this added to her financial wealth which Lizzie invested. She purchased $2,500 worth of stock in Evans, Snider, Bewell Cattle Company of Chicago, Illinois. In three years, Lizzie sold her stock for $20,000. On June 1, 1871, this resourceful woman bought a herd of cattle, branded them with her own brand (CY) and registered it in the brand book at Travis County, Texas. Her wealth grew. Finally, in 1879, having fallen in love with Hezikiah G. Williams, 36-year old Lizzie married. He was a devout preacher and a lonely widower with several children. She insisted on a pre-nuptial agreement "that all of her property remained hers." Twice, in the fall of 1879 and again in 1880, Lizzie and Hezikiah drove their cattle herd up the Chisholm Trail to Kansas, becoming "the first woman to drive her own herd up the trail." Lizzie Johnson Williams died in 1924 at the age of 84-years old. Her estate was more than $200,000

---

[172] They Called It Content by Juanita Daniel Zachry; Frontier Times, March 1971, p. 43

[173] Cowboy Culture: A Saga of Five Centuries by David Dary, p. 261; Avon Books, 1981

including several pieces of real estate in Austin, Texas. She was the epitome of one who believed women should have equal rights both in the home and work place.

Perhaps another was stagecoach driver, Sadie Orchard owner of the Lake Valley, Hillsboro & Kingston Stage Line--the "only woman stage driver in New Mexico...who owned the business with her husband." [174] This illustrious female stage driver, "a tiny, one-hundred pound woman, dressed in silks and jewels and rode sidesaddle around town like a grand lady." Her actions were course and language intemperate A rare photo depicts her wearing a riding outfit consisting of a tall silk hat, butter soft leather gloves, bouffant-sleeved blouse and a bustled skirt. She was "a daring, flamboyant woman ...[with] a colorful personality and aggressive manner [which] so overshadowed her husband that history has slighted him; we do not even know his first name." Legal documents, as a matter of fact, refer to him as merely "Sadie's husband." Sadie hailed from London, England where she'd been born in 1861 as Sara Jane Creech. As a child, she spent considerable time on the London docks amid the sailors who came and went. When she showed up in Kingston, New Mexico in 1885, she opened a whorehouse on Virtue Avenue. How she must have had a good laugh out of that one, no doubt! Business boomed from the start and Sadie was the local celebrity. Afterwards, she met and married "Mr." Orchard and they began the stage line.

"I could kick the foot brake with the best of them," she was often heard to brag with laughter. Before long Sadie and Mr. Orchard opened a hotel and eating establishment in Hillsboro. The hotel was most accommodating for single men frequenting the business. Each room had an outside entrance so 'gentlemen' might entertain lady visitors. Sadie possessed a heart of gold. She helped the people of Kingston, New Mexico raise $1,500 to build the first church the town ever had plus frequently aiding the sick, the poor and the lonely. Sadie died during the middle of World War II in 1943. During her seventy-eight-years, she demonstrated women were equal in the matter of employment.

Julia Bulette also felt females had a right to pursue any career they desired. Julia, like the subject of this chapter, was interested in fire fighting. She came to Virginia City, Nevada soon after the discovery of the famous Comstock Lode. Several miners claimed they'd known her from New Orleans while some thought her French or even English. The combination of her beauty, the scarcity of her commodity, and the affluent condition of her customers explains the magnitude of the fortune she accumulated during the next

---

174   Sadie's Mountain Pride by Jacqueline Dorgan Meketa; Old West, Spring, 1993, p. 28-31

three years. Using her brain, as well as other anatomical parts, she gained a tremendous amount of wealth and invested in building "the first magnificent structure in Virginia City." Dubbed Julia's Palace, the house on D Street had "rococo ornamentation [and] was an oasis in a community of drab shacks and cheerless rooming houses." Julia allowed no "disorderly conduct" and served her guests imported French wines and cooking. She bedecked herself in the latest Paris fashions including sable muffs and scarves and toured the streets of Virginia City in a "lacquered brougham which bore a painted escutcheon on the panel--four aces crowned by a lion couchant."

Her greatest honor came on July 4, 1861, when she was made Queen of the Independence Day parade. She was given a fireman's hat for a crown, a brass fire trumpet filled with fresh roses and sat up front in the new fire truck while red shirted firemen marched behind. She considered her position of great privilege, donating considerable money to the local fire company for purchasing new equipment. If the fire engine were on a run she would rush from her Palace to the scene of the fire. Many a driver purposely slowed the fire engine so she could hop aboard. Julia often jumped in and lent a hand at working a water pump. On January 20, 1867, she was robbed, severely beaten, strangled and shot to death, dying as flamboyantly as she lived. [175]

But our story is not about Julia or these other women. Instead, it's about another woman obsessed with chasing fire wagons to local fires. One who deemed it her God-given right to aspire to whatever career she wanted to pursue. A woman who rocked San Francisco with her antics and escapades amid the blazing infernos of a town known for its hellish fires. On May 20, 1851, the vessel *Tennessee* docked in San Francisco, California. Aboard that crusty ship was Doctor Hitchcock and his family. The doctor was a graduate of the University of Maryland and a well-known army surgeon. His wife, Martha, an educated woman, was a talented journalist. She'd been a Southern belle, growing up on a Virginia plantation having already inherited a considerable fortune from the family estate. Thus, the Hitchcock's lived stylishly amid the fashionable Oriental Hotel and rubbed elbows with San Francisco's high society. The 8-year old daughter Lillie accompanied the Hitchcock's. She was "a happy, talkative girl with smiling eyes and an appetite for adventure." [176] The impressionable child, curly chestnut hair

---

[175] The Gentle Tamers:Women of the Old Wild West by Dee Brown, p. 80-83; Univ. of Nebraska, 1958

[176] Lillie No. 5: San Francisco's First Firewoman by Jan Holden; Old West, Spring, 1991; p. 50-53. All information, unless otherwise noted, about Lillie is from this article.

cascading to her shoulders, was different from most girls her age. She intelligently conversed with adults and joyfully played with other children. But Lillie *really* enjoyed chasing fire wagons speeding along San Francisco's wood-planked streets.

On December 23, 1851, playing amid the uncompleted Fitzmaurice Hotel, Lillie became trapped by a blazing inferno. A passing citizen shouted the alarm and the Knickerbocker Five fire wagon arrived. Lillie was unable to escape as raging fire enveloped, not only rooms, but the stairway. Realizing she was trapped, fireman John Boynton took his ax, chopped a hole in the roof, climbed down a rope into the burning menace where Lillie was screaming and rescued the child. The Hitchcock's, so happy Boynton rescued their daughter, donated one thousand dollars to the Knickerbocker station for more equipment. Lillie immediately befriended the members of the fire fighting group and, at future fires, stood to the sidelines, cheering them as they fought amid the tortures of hades. The firefighters adored her and soon made her their mascot.

Doctor Hitchcock didn't find her infatuation toward the firemen disturbing. However, Martha, who home tutored the child, sent her to a boarding school at the age of fifteen. So in 1858, Lillie moved to the convent in San Jose, California. But the girl with the "smiling eyes and appetite for adventure" had other plans, indeed. Her first stunt was a "melodramatic hunger strike." Her health alarmed the Catholic Sisters. The parents were immediately notified and Lillie refused to cease her rebellion unless allowed to return home. Doctor Hitchcock and Martha surrendered and Lillie returned to San Francisco. But there was one hitch. Lillie was to stop chasing fire wagon's enroute to local fires. She tried. She really did. But to no avail. In 1860, 17-year old Lillie was to be a bridesmaid at a wedding for a family friend. The day of the rehearsal, as Lillie assisted the wedding arrangements, she heard the fire bell off in the distance. She leapt to her feet. With chestnut hair bouncing, her clothing waving and flapping in the breeze, she ran into the street and briskly toward that area where the smoke was thickest. Needless to say, the wedding was conducted without her the following day.

The following year, of course, the War for Southern Independence erupted in the East. Lillie and her mother, despite military law forbidding the helping of Southern sympathizers, aided several to flee San Francisco and journey back to the Confederacy where they bravely fought. Fearing for his daughter and wife, Doctor Hitchcock arranged for Martha and Lillie to leave for Paris. Before leaving, Lillie met with the *Bulletin's* editor, persuading him to let her be the foreign correspondent from Paris. Lillie sent several articles about "her daily experiences and adventures" in France, signing them *Lillie Hitchcock 5*--still considering fire fighting as her true vocation.

"We had a fire, and such a fire!" She wrote of her first morning in Paris. "We were just sitting down to a comfortable breakfast of beefsteak, potatoes, cold coffee and butter with not an atom of salt in it, artistically served in the shape of leaves, when our femme de chambre rushed into the room, horror on her face. She said the whole Palace Vendome was on fire." Lillie abandoned breakfast and secured the report firsthand giving detailed accounts of the blaze and the firefighters conduct. Her graphic detailed accuracy combined with fiery passion for her assignment brought Lillie a large following back in San Francisco. Amid these devotees was Howard Coit, son of well-known surgeon Benjamin Coit.

The Hitchcock ladies returned to San Francisco in 1863. Musicians and firefighters were on hand to welcome Lillie home, rolling out the red carpet for their heroine's arrival. Mrs. Hitchcock was disheartened, loosing her daughter to this mad world of rowdy firemen ready "to pop a cork." Upon arrival, Lillie was awarded "a beautiful certificate making her an honorary member," given a small gold pin in the shape of the number "5" and an official helmet. She dressed in a bright red shirt and a black silk skirt and continued to sign her name with the number "5" next to it. Even worse, in Mrs. Hitchcock's opinion, Lillie started dating Howard Coit. Then in late November 1868, to mother's horror, they were married at St. James Church. A furious mother and a father watched as the Knickerbocker Fire fighting company serenaded the newly-weds. Problems soon developed, however, within their happy marriage. Lillie couldn't forsake her passionate excitement for the rowdy life, the fires, the parades and the champagne-soaked dinners. Howard, on the other hand, only wanted a wife.

Both took an extended trip to Europe. This didn't help. They returned to San Francisco and separated. Neither sought a divorce. They remained married until Howard died at the age of 47-years old. He left her a fortune of over $250,000 but a fortune wasn't what she wanted. Lillie withdrew. She resigned her post with the Fire Fighters, having attended over one hundred fires in her career. She kept in touch and, if one was sick, visited him with an armful of roses and a box of cigars, her presence a healing balm. Lillie's popularity grew in the bay city area. Newspaper editors and reporters constantly clamored for any tidbit of news about Lillie Coit. Every socialite was interested in the rebellious lady's activities. [177] In 1904, two years before San Francisco's disastrous earthquake, Lillie was forced into a twenty year exile. Living in the Palace Hotel, entertaining guests amid the atmosphere of the widow's sitting room, Lillie was visited by an old family friend, Major J. W. McClung.

Lillie "5"

They were enjoying a cup of tea when Alexander Garnett burst into the room carrying a six-shooter. Garnett, a distant relative of Lillie's mother, aimed the gun at Lillie and fired. The bullet went wild as McClung jumped to his feet and charged the pistol-

177   Silver Hillside: The Life & Times of Virginia City by Barbara Richnak; p. 95; Comstock-Nevada Publishing Co., 1984. See also The Spectacular San Franciscans by Julia Cooley Altrocchi; p. 199-200; Dutton & Co., 1949.

wielding maniac. The gun again discharged during the struggle and the projectile penetrated McClung's lower stomach. Lillie rushed over to aid the major as Garnett dropped the gun and fled. Shocked, Lillie received word the following day McClung had died. It was weeks before she could testify at any trial. Garnett was eventually found guilty and sentenced to a mental hospital in Virginia. Afterwards, Lillie packed her bags, left San Francisco and went to Paris. She stayed until August 1923, refusing to return until word came that Garnett had died while in the institution. [178] Though Lillie spent the remainder of her life entertaining friends in San Francisco, things had changed. The old friends, the volunteer firefighters, were gone or all dead. Lillie joined them in death on July 22, 1929, leaving the city of San Francisco $100,000 to be used to "beautify the city." The city council decided to erect a tall, fluted concrete tower encircled by windows. Since then millions of residents and tourists alike have viewed the 540-feet structure known as Coit Tower gazing out upon the bay area.

What best can be said about Lillie Hitchcock Coit?

She vehemently defiled the old Victorian "code of proper conduct for young ladies," becoming the "first female member of the city's volunteer fire department." She possessed an unusually convincing character, believing women not only 'should be' but 'were' equal to men when it came to employment. She experienced everyday of her natural life not only teaching this truth but practicing it for all to see. Lillie was the picturesque epitome of equal rights for women. A photo showing her clutching her shawl over her right shoulder with her right hand and a bottle of champagne in her left depicts her a beautiful example! [179]

---

[178] No reason was found by this author as to why he wanted to shoot Lillie or why she stayed away until after his death.

[179] This photo is located in the Wells, Fargo history room in San Francisco, California.

Lillie Hitchcock Hoit:
Social Profile on Chapter Six
by
Virginia C. Nelson-L'Aloge, M. A.

How can we, women of today, truly know what it was like to be caged in a life-style that belittled our intelligence while often being set upon a pedestal all at the same time? Those of us born before 1960 have more of an idea of what that is like than those fortunate women born thereafter. Ours is often a story similar to those presented in this chapter. But these are the forerunners, these are the mold breakers!

The most important thing for people, any people, is to have a choice. A person's sex has no bearing on the need or choice--especially as to how they live their lives or how they earn their living. For century's women had no choice. They were born and educated to cook, sew, garden, clean, wash clothes, be mistress to the man and then birth and rear the children. If a woman so chooses then that is great. In fact, now in today's society, some men are taking the role of homemakers and raiser of the children. More often than that occurring, the choice is for the male and female to share that aspect of their lives as they pursue career choices contributing to the income. There are, of course, some who still advocate *roles* for men and women.

One of the questions presented in this chapter is that, if in order to do what she had to do, she disguised herself as a man. The fact is that Josephine Monaghan, Charley Parkhurst and Loreta Janeta Velazquez [alias Harry T. Buford] dressed the part of a man. What would have happened had these women attempted to do what they did presenting themselves as a woman? How much credit or respect, in fact, how much safety would there have been, without the disguise? Absolutely none! There were no equal rights for *these* women. A woman drive a stagecoach? A stagecoach then was equivalent to women driving a truck today. There are still problems with women driving a truck today in some cases. The attitude then is still repeated by some today: "Why don't they stay in their places?" Doors are still often closed.

Lucy Hobbs Taylor wanted to be a dentist. After many attempts at getting an apprenticeship she finally found a male dentist to "allow her to *clean* his office and watch!" *Clean his office* in order to watch--is this how a male would have had to learn? Again the answer is an emphatic No! But to break into a heretofore male profession-- woman, then and now, must be persistent and not take no for an answer. If she had the talent she must prove herself over and over again. Lucy, and others like her, trailblazed new trails so that we can follow their shining examples.

Nancy Parker, on the other hand, invested wisely and protected herself financially by purchasing cattle. Because she owned them she was able to drive them to market. The same is true of Sadie Orchard. She and her husband owned the business. What sets them apart from the other women previously discussed? They were married so they had their husband's protection. A single woman on her own, however, so often impersonated a man to survive. These women all recognized they were intelligent and resourceful. Most importantly they were determined! That's what it takes even now. Many times these women were ridiculed and looked down at by other women who lacked their courage. They were even laughed out of town.

Lillie Hitchcock was a girl of "good family." She almost died in a fire but was rescued by a fireman. It is perfectly logical that this so impressed young Lillie she had to see if others were rescued also. She was obsessed with fires and firemen. She was so grateful to firemen she spent her lifetime devoted to them. Her frustration was she wanted to be a fire fighter but was not able to do it because she was a female. How many people today get their interest peaked by an early childhood experience?

So many women and men, then as well as now, defy convention because they have had an experience that impresses them. Whether they were male or female did not enter into it. If they have a beloved pet saved they often want to be a veterinarian. If they are impressed with the construction of a bridge they often want to build bridges. Many people I counseled wanted to be one when finished with their counseling. I am happy to say that this is the case today. Today the opportunity is there. But this was not the case with Lillie. She was made honorary fireman but was not allowed to be one. And for Lillie, as is true for so many women who defied the norm, they lost out. They could neither be who and what they wanted to be because they were women and, unfortunately, they were rejected as women because of their not being socially acceptable anymore. They no longer fit into the neat little women's role created for them by society.

110

It is decidedly better today than even twenty years ago. Pay is becoming equal as is the opening of work opportunities but we must remember we are women. We no longer have to act like a man to work in our chosen profession. The women of this chapter, for the most part, gave up so much to do what they chose in their lives. This took persistence, courage and tenacity to accomplish. They truly were trailblazers!

Such ads as these in the Denver Daily Tribune appealed to Mrs. Hitchcock.

Sarah Amanda McDaniel:
Social Profile on Chapter Seven
by
Virginia C. Nelson-L'Aloge, M. A.

We come upon a woman, Sarah Amanda McDaniel, whom it appears did not set a very positive example for women. The possibility is she cannot be looked at as a heroine. She, apparently, acted out of purely selfish motives. Or was she set up? Then is the question: "What really happened?" The men of her time could not believe, or did not want to believe, this beautiful, sweet looking woman was capable of murder or conspiring to murder anyone--least of all her husband and protector. The role of woman was life-giver not life-taker. Men were the hunters. Men were the predators. Women were submissive, the gentle ones. Their 'roles' were clear.

To set her husband up as a target and have her lover kill him is not a new theme then or now. Motivations can vary. Did Sarah do this to her husband or did O'Neil act on his own hoping to get a rich widow? That also occurs--then and now. We shall now explore the two possibilities. If Sarah indeed was not only knowledgeable but instrumental in her husband's death what could be the motivation? Little is known of Lewis McDaniel so we are left with exploring suppositions. We do know that he was considerably older than she. Many marriages are perfectly happy with either spouse being older than the other. Perhaps Sarah or her child was secretly mistreated or abused in the marriage. There is a question of did she take a younger lover because she was not satisfied in the bedroom? Or it may be as simple as that she indeed was a psychopath without conscience.

It is hard to believe that any woman who loved her husband, awakened from a very sound sleep, would not react to the fact he had just been violently murdered! Yet, this same woman showed emotion and was "visibly shaken" when the jury stated *she* was not guilty. One with no conscience is very involved with self-welfare and self-safety over and above all others. They *use* other people to fill their owns needs. There is no evidence that she cared for O'Neil once the dirty deed was done. She *dumped* him royally! Whatever her motivation she showed no emotion as far as he was concerned. Contrast Sarah's reaction with that of Laura Bullion for Ben. Laura loved Ben, she wrote to him, she followed him, she was true to him. When he died Laura was heart-broken.

It is said that Mr. McDaniel and O'Neil had "words" about Sarah. Neighbors knew of O'Neil's comings and goings from the McDaniel house. The evidence that O'Neil was guilty is strong. Sarah became "well off financially as a result of her husband's death." O'Neil was no longer needed. Sarah was now free of both men.

What if, however, she did not conspire with O'Neil to have McDaniel murdered? Perhaps she was unhappy with her husband, sought excitement and so merely had an affair with O'Neil. Her husband told him to stay away from him. What if O'Neil wanted Sarah and decided to kill McDaniel freeing Sarah for himself? He must have also known that McDaniel's estate was considerable.

If Sarah did not conspire with O'Neil what would have caused her reactions to be as they were? If she were unhappy in her marriage the death of her husband would have been a relief. No mention is made as to her upbringing. Perhaps she was raised in a stoic family, one where showing emotions was not acceptable, so it was natural for her to not show emotion. Often if someone has endured traumas over a long period of time they become numb and feelings are not acknowledged or felt. If she were innocent, being jailed and awaiting trial would have been traumatic in itself. Knowing that if found guilty hanging was probable would make anyone 'weak-kneed' when 'not guilty' was pronounced. One cannot help but wonder about the fact that she did not become a carefree widow. She choose to be low-profile for the rest of her life. She choose to be quiet and cause no further focus on her life. This could be the result of either guilt, shame or both. It could also be the reaction to being severely traumatized.

Divorce was not an option that society would accept. Divorce meant, especially for a woman, isolation in society. The proof needed for a divorce was often difficult to obtain, particularly for a woman. If her husband objected to the divorce, and was not guilty of adultery, she would be penniless. As previously stated, women were not prepared for or seldom allowed to earn a living in any way but laundress, maid, servant, nanny, school teacher or prostitute. Most barely existed on meager wages. Divorce then was not a positive option. For a woman to have a descent life-style she had to be married, under a man's protection or, in rare cases, rich herself.

Love is a motivation for people who do things they normally would not do. So is hate or intense fear. Sometimes greed enters into the formula. Sometimes it is a shifting and combining of all of them. Always is the belief things cannot go on as they are. Always is the belief that to do something is to survive. That is true even in crimes of passion where it is a spontaneous thing.

The murder of Lewis McDaniel was premeditated. He was totally unaware of that danger. Whoever was responsible is dealing now with their Maker. But does hanging absolve one of the crime or does it simply multiply the crime? Who of us can make that judgment? Is the hangman as guilty as the murderer he hangs? Is the one who plants the murder's seed--nurturing it to fruition through the actions of another--as guilty of murder as the one who executes the murder? Love or the lack of love *is* a motivation. Who shoulders the responsibility for this crime?

Does the pious society who would then not allow divorce go guiltless?

THE LOVE TRIANGLE

OF

SARAH AMANDA MCDANIEL?

The teaming up with male gunfighters, highwaymen and outlaws was certainly not foreign to Old West women. Many reasons could be given for these unions. Love, money, adventure and greed for a position in life are among but a few. Several women have already been lauded by authors. Such famous and not so famous attachments as Big Nose Kate to Doc Holliday, Ann Walker [alias Nancy Slaughter] to William C. Quantrill, Calamity Jane to Wild Bill Hickcock and Belle Starr to Cole Younger. [180] Love has been, and probably always will be, the main motivating force behind these alliances. Some couplings demonstrated the strength of a woman's love for a man--even an outlaw. One such example follows:

Laura Bullion, alias Della Rose, was the oldest of three children. [181] Her father and mother were J. Henry Bullion and Fereby Byler and were married September 5, 1875. Laura was born somewhere in Arkansas the following year. Eventually, she moved to live with her grandparents near Knickerbocker, Texas. Her early academic education was somewhat limited. "I never got much schooling, 'cept a little now and then in the district school," she once told folks. Nevertheless, love letters she later wrote during her life proved she was literate and enjoyed reading. It is these letters and the outlaw to whom

---

[180]   The Gentle Tamer by Dee Brown, p. 263; Univ. of Nebraska, 1958. Brown states Ann was "more renown for her nymphomaniacal tendencies than for her freebooting accomplishments.

[181]   The Thorny Rose by Carolyn Bullion McBryde; True West, Apr. 1992, p. 21-27

she wrote them that have given her a place in the history of the Old West. For Laura Bullion was the girlfriend of noted gunfighter and highwayman, Ben Kilpatrick.

Kilpatrick was none other than a famed member of the notorious Wild Bunch. About six months after the turn of the century, Kilpatrick and the Wild Bunch robbed the Great Northern Railroad train. Later that year, in St. Louis, Missouri, Ben was fined one dollar and sentenced to fifteen years in prison for "passing altered [payroll] bank notes." [182] At the same time, Laura was arrested in St. Louis and convicted. She had met lover and co-outlaw Ben Kilpatrick by way of Aunt Viana Byler's marriage to Will Carver. That marriage was in July 1891. One year later, Viana died. That was how she met Carver who, in time, introduced her to Kilpatrick, Kid Curry, Sam and Black Jack Ketchum. [183] While on the run, Ben sought hiding places with Butch Cassidy and the Sundance Kid.

"Part of the time I lived out and part of the time I helped at home, but you all know how it is in a small country place--they ain't much for a girl to do and when a girl ain't got no parent to look after her and tell her how to do right," Laura told the reporter at the San Angelo *Standard Times*, "she just naturally gets to running wild." With the death of Carver on April 2, 1901, Ben adopted the young girl under his wing. When Kilpatrick left Sonora after Carver's death, he took Laura and before long they were lovers. After the Great Northern train robbery, Laura and Ben fled to St. Louis, living at the Laclede Hotel as Mr. and Mrs. J. D. Rose when a Pinkerton man spotted Ben and gave pursuit. Kilpatrick was arrested in a whore house later that day and it was discovered he had a key in his possession. That key fit the lock to the hotel room. The Pinkerton man arrived in the nick of time to catch Laura leaving--with $7,500 worth of stolen notes.

Found guilty, Laura 'Della Rose' Bullion was sentenced to five years in the Missouri State Penitentiary at Jefferson City. Ben was sent to the federal prison in Atlanta, Georgia. Despite the great distance, she wrote several letters to him "always expressing more concern for Ben than for herself." She repeatedly affirmed her "greatest joy was to receive a letter or gift from Ben." At one point, Ben sent her a small lead pencil. "I received the little lead pencil you sent," she wrote back. "It just simply could not be prettier. I think it is too sweet to be used...I would not take anything for it." Released on September 19, 1905, for good behavior, she immediately journeyed to Atlanta, paying her

---

[182]   The Tall Texan by Dale T. Schoenberger; True West, Apr. 1992, p. 20

[183]   For more information on Sam and Black Jack Ketchum, refer to Knights of the Sixgun by Bob L'Aloge; Yucca Tree Press, 1991

fare from prison funds she'd earned. "Innuendoes in several of her letters...before leaving prison suggested Laura made the money to pay her travel expenses by prostitution." Ironically, her looks and performance were undoubtedly beneficial as she was able to purchase half-interest in a rooming house the following week.

Financed by her risque funding, time was provided to obtain a pardon for Ben. Finally, to her joy, Ben was released on June 11, 1911. He was immediately arrested again, however, before Laura could so much as kiss him. With unquenched passion seeking satisfaction inside her heart, Laura dejectedly followed Ben and the lawmen to Concho County, Texas. Her outlaw paramour was placed on trial for the murder of Oliver Thornton, acquitted and Laura finally had him to herself. But on March 12, 1912, Ben robbed the Southern Pacific train in Texas. Though no evidence at the time, many suspected Laura of holding the get-away horses for Ben and Ole Beck--his accomplice. No doubt Ben should have heeded her warning for during the robbery, he was shot dead. Laura was heart-broken.

Certainly amid these many female/male teams, a couple of questions need to be answered. Would a woman betray her man to the law? Or would a woman murder the man she'd married? Both are answered in the following two non-fictional accounts.

Rosa Lewis, wife of Ras Christianson, alias Diamond Dick, destitutely stood sobbing at the uncurtained window of their ranch house, listening to her husband agree to again join forces with the McCarty's in another hold-up. Rosa was tired of the 'jobs.' She pleaded for him to quit hanging out with those good-for-nothing McCarty's. Further still, on more than one occasion, he'd promised to quit as soon as he had enough money to start over somewhere else. Always the same old story, she thought. Rosa kept hoping he'd turn them down and tell the four brothers to ride on and forget the idea. [184] But Ras was gazing off into space, thinking about the money.

"Twenty thousand dollars is exactly what I've been looking for. Did you boys case the bank completely?" Ras asked.

"We was all through it yesterday. Just come from there today, straight here," George admitted.

---

[184]   Ben Snipes and the Great Roslyn Bank Robbery of 1892 by Bob L'Aloge; BJS Brand Books, 1993

"What did you find? Did you check for a getaway plan and what did it look like?" Ras inquired. He was a notorious planner and the infamous McCarty's had often relied on his skill in successfully pulling off several robberies.

Rosa heard George tell Ras the job looked easy for five men. Finally, to her disappointment, Ras agreed he'd ride with them on one more bank robbery. Their destination was the Snipes Bank in Roslyn, Washington. Ras turned and strolled back toward the house. Sarah, his sister-in-law, met him at the front door. She despised him, wishing Rosa would take the baby, leave him and go back to Utah with her.

"You lied to Rosa and your baby," she snarled at him. "You dirty, low-down, thieving outlaw. You'll never change. Crooks like you never do."

"Do you realize what would happen to your sister Rosa and to your little niece Hayda, if anyone dropped the slightest hint about me?"

Diamond Dick had just supplied his sister-in-law with the ammunition needed. From that point on, Sarah used every opportunity to persuade Rosa to betray Ras. And betray him she did. Ras and the McCarty's robbed the Roslyn bank in September of 1892. On May 11, 1893, the *Herald* newspaper in nearby Yakima, Washington, published a copy of an affidavit signed by Rosa Lewis--wife of alias Diamond Dick.

It read:

> *"I am the living witness that George McCarty, Billy McCarty, Ras Lewis alias Ras Christianson, Tom McCarty alias Williams, Fred McCarty and Nellie McCarty are the only individuals interested in the above robbery. This, your honor, and gentlemen of the jury, I swear by the power of all heaven, and the rights of our government as an honest citizen, the wife of Ras Lewis alias Christianson.*
>
> *"Now, as for dates, as near as I remember about the 10th of September, they first met at my house planning the robbery. They left about the 12th. In about two weeks Ras Lewis went to where they were and returned the night of either the 1st or 2nd of October. That was the last I saw of them until November 12, 1892, when Billy, Tom and Fred McCarty come there to plan another robbery and would of went but for my interference. I swear to what my sister, Sarah J. Morgan, has said, that it is the truth and the truth only, so help me God.*
>
> *"I am also witness for five other robberies--train, bank and store.*
>
> *(Signed)*
>
> Rosa Lewis
>
> *Subscribed and sworn to before me this 1st day of May, A. D., 1893.*
>
> J. L. May
> Notary Public.

Thus, it's feasible a woman, teamed up with a man, under certain circumstances would betray him to the law. But would a woman murder the man she had married?

"No woman would kill the man she was married to!" Mrs. Josiah Pottss told a jury in 1888. [185]   Mrs. Pottss, on trial for the murder of Miles Fawcett, lived in a cabin near Carlin, Nevada. Miles was a mechanic for the Southern Pacific Railroad. Sometime in January 1888, believed to be the fifth, Miles went to the Pottss house in his buckboard. He climbed out, tied the animals to the tie rack and went inside. He never came out alive. But Josiah Pottss came out of the house. He climbed into Miles' rig and drove away, claiming Miles had been ordered back to San Jose, California.

Nine months later, the Josiah Pottss family moved away from the old house. Another couple, named Brewer, took occupancy. Noises prompted them to search out the dirt floor of the basement where they discovered the remains of a body. It was Miles Fawcett. The Pottss' were expedited back to Carlin, Nevada and placed on trial for murdering Miles. Both pleaded not guilty. Both were convicted. The judge sentenced her to hang and, on the scheduled day of execution, at approximately 10:27 a.m., it was done unto her. But hanging a woman stirred up public sentiment. A newsman from a San Francisco paper was curious about Mrs. Pottss statement. The one stated, *"No woman would kill the man she was married to!"* The journalist checked into the facts discovering Mrs. Pottss had contracted with "a marriage broker to find her a husband." Proof was further found that Miles had indeed married a woman whose name was given as Elisabeth Atherton. Miss Atherton gave her age as thirty-eight and her former address as London, England. Miles hired a detective, W. Mathews, to investigate "a debt amounting to $100 owed to a marriage broker." This was owed by Miles' new wife. Further still, she'd used an alias--Miss Atherton. Fawcett also learned, through Mathews, his new wife was still married to Josiah Pottss of Carlin, Nevada. Mrs. Miles Fawcett stayed with Fawcett for a while longer. They lived in San Francisco and then in Fresno. That was when she left him and went back to Josiah.

But Miles Fawcett was still in love with her. He sold out and trailed after her. He set himself up to visit her often. Apparently, and this can only be surmised, Pottss had no idea that while she was away, she had married Fawcett. Growing jealous, Josiah Pottss "began to be suspicious at the frequency of Fawcett's visits and the way he looked at Mrs. Pottss." Fawcett even brought his laundry over for Mrs. Pottss to wash. This upset

---

185   Too Many Husbands by Donald Everett; Frontier Times, Jan. 1971, p. 45-46

Pottss and he'd sulk. Both Pottss' claimed Miles had confronted them, become despondent at learning she no longer "loved him," and committed suicide. They had buried him in the basement from fear of being accused of murder. According to her that is what had prompted her statement about murdering the man she'd married. The consensus was one of two reasons for Miles' death. Mrs. Pottss murdered him to gain his estate or he'd threatened to expose her and she killed him to silence him. Who knows?

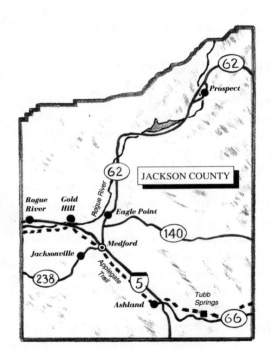

So it is, as seen by these examples, women in the Old West were subject to betraying their men- -even to the point of murder. So with this in mind, let us again asked: "Would a woman murder the man she's married to?" This chapter is about an alleged love triangle concluded in murder. It is an episode taking place between Lewis McDaniel, Sarah A. McDaniel and Lewis O'Neil. [186] It occurred in Ashland, Oregon in late 1884, and these are the known facts about the "love triangle of Sarah Amanda McDaniel."

Prior to 7:30 p. m., Thursday, November 20, 1884, the enigmatic union of Amanda and Lewis O'Neil manifested itself completely in the murder of Lewis McDaniel-- husband to Amanda.

No one gave much thought to the "loud report" heard in the town of Ashland that evening in late November. One resident, Clarence Lane, stated he "thought old man

---

[186] Bizarre Case of the Church Street Murder by Gary Meier; Old West, Summer 1991, p. 42-46

Collidge was shooting at cats again." [187] Most thought it nothing more than a continuance of the earlier celebration for president-elect Grover Cleveland. After all, the Republicans in town were still joyous over the victory. Nevertheless, as Anson W. Jacobs was heading home that evening, [188] he heard a "raspy breathing" of what he thought to be a drunk. Investigation proved otherwise. It was the dying Lewis McDaniel--blood-soaked and face down in the street. That is, that part of his face not blasted away by a shotgun at close range. Jacobs ran to Main Street and shouted the alarm. A crowd gathered where McDaniel lay dying. Several doctors were summoned but found they could do nothing because "the bullets had torn the bones of the face, shattered the front part of the skull and penetrated the cerebrum or front part of the brain, which oozed out from the wounds in the forehead." [189]

Less than thirty minutes later, Mr. McDaniel, described as "an old citizen of the county and a resident of Ashland for nearly a year past," [190] was pronounced dead. Unfortunately, he "died without speaking." Worse still, there were no eye-witnesses. The time: 8:19 p.m. at the latest. Someone went to the McDaniel house about 100 to 150 feet away from the murder site. They banged loudly on the door. No one answered. They banged again. Still no one came to the door. Could it be no one was home? Or, could it be Mrs. McDaniel and her ten-year-old boy had gone to bed early? Again and again they knocked until "it was nine o'clock." A total of 40-minutes elapsed before Mrs. McDaniel and her son "could be awakened and told the terrible news." [191] Mrs. Sarah A. McDaniel's [192] reaction to the news prompted authorities and others to become extremely suspicious of her. She expressed hardly any grief or minute emotion over the news. The *Ashland Tidings* editor felt Sarah possessed "a great lack of sensitivity or a wonderful control over her feelings." [193] Conjecture grew. Presuppositions came easily

---

[187]   On Trial For Murder by Larry Derry, p. 1; Term Paper presented to Dr. Frank Haines, December 1961. Mr. Derry conducted a personal interview with Clarence Lane on November 18, 1961.

[188]   Derry states Anson W. Jacobs "was walking *toward* town..." p. 1

[189]   Ashland Tidings, Nov. 28, 1884

[190]   Ashland Tidings, Nov. 21, 1884

[191]   Derry, p. 2

[192]   The name of Sarah was provided by Jeanine Jenkins during her research she conducted for me at the Jackson County, Oregon, courthouse. She discovered it among some of the records.

[193]   Ashland Tidings, Nov. 28, 1884

due to many troubles the victim "was known to have had with various people." [194] One thing was certain. The motive wasn't robbery. McDaniel still had a sum of money.

Sheriff Abraham S. Jacobs and his men investigated the events leading up to the murder. They determined McDaniel had been in the shooting gallery at Church and Main Streets. He'd leisurely walked up Church Street toward his home "with his hands in his pockets." [195] Approximately 150-feet from the front gate to his residence, an unknown assailant, thought to be "crouching in the dark behind a fence," shot him dead. The shotgun blast had blown away his face. The assassin had disappeared. Meanwhile, inside the house, Sarah had 'supposedly' gone to bed. She confessed she clearly "heard a gun discharge [but] thought someone was firing to celebrate the election result." She claimed she'd not heard the crowd of spectators gathering about her dying husband's body. She knew nothing, she swore, until she'd been "roused from her sleep." Like wise, she knew of "no one who would want to kill her husband."

Lawmen John Taylor and Enos Walrad questioned several people standing around. They learned Lewis O'Neil, "a married ne'er-do-well with six children, had been *dallying* with Mrs. McDaniel of late." Neighbors related how "certain things were definitely seen going on between Sarah and O'Neil right there in the McDaniel house when the husband was away." This raised questions. Was it just gossip? Or was it true? Had Sarah been 'carrying on' in an unwomanly manner for the 1880's? Was there some other reason behind the closed door antics of this couple? The deputies discovered the husband and O'Neil had words about Mrs. McDaniel. The husband had told the no-good scoundrel to stay away from his wife. The deputies wondered if Mrs. McDaniel complained about O'Neil's harassing her? Or had McDaniel learned Sarah was having an affair and allowed his actions to be governed by jealousy? Had he and his wife argued about O'Neil being at the house so much? The lawmen knew they would have to find out for sure before drawing any conclusion. [196]

The lawmen learned another important thing in their early investigation. For the past few nights, O'Neil had been seen loitering about the area. Everything clearly pointed to the idea Lewis O'Neil had murdered McDaniel with a shotgun blast to the face. After all,

---

[194]   Ashland Tidings, Nov. 21, 1884

[195]   Ashland Tidings, Nov. 21, 1884

[196]   Ashland Tidings, Nov. 28, 1884, states that "the grounds of suspicion in [O'Neil's] case were that he was known to have had trouble with McDaniel, who had forbidden him to visit his house, not liking his intimacy with his family."

"more likely than anyone else... he had a motive for the crime." [197]   Angry citizens demanded O'Neil be arrested for the murder. Later that night, at High and Taylor's saloon, the suspect was taken into custody by Taylor and Walrad. The deputies ordered him to throw up his hands. He didn't appear to be surprised they had come to arrest him nor did he ask why until after he'd been incarcerated.

The following day, November 21, 1884, Justice Eubanks was appointed by Coroner Inlow to investigate the murder. Eubanks appointed an investigative jury consisting of: H. C. Hill, Charles Wolters, T. Noonan, Heaton Fox, B. F. Meyer and his son, J. S. Eubanks Jr. Two local physicians, Doctors Parson and Songer, were asked to conduct the autopsy. Parson and Songer found seven wounds were about the face and neck. These wounds were caused by a shotgun fired from the left side and traveled up and to the back of the victim's head. The murderer, it was estimated, had been approximately twenty feet away, crouching behind some shrubs. [198]   Sheriff Jacobs took over the investigation discovering a set of boot prints amid the soft mud around the fenced area where the shot was fired. He placed a boot belonging to O'Neil "in the imprints and they fit perfectly." He followed the tracks through two empty lots, down a hill to Granite Street, through a meadow to Main Street and near the Reoser Building. That is where O'Neil had "been sighted before entering the saloon" where he was later arrested.

November 22, a Saturday, Mr. McDaniel was buried. The newspaper reported it "was attended by very few persons besides the family, as no public notice of the time had been given." John McDaniel, the "brother of the late Lewis McDaniel," attended as he was in town from his home at Little Butte. He expressed "a determination to have the mystery of the murder solved, if possible." [199]

On Sunday, November 23, the sheriff and deputies located a double-barreled shotgun. The weapon had been taken apart and thrown into shrubs at the Coolidge Nursery, situated about one hundred yards from the McDaniel house. The alleged murder weapon was a double-barreled, 16-gauge "old fashioned muzzle loading type." [200]   One barrel was loaded. One was empty and had been recently fired. The wadding used to tamp into the barrel had been torn from the *Ashland Tidings* newspaper. A search of O'Neil's room

---

197   Ashland Tidings, Nov. 28, 1884

198   Ashland Tidings, Nov. 28, 1884

199   Ashland Tidings, Nov. 28, 1884

200   Derry, p. 4

revealed a newspaper, with a section torn from its pages, matching the piece used as shotgun wadding. The evidence was certainly adding up and it all pointed in one direction. Ownership of the shotgun was said to be that of George O'Neil--brother to Lewis. George, however, claimed he'd sold the gun to his brother sometime before the murder occurred. Likewise, Lewis claimed he'd later sold the weapon, distinguished by "an alligator's head carved in the stock," to another man.

For six days the jury examined evidence. On the 26th, the panel announced a decision. "We hereby charge the said Lewis O'Neil with the murder of said Lewis McDaniel." The seventh day, O'Neil was arraigned before Justice Eubanks. Attorney J. T. Bowditch represented him and O'Neil was taken to the county jail at Jacksonville. Trial was scheduled for February 27, 1885. The jury consisted of Levi Gartman, Jacob Bowman, Thomas Martin, Benjamin Carter, W. H. Bailey, J. D. Neathamer, J. S. Morgan, E. S. Trimble, J. H. Griffis, James McDonough, George Mergle and John E. Pelton. Twenty-eight names were chosen before reaching a decision of these twelve. District Attorney Kent presented his case with precision showing evidence that O'Neil owned the shotgun believed to be the murder weapon. A witness was presented that said he'd seen the gun in the possession of George O'Neil. Since George, age 72, was too ill to attend the trial, the judge conveyed the court to Grave Creek and George was questioned. He testified he'd sold the gun to his brother sometime earlier. Lewis O'Neil, on the other hand, claimed he'd sold the gun also. But Wesley Kahler and James Neil, his attorney's, were unable to prove this. During all this, surprisingly, Sarah kept "a low profile in Ashland, making an effort to appear bereaved, and tending to the administration of her late husband's estate, a source of considerable financial gain to her." On Thursday evening, March 12, at about 9:30 p.m., the jury was given charge of the case. In less than 90-minutes, they returned to the courtroom.

"O'Neil evinced little if any feeling when the verdict was rendered, but on entering his cell gave vent to a volley of oaths at the expense of the jury and the prosecution," claimed the *Ashland Tidings* on March 20, 1885.

The defense attorney requested a new trial after the guilty verdict was read in the courtroom that evening. Judge Webster told O'Neil and his lawyer he would take the motion into consideration and announce his decision on the following Monday. Monday came. But it wasn't until Monday, March 23, Webster announced his decision for a new trial. He denied the motion and O'Neil was given a chance to say what he desired. The murderer proclaimed his innocence. Judge Webster then pronounced sentence on O'Neil and appointed May 21, 1885, as the day he was to be "hung by the neck until dead."

O'Neil was informed by his attorney he had two chances left of saving his life. That is, a pardon from the governor or an appeal to the Supreme Court of Oregon. O'Neil was taken back to his cell to wait. Back in his cell, he chatted informally with fellow prisoners. Two of these, John Crimmons and Levi Grigsby, were extremely interested in what the convicted murderer said. Sometime prior to April 10, 1885, O'Neil told these prisoners Amanda had helped him murder her husband. Crimmons and Grigsby told the authorities--in hopes such assistance would aid them in charges they were facing. On April 10, Mrs. McDaniel was arrested at Eagle Point, Oregon, at the home of her sister-- Mrs. Fryer, placed in jail and held without bond for "complicity before the fact in the murder of her husband." But due to some legal technicality, the charge was changed to being an accessory in the murder. Sarah was officially indicted by the Grand Jury on October 20, 1885. [201] The indictment read as follows:

In the Circuit Court of the State of Oregon for Jackson County

Amanda McDaniel is accused by the Grand Jury of the County of Jackson and State of Oregon by this indictment of the crime of murder, committed as follows:

The said Amanda McDaniel and one Lewis O'Neil on the 20th day of November A. D. 1884 in the county of Jackson and State of Oregon Purposely and of deliberate and premeditated malice killed Lewis McDaniel by then and there shooting him with a gun contrary to the Statute in such cases and against the peace and dignity of the State of Oregon.

Dated at Jacksonville Oregon on the 20th day of October A. D. 1885

She was held for over six months, after her arrest, before placed on trial on November 16, 1885--lacking four days being one full year after the murder of her husband. Sarah's Jacksonville jail cell was a little way from the cubicle occupied by "her convicted lover," Lewis O'Neil. The very next day, J. J. Fryer, her brother-in-law, was also arrested on a charge of suppressing evidence that "would have implicated Mrs. McDaniel." Supposedly, Fryer attempted to bribe possible witnesses, attempting to get them to leave the countryside. A lack of evidence, however, allowed him to go free later that day. The witnesses who testified were: Thomas E. Nichols, J. H. Hyzer, Eugene Walrod, J. D.

---

[201] Most sources say it was in May 1885 but the indictment, signed by District Attorney Kent, is dated October 20, 1885.

Gray, James Pease, Phillip Mullen, Mrs. Nora Walrod, Mrs. M. J. Goodyear, C. D. Morgan, H. Farlow, Mrs. A. S. Jacobs (the Sheriff's wife), N. R. Parsons, John A. Gridley, S. D. Taylor, Dr. J. S. Parsons, Louisa Gridley, J. N. Banks and Levi Grigby.

SARAH AMANDA MCDANIEL

In the meantime, Lewis O'Neil managed to raise enough money to take his case to the Oregon Supreme Court. As a result, Judge Webster granted a stay of execution. Rumors, however, circulated through town that if he was not hanged according to Webster's March 21st decision, the vigilantes would lynch the murderer. Sheriff Jacobs made preparations for such an event but nothing came of the rumors. Finally, Mrs. McDaniel's trial was called. Seven members of the Grand Jury were chosen to sit in judgment of Mrs. McDaniel. The other five were selected from a list of twenty-four people. Those who were finally approved were Ulm Mayfield, Squire Walton, G. W. Howard (both of Medford), J. W. Plymire (of Manzanita), Rufus Cox, C. Turpin (both of Little Butte), Ralph Dean (of Willow Springs), Frank Parker, B. F. Miller (both of Rock Point), Tom Miller, J. T. Layton (both of Applegate) and T. J. Keaton (of Roosmen's Creek). [202]

The court records available don't reveal much about Amanda's trial. On November 18th, for example, they reflect the jury of "twelve in number, good and lawful men of the County duly sworn and impaneled...to try this cause and having sat and heard the opening statements of Counsel for both sides of the Court adjourned until the coming in of the Court tomorrow morning." The following day, the jury "sat and heard a portion of the evidence." Nothing is said in the court records about what the evidence was or the names of the witnesses. By Saturday, November 21, the "jury, having sat and heard all the evidence in this cause offered by both parties were under charge of the Court." The court didn't meet on Sunday but did again on Monday. On Tuesday, November 24th the jury was allowed to retire "to deliberate upon their verdict." That was at ten o'clock that morning. Twenty-two hours later, the jury finally reached a verdict. The foreman, G. S. Walton, was asked to read that verdict.

"We, the jury in the above entitled action, find the defendant, Amanda McDaniel 'not guilty' as charged in the indictment." Sarah was visibly shaken at the verdict. If by some chance she was guilty, the law could no longer touch her, for no one is to be tried twice for the same crime. [203] The prosecution relied upon two outlaws who testified Lewis O'Neil had confessed his guilt to them and implicated Sarah. Sarah A. McDaniel was released and she returned to her secluded life in Ashland, Oregon. But on March 11, 1886, the evening prior to the hanging of O'Neil, Sarah McDaniel "was seen to leave Ashland for parts unknown."

O'Neil's attempt before the Oregon Supreme Court failed to overturn his verdict. Justice Lord and Thayer concurred with the Circuit Court and Justice Waldo dissented. O'Neil was informed of their decision and remarked he "hoped that the persons who had

---

202   Ashland Tidings, November 20, 1885

203   This author conducted two interviews with Jeanine Jenkins, an employee of the Jackson County, Oregon court house on July 6-7, 1993.

sworn his life away would get their reward in hell." [204]   Through his attorney's, O'Neil again pleaded with the Oregon Supreme Court in January of 1886. Again he was denied. Back in his cell, the murderer threatened to go on a hunger strike. Many were afraid he'd die before the hanging as he stuck to his hunger strike like an adept cuttin' horse clings to maverick longhorns. An unidentified citizen came into the jail in January of 1886 to see when the next sentencing would be on O'Neil.

"Say, you're right damn anxious to hear a man sentenced to be hung!" O'Neil shouted from within his cell. [205]

Sentencing came on January 26, 1886. Judge Webster sat before O'Neil and pronounced the sentence he should be hung by the neck until dead. The execution was to be carried out on Friday, March 12, 1886--between ten o'clock in the morning and two o'clock in the afternoon. March 11th, O'Neil got word through a Catholic nun that he wanted to see Father Blanchet. The nun, from the Sisters of Mercy in Jacksonville, told the priest he was requested and Blanchet went to see Lewis. O'Neil took confession. Only God, the priest and Lewis knew what was said. The following day, a crowd gathered within the enclosure's confines built to shield the hanging from uninvited guests. Newspaper reporters were given "a station in one of the clerk's rooms where everything said upon the gallows could be heard." Father Blanchet arrived and entered O'Neil's cell about 1:30 p.m. They talked. Shortly before leaving the jail cell, O'Neil asked he be allowed to consume "a stimulant, which was given him." [206]   At ten minutes after two in the afternoon, Sheriff Jacobs came out of the jail. O'Neil followed closely. Behind O'Neil were Deputy Steadman and Mr. Moon. O'Neil solemnly shuffled up the steps without raising his eyes to the crowd. Sheriff Jacobs read the death warrant and inquired if Lewis had anything to say. His lips moved but nothing came out.

"Mr. O'Neil has nothing to say!" Father Blanchet remarked.

Father Blanchet gave O'Neil a crucifix. The murderer kissed the religious article and repeated the words to a prayer Blanchet was reciting. His hands were tied behind his back. Then his ankles were secured. A black hood was placed over his head followed by the hangman's noose. Sheriff Jacobs stepped over and sprung the trap door. The time was 2:15 p.m. Doctor Aiken placed his finger on O'Neil's pulse while Doctor Robinson

---

[204]   Jacksonville Democratic Times, December 14, 1885

[205]   Derry, p. 13

[206]   Ashland Tidings, March 19, 1886

gripped the left arm to steady the dangling body. Eight eternal minutes later, he was pronounced dead. Twelve minutes after that, they cut his body down. It was placed in a pine box and buried in the "county pauper section of the Jacksonville Cemetery--between plot numbers one and six." [207]

Lewis O'Neil was hanged while over 20-armed members of the Jacksonville volunteer fire department served as guards. About 200 tickets were issued by Sheriff Jacobs for people to attend and witness the hanging. Several in attendance were women and two or three children. The rope strangling Lewis O'Neil was cut into small pieces and each received a portion as a souvenir. The newspapers concluded "O'Neil's mental organization was evidently of a stolid character, morally abnormal, and he was incapable of recognizing the value of life. He did not act the bravado and try to make a criminal hero of himself; neither was he overpowered by the dread of death--a murky mind--a dangerous man to society. He was one whom it would have been perilous to turn loose after the trial for murder." [208]

So whatever became of Sarah Amanda McDaniel?

She moved to the community of Talent, remarried, and there, in southern Oregon, ran a cafe for some years. Her name, however, does appear once more in court. On June 28, 1886, attorney J. R. Neil filed suit against her and J. J. Fryer--her brother-in-law. The suit was an "action to recover money" in the sum of $180.94 plus $19.14 court costs. This was the balance owed him on a promissory note dated May 16, 1885. Neil stated she'd already paid him "$25.00 on July 11, 1885 and $60.00 on September 15, 1885 and $100.00 on November 25, 1885." A summons was issued that June day. On the back, in what is the allegedly the handwriting of J. J. Fryer, are these words:

"I J. J. Fryer as the within named defendant's hereby acknowledge service of the within complaint and summons on me in Jackson County Oregon on this the 28th day of June 1886 and waive my right to copy thereof." The words "I Amanda McDaniel and" appeared prior to this statement and had been scratched out--apparently by Fryer. Also on the back is written the following: [209]

"I, A. S. Jacobs, Sheriff of Jackson County...hereby certify that...on the 1st day of July, 1886, I served the within summons on the within named Amanda McDaniel, one of

---

207   Jacksonville Cemetery Records, p. 553

208   Ashland Tidings, March 19, 1886

209   See appendix for all court records pertaining to Sarah A. McDaniel.

the defendants in the within entitled action by delivering to her personally a true copy thereof together with a copy of the complaint." It was signed by Jacobs. A judgment was rendered on August 2, 1886. J. J. Fryer and Sarah McDaniel were found guilty and ordered to pay attorney J. R. Neil. Sarah seems to have faded into the history of Jackson County after that. Perhaps it is just as well.

So did Sarah A. McDaniel conspire to murder her husband?

Let's briefly review the factual highlights.

1. McDaniel was shot shortly before 7:30 p.m. and it was between "fifteen and twenty minutes" before he was found. He was pronounced dead less than thirty minutes later--8:19 p.m. at the latest. Where was Sarah McDaniel between the time of 8:19 p.m. and 9:00 p.m. on the night of the murder--a total of 41 minutes? She confessed to *hearing* the shotgun blast that killed her husband but stated she and her 10-year old son were both in bed asleep prior to the arrival of the death news.

2. O'Neil was brought to trial and his entire "conviction...rested upon *circumstantial evidence.*" [210] Amanda, on the other hand, was brought to trial and although "there was *strong circumstantial evidence against* [her]" there was "not quite enough evidence to remove all doubt of guilt." [211] It must have been more advantageous to be the "comely young wife." [212]

3. All sources point to the fact O'Neil and Amanda was having an affair. "O'Neil had been intimate with the wife," stated the *Ashland Tidings* on March 19, 1886. The newspaper also stated O'Neil had "*crooked relations with the family* of the murdered man." [213] But exactly what those "crooked relations" were we are not told.

4. Again, all sources confirm McDaniel knew of this "intimate association or affair and warned O'Neil to keep away from Amanda."

5. As to why Amanda showed "very little sign of grief" when told about her husband being murdered we can only guess. Perhaps, like others, her constitution was such she

---

[210]   Ashland Tidings, Mar. 12, 1886

[211]   Ashland Tidings, Nov. 27, 1885

[212]   Meier, p. 42

[213]   Ashland Tidings, Nov. 28, 1884

was able to control her emotions. Or perhaps, she'd arranged the murder herself. The answer lies somewhere in between--if not one of these.

6. No one in Ashland, Oregon knows what became of the 10-year-old boy or if he knew anything.

Before the execution of O'Neil there was something that happened which stirs the boiling cauldron of curiosity. O'Neil wrote this letter to her.

> Mandy,

> ...*Now you have been tried and come clear, and it is in your power to save my life. You can do it by coming to town and swear that you did the killing...That would clear me, and the law could not hurt you as it says plainly that no man's life shall be put in jeopardy twice for the same offense. Then I could employ one of the best lawyers in California and come on the State of Oregon for heavy damages, and I would divide equally, or if that was not enough, I would give you all, so I hope you will not delay as I know you can save my life and the disgrace will be no worse on you than it is now.*

This letter was later published in the *Ashland Tidings*. [214] So let us present the following hypothesis based upon the known facts.

Perhaps the young and beautiful [215] Sarah married the 'older' Lewis McDaniel for the security he offered her and her son. At some point, she grew tired of him and his ways, realizing if he were no longer around she could have it all. But Sarah could ill afford to do the dirty deed herself. What she needed was a man to do the work for her. Thus, through her feminine charms and by bestowing upon O'Neil favors and such, she knew she could get him to do her demonic bidding. After all, if approached in just the right way, a man was often willing to commit murder for the woman that loved him.

---

[214]   Ashland Tidings, Mar. 19, 1886
[215]   Meier, p. 42

Through some connection, Sarah found in Lewis O'Neil what she was looking for in a man. He was already burdened down by a family he most likely didn't want and more than willing to find in her the extra-marital affair his lustful heart was seeking. At first she innocently teased him with her dark flirtatious eyes and beguiling ways. As the affair with O'Neil grew more intense, however, the vulpine female casually dropped hints she might marry him if it only wasn't for Mr. McDaniel. Once the seed of desire was planted, the idea germinated and soon took root and grew within the sordid mind of Lewis O'Neil. Here was his chance to get away from the drudgery of his large family and nagging wife who never seemed to understand him. To escape with a beautiful, vivacious, sexually attractive woman. Reveling in the thought of her worldly charms, he agreed he'd become her 'knight in shining armor, rescuing the damsel in distress' from an unbearable marriage. So he waited in the shadows for McDaniel to appear and, encouraged by lust, he shot her husband dead and ran back to the McDaniel house.

"Mrs. McDaniel [was] an accessory in the crime, and it was generally believed that an immediate and thorough search of the house in which she was living would have disclosed convincing evidence of her connection with the murder. It was generally believed that she received the gun from O'Neil immediately after the shooting." Then, during the mysterious 40-minute absence of Sarah Amanda McDaniel, under the cloak of darkness, Amanda left the house with the shotgun and "concealed" both pieces of the murder weapon at two different locations. She returned to the house and entered through the back door in time to hear the knocking at the front. She quickly ruffled herself as though she'd been asleep and rushed to answer the door. As for the boy, he'd been sent to bed a considerable time earlier and had no idea of what was happening around him.

O'Neil, after disposing of the weapon through Amanda, headed downtown to throw off suspicion from Amanda and himself. But it didn't work. People suspected him from the start. So he was arrested and placed in jail. Then came his trial. O'Neil did admit "before his trial that he shot McDaniel and that Mrs. McDaniel was waiting near and took the gun, while he started off at once." [216] Mrs. McDaniel, realizing the fulfillment of her dream, played the innocent. O'Neil had meant nothing to her except a means to an end and so she dumped him upon the courts to rid her of the "ne're-do'well." They did. But O'Neil, realizing the betrayal, decided to spill the goods on her. She was arrested and tried and, from behind those same innocent eyes, looked out upon a jury who acquitted

---

[216]   Ashland Tidings, April 17, 1885

her. Sarah was at last free to inherit her dead husband's estate and to do as she pleased. Better still, having been tried herself for the crime and acquitted, they could never convict her. Knowing this to be true, O'Neil wrote Sarah begging her to admit her role in the murder. His plea, however, fell on deaf ears. The love triangle of Sarah Amanda McDaniel had provided her with the perfect murder.

Or did it?

LEADVILLE'S ADMIRABLE FIRST LADY

"Leadville never sleeps," wrote the local *Chronicle* editor in a segment of articles subtitled 'Midnight Notes.' "The theaters close at three in the morning. The dance houses and liquoring shops are never shut. The highwayman patrols the street in quest of drunken prey. The policeman treads his beat to and fro. The music at the beer halls is grinding low. A party of carousers is reeling through the streets. A mail coach has just arrived. There is a merry party opposite the public school. A sick man is groaning in the agonies of death...Three shots are heard down below the old court house. A woman screams. There is a fight in a State Street casino. The sky is cloudless...Another shot is heard down near the city jail. A big forest fire lights up the mountains at the head of Iowa Gulch...The clock on the Grand Hotel points to one. Shots are heard from Carbonate Hill. The roar of revelry is on the increase. The streets are full of drunken carousers taking in the town." [217]

Author, illustrator, mother and engineer's wife, Mary Hallock Foote, described the town as "a senseless, rootless place" while Helen Hunt Jackson defined it as "unnatural." Jackson added that "grass would not grow there and cats could not live." [218] It was the kind of town a man could get practically anything--providing he was not particular as to what it cost or what he had to give up to obtain it. One such "unnatural" example was that of a woman named Josephine Lockwood Patton who was traded for a silver mine.

---

[217]   The Gold Rush: The Search for Treasure In the American West by George F. Willison, p. 172; Indian Head Books, 1992

[218]   Beyond Baby Doe: Child Rearing on the Mining Frontier by Elliott West, p. 182; The Women's West edited by Susan Armitage and Elizabeth Jameson; Univ. of Okla. 1987

J. D. Patton married Josephine Lockwood in April 1878, at St. Louis, Missouri. Their marriage ceremony, conducted by Reverend James Ferguson, was at the Third Methodist Church. The happily married couple lived in St. Louis until Patton was infected by gold and silver fever. They packed their bags and moved to Colorado on March 26, 1879. Arriving in Denver, the couple staid a couple of weeks and enjoyed the finer things the booming town offered. It was mid-April 1879, before they arrived in Leadville. They moved into a small cottage on Carbonate Avenue and, on September 1, 1879, moved into the Peet Hotel on Elm Street. Here they "lived quite happily." Leastwise, that's what we are led to believe as we are not told otherwise. The idea anything might be amiss started when John M. Hamilton, part time miner and cook, went to work as a cook for the Patton's at the Peet Hotel. He was paid seventy-five dollars a month and board for his expertise as a chef. Sometime in the fall of 1879, he discovered and laid claim to the Mountain Belle Mine in Tennessee Park--expected "to develop...into considerable value."

Patton, who had not lost his fever, wanted the mine for his own. However, he did not possess the "requisite amount of money to pay for the same." For weeks the two haggled and bartered over the selling price. Hamilton wanted more than Patton could give. Patton, in turn, did all to *Jew the miner down* in price. Finally, after several weeks, "Hamilton said to Patton that he would give him the mine for his wife." Patton went straight to Josephine. "He took his wife into their bedroom, where they held a long conference over the proposed trade." We're not informed how long they stayed in the bedroom nor what transpired between them. We are not told if Josephine objected nor, by now, if she even wanted her marriage to Patton. We're not told if Hamilton and Josephine were having an affair behind Patton's back? It is obviously clear Hamilton wanted the woman. But we're not told if Josephine liked, disliked or loved Hamilton. Nor are we told if J. D. and Josephine might have conspired to gain control of the mine and then later renege. We are merely informed they emerged at last.

Patton approached Hamilton. The two men clasped hands and shook as Patton informed Hamilton "that both himself and his wife had consented to the trade, and that the wife should be his as soon as the necessary papers could be drawn up and executed." J. D. Patton, Josephine Patton and John M. Hamilton, having come to an agreement about the terms and conditions, left the Peet Hotel and went over to the office of L. P. Palmer-- the recorder. Palmer drew up "a quit claim deed from Hamilton, conveying his Mountain Belle Mine to Patton and one from Patton conveying his wife to Hamilton." The proper papers were notarized and, without any given sign of regret, Patton took his wife by the hand and gave her over to Hamilton as Hamilton turned over the papers to his silver mine. Josephine then "locked arms with her new husband, and the three returned to the Elm Street boarding house." The purchased wife "very carefully packed her personal effects, kissed her [former] husband an affectionate farewell [and]...an hour later, seated with her new husband and trunk, in an express wagon, she was driven to a furnished room on Third Street." That is where John M. Hamilton and his new wife, Josephine, took up their abode. The story apparently has a happy ending as the reporter who covered the story concluded by stating "all parties look upon the transaction as being final and forever!" Such was the style and way of life in Leadville, Colorado. [219]

These descriptions of life in Leadville, though maybe uncouth, are mild. Miners, gamblers, barkeepers, teamsters, lumberjacks, smelter hands, Jewish storekeepers, blacksmiths, carpenters, engineers, lawyers, doctors, preachers, temperance lecturers, actors, school teachers, prostitutes, bankers, pickpockets, footpads and highwaymen of every sort flocked into Leadville as the 1870's rapidly ended. Everyone was welcome, it seemed. Everyone but Indians and Chinese, that is. Despite warnings issued, three Chinese came to town, were captured upon arrival by vigilantes, shot dead and dumped in an abandoned mine--not found until several months later. [220] Yet, amid the pistols and petticoats of this uproarious hell-hole emerged a staunch woman--Augusta L. Pierce Tabor; and, for one brief shining moment, she was Leadville's admirable First Lady.

"It was as a pioneer that [Augusta] really shone and as a pioneer that she made her greatest contribution to western history." [221] Augusta met Horace Austin Warner Tabor in August 1853. She was merely 20-years old when she courted the Holland, Vermont stone-cutter--two years her senior. He'd come to work for her father in Maine. It took him two years to "fall in love with the boss's daughter...She was the one who listened eagerly to his plans for the future and the one who encouraged him to pursue his dreams. She knew what it was like to have a roving spirit held prisoner in a frail body." [222]

On March 13, 1855, Horace went west with the aid of the New England Emigrant Aid Society. The society was the impulsive brain child of what had formerly been the Massachusetts Aid Society, incorporated by Eli Thayer, on April 26, 1854, back in

---

219   Arizona Daily Star, May 14, 1880
220   Willison, p. 173
221   Pioneer Pathways by Betty Moynihan; True West, January 1993; p. 42-47
222   Moynihan, p. 43

Worcester, Massachusetts. Its purpose was to "raise capital, advertise the advantages of Kansas, recruit well-organized bodies of settlers, and send them west to...build mills, hotels, schools, and churches." Thayer was forced to change the name of the society when "the fear of stockholders that they would have a pecuniary liability for all obligations" demanded he reorganize. [223] The society was pro-abolition and offered to provide transportation to young men who would support their cause while living in Kansas. So Horace left Boston and, about two weeks later, arrived in Lawrence, Kansas. For the next two years he worked the land and supported the abolitionist movement. [224] In January 1857, he returned to Maine.

"On January 31, 1857," Augusta wrote, "we were married in the room where we first met." [225] Horace's background was relatively simplistic in that he was born in 1830 to Sarah (Ferrin) and Cornelius Tabor--described as a "small farmer and country schoolmaster." [226] He learned his trade from an older brother who lived in Quincy, Massachusetts. On the other hand, Augusta was among seven daughters and three sons born to William Pierce and his wife, Lucy. She was born in Augusta, Maine on March 29, 1833. [227] William was a stone contractor, most noted for building the state insane asylum. Thus, being rather affluent, she grew up in the lap of a well-to-do family. She was "a frail and delicate girl, she was rather angular perhaps both in figure and manner...but whatever Augusta may have wanted in physical strength, comeliness and charm, none ever denied her remarkable moral stamina, steadfast loyalty and great unpretentious courage."

Accounts are scarce about the few months in life after marriage. But at one point they "journeyed by train to its terminus at St. Louis and thence by five-day boat to Westport (Kansas City). We purchased a yoke of oxen, a wagon, a few farming tools, some seed, took my trunks and started westward," Augusta recalled. [228] The couple spent time farming in Kansas before "the news of gold in Colorado broke [and] the Tabors joined

---

[223]   Ordeal of the Union: A House Dividing 1852-1857 by Allan Nevins, p. 307-308; Charles Schribners Son's, 1947

[224]   Moynihan, p. 43

[225]   Augusta Tabor: Her Side of the Scandal by Caroline Bancroft, p. 5; Bancroft Books, 1983. See also Tales of the Colorado Pioneers by Alice Polk Hill

[226]   Willison, p. 35

[227]   Moynihan, p. 42

[228]   Ibid., p. 36

the rush." [229] While at this Kansas farm, at Zeandale near Manhattan, they moved into an abandoned homestead and set up housekeeping. Augusta easily recalled those melancholy days at the Kansas farm. "To add to the desolation of the place the wind took a new start. Our only furniture was a number 7 cook stove, a dilapidated trunk and a rough bedstead made of poles, on which was an old tick filled with prairie grass. I sat down upon the trunk and cried. I had not been deceived in coming to this place. I knew perfectly well that the country was new, that there were no saw mills near and no money in the territory. But I was homesick and could not conceal it from the others." [230]

Before and after: (left) The East heard of the Cherry Creek gold "strikes" in articles such as this one in The New York Times, January 3, 1859, which contained almost no truth whatever. (Right) This New York Times article broke the truth about the gold rush on April 20, 1859. Ironically, the Pike's Peak rush would be redeemed by bona fide gold strikes in just three more weeks.

"In those early years of self-sacrifice, hard labor, and economy, [Augusta] laid the foundation for Mr. Tabor's immense wealth. Had [she] not stayed with him and worked by his side, he would have been discouraged, returned to the stone-cutting trade and so lost his big opportunity." [231] While in Kansas, she cried and mourned the irksome days and dismal nights away thinking about past pleasures. Yet, fearing the future uncertainties, this stalwart woman prepared for greater hardships ahead. In her darkest hour, it was as though Augusta wiped her eyes, doubled up her fist and, clenching the

---

229   Bancroft, p. 5

230   Willison, p. 36

231   Bancroft, p. 16

barren dirt within the palm of her calloused hand, swore she would endure and never surrender to the hardships facing her. That first summer in Kansas saw "a searing drought [preventing] growth and turning the soil to choking dust." In October 1857, Nathaniel Maxcy Tabor, Horace and Augusta's only child, was born amid the barren Kansas prairie. Augusta made only one entry that day in her diary: "Baby came." [232]

"In February 1859, Horace Tabor heard of Pike's Peak through someone in Green Russell's party who was returning, and at once decided to try his luck in the new El Dorado. He told me I might go home to Maine, but I refused to leave him, and upon reflection," Augusta recalled, "he thought it would be more profitable to take me, as in that case the two men would go along and board with us, and the money they paid would keep us all." Horace worked at Fort Riley during the months of March and April 1859. The date of April 5, 1859, [233] is listed when the Tabors "set out in an ox-drawn covered wagon with two men friends and their sixteen-month-old baby son, Nathaniel Maxcy." They journeyed up the Republican River amid lush green prairies where crimson anemones and blue larkspur grew wild. Eventually the timber along the creeks and rivers diminished entirely and they traveled through barren prairie. Nothing in sight but buffaloes, antelope and Indians. Up ahead a tornado overturned "heavy freight wagons, blew a light buggy into fragments, tore open boxes and scattered dry goods for several miles and rolled a cooking stove forty to fifty yards." The survivors dubbed it Hurricane Creek. The Tabors soon passed by and witnessed the scene but they themselves encountered no storms of any magnitude.

"Indians followed us all the time and, though friendly, were continually begging and stealing," Augusta related. "Every Sunday we rested, if rest it could be called. The men were hunting, while I stayed to guard the camp, wash the soiled linen and cook for the following week. My babe was teething and suffering from fever and ague, and required constant attention day and night. I was weak and feeble, having suffered all the time I lived in Kansas with the ague. My weight was only ninety pounds...What I endured on that journey only the women who crossed the plains in '59 can realize." [234]

It took them until June 20 to reach Denver. They spent two weeks allowing the oxen to rest from the long journey before traveling on to Golden, Colorado. They stayed but a

---

232   Moynihan, p. 44
233   Willison states the date they left Zeandale, Kansas was May 5th instead of April 5th.
234   Ibid., p. 38-39

short time before deciding to move "on to Gregory Diggings, now Central City....Leaving me and my sick child in the 7 by 9 tent, that my hands had made, the men took a supply of provisions on their backs, a few blankets, and bidding me be good to myself, left on the morning of the glorious Fourth...Twelve miles from a human soul save my babe. The only sound I heard was the lowing of the cattle, and they, poor things, seemed to feel the loneliness of the situation and kept unusually quiet. Every morning and evening I had a 'round-up' all to myself." [235] Three weeks later, Horace returned. But on July 26, 1859, they again loaded up and headed for the mountains. They journeyed by way of Russell Gulch and up to Payne's Bar--now Idaho Springs. Augusta spoke about life on the trail.

"The road was a mere trail," Augusta recalled. "Every few rods we were obliged to stop and widen it. Many times we unloaded the wagon and by pushing it, helped the cattle up the hills. Often night overtook us where it was impossible to find a level place

---

[235]   Bancroft, p. 5

to spread a blanket. Under such circumstances we drove stakes into the ground, rolled a log against them and lay with our feet against the log. Sometimes the hill was so steep that we slept almost upright. We were nearly three weeks cutting our way through Russell's Gulch in Payne's Bar." [236]

The elements of nature definitely affected her. "Ours was the first wagon through and I was the first white woman there, if white I could be called, after camping out three months," Augusta related sometime later. The men quickly erected a log hut and stretched the 7'x9' tent across the top for a roof. Horace prospected during the day while Augusta baked bread and pies, cooked meals and sold milk from the family cow. Horace was having no luck with finding gold but she was making money hands over heels with the hungry miners. She spoke about this lifestyle. "Here one of our party, Mr. Maxcy had an attack of mountain fever, and for four weeks he lay, very ill, at the door of our tent, in a wagon bed, I acting as physician and nurse. A miner with a gunshot wound through his hand was also brought to my door for attention." [237]

Horace staked a claim at the creek near the Jackson diggings. He worked hard but, like before, to no avail. Even the diggings by Jackson came to nothing as the summer progressed. George Jackson had one curious friend who, no doubt, Augusta must have seen wandering from saloon to saloon as she walked about the camp. If she didn't see him, then it is certain Horace did. The other miners called him Old Phil the Cannibal. He was "a filthy monster...trailed by a large mangy dog almost as dangerous as his master." Phil was a fugitive from the law back in Philadelphia. He'd committed several brutal murders and openly boasted of the incidents to those who listened. He even admitted to "having, in emergency, turned cannibal...Said he had killed and eaten two Indians and one white man (French). Upon being asked about the taste of human flesh, he answered that the head, hands and feet, when thoroughly cooked, tasted good--not unlike pork, but the other portions of the body he did not like; they were too grisly and tough." [238]

Chicago Creek area was the same and, in no time at all, it appeared to be dying. The miners were restless, many wanting to move on. Augusta soon made enough money to buy the homestead back in Kansas. But providence had decided she would never again live there. Instead, they went to Denver to spend the winter. She spoke of the first snow

---

[236]   Willison, p. 58-59

[237]   Willison, p. 59

[238]   WIllison, p. 80

and fleeing the mountains in late September 1859. "With the first snow came an old miner to our camp who told dreadful tales of snow slides and advised Mr. Tabor to take me out of the mountains immediately. Those who know anything of the surroundings of Idaho Springs will smile at the idea of a snow slide there. But we, in our ignorance of the mountains, believed all the old miner said, and left for Denver." [239] About Denver she added: "I had been very successful with my bakery in camp, making enough to pay for the farm in Kansas and to keep us through the winter. Arriving in Denver, we rented a room over a store. It was the first roof I had slept under for six months...I took in a few boarders." [240] The store, Vasquez's, was located on Ferry Street. [241]

Horace returned to his claim to find claim jumpers had taken over. Rather than fight, he moved farther into the wilderness. Somewhere along the Arkansas River looked good, he thought. [242] "So he lost all his summer's work and had to sell the cow to buy supplies for the new camp," Augusta remembered. He returned to Augusta and the child in Denver to make plans. Eventually, on a cold blustery February morning, Horace loaded them into their battered old wagon, hitched the team of scrawny oxen and drove off with fellow boarders toward Pike's Peak. Augusta recorded in her diary:

"*March 1st: The sun arose bright and beautiful, not a cloud to be seen...Breakfast of venison ham and sassafras tea. This I call a poor apology for coffee. We camped for noon at the mill. The wind blew very high. I had a walk after dinner. At night we camped on plum creek. The wind blew all night.*

"*March 2nd: Morning is very windy...[the baby] has a bad cold and is very cross, breakfast of venison ham and coffee. We stopped under a hill to break the wind of and to have dinner...4 o'clock we camped for the night beside a log cabin in which lived a woman and five raged [sic] dirty chuldren[sic]. Here the prairie caught a fire, and the men worked an hour or so in trying to keep the fire from a small hay stack, but in vain. We retired early as usual, and slept sound until the sun was up on the day.*

"*March 3rd: Windy and cold, I kept the bed al [sic] the morning. At noon we stopped at a ranch and built a fire in a cabin but the smoke was so bad we were oblige to move it out side. The wind is still blowing hard, have kept the bed al [sic] the afternoon...4*

---

239   Willison, p. 73
240   Willison, p. 73
241   Moynihan, p. 46
242   Bancroft, p. 6

Sunday. The wind is still blowing we came near to the mountains and passed some natural monuments, some nearly white as marble and standing thirty or forty feet. We drove into a beautiful valley and halted for noon. There a man overtook us with some cows, and kindly offered us some milk which was thankfully received as we had had no milk for coffee since we left civilization." [243]

After prospecting Fontaine qui Bouille and some of the other creeks in the immediate area, Horace, Augusta, the child and the boarders moved on. They followed the trail through Ute Pass, taking them a month before reaching South Park. [244] "I shall never forget my first vision of the park," she recalled. "The sun was just setting. I can only describe it by saying it was one of Colorado's sunsets. Those who have seen them know how glorious they are. Those who have not cannot imagine how gorgeously beautiful they are." [245] A few days later, they found Salt Creek. Likewise, as the name implied, the water was unfit for consumption. That night was extremely cold. A stray burro came clomping its way into camp to warm itself by the dying embers of the fire. By the next morning "his fetlocks [were] burned off." Augusta adopted it as a pet to keep her company while the men were doing what they'd come to do. [246]

---

[243]   Willison, p. 137-138

[244]   Willison says it took them only two weeks. p. 139

[245]   Bancroft, p. 6

[246]   Willison, p. 139

The following day they moved on to a better water supply. One prospector remembered another group of miners who'd left Denver before them and headed for this area, also. Horace and the others quickly shouldered their weapons and went looking for the others. Meanwhile, Augusta was left behind to fend for herself and the child. By the next morning, the men were back in camp. What to do, they wondered? Where to go? Where to look? One suggested they "throw a stick into the air and proceed in whatever direction it happens to fall." [247] They did. The stick pointed southwest. A couple of days later they arrived in the Arkansas Valley. A host of mishaps slowed their crossing over the icy, roaring torrent. Horace and the others moved along the river to Cache Creek and all staked their claims. They found gold but the texture was so fine it wasn't worth the trouble. Further still, it was mixed with a heavy black sand that didn't appear to be worth much. Augusta detailed the hardships and loneliness here when she wrote: "For four weeks we worked there. Our supplies were almost gone and we felt discouraged. It had been a long year since we had heard of the loved ones at home." [248]

At one crossing, Augusta and the child nearly drowned. In crossing the wagon slipped from a rock ledge and went swirling down the swift river in the deepest part of the channel. She acted quickly, seized some willow branches under an abrupt bank and, despite the raging waters, managed to hold on until she and the child were rescued.

On May 8, 1860, after several weeks of little success, they arrived at California Gulch. Food was low. They decided it was time to butcher the oxen that had brought them all the way from Kansas three years before. [249] Once more she was the first woman to be in this particular camp. Likewise, as before, the men built her a log cabin with a sod roof, a dirt floor and no windows. As before, Augusta went into business doing what *women* did best in those days. Upon arrival, no more than fifty miners were working in the hard and bitter snow. Augusta found little to feed her family except "poor beef and dried apples." Within a few weeks, ten thousand men had moved into California Gulch and Augusta was appointed postmistress of the first post office. The camp's growing population christened the town Boughtown; afterwards, changing it to Oro City. Days passed and, despite hard times, Augusta felt most happy that summer.

---

[247]   Willison, p. 140

[248]   WIllison, p. 140

[249]   Bancroft, p. 6

In camp Augusta found the miners were a rough and cussed lot, not over-tolerant of others' ill-manners. One day, after a torrential downpour in Oro City, an interloper came galloping through the town splashing mud everywhere. A miner pulled his six-shooter.

"Hold on thar, stranger! When you go through this yar town, go slow so's folk kin take a look at you!"

The rider continued on his way up the gulch. On his way back, however, he was walking his horse. Suddenly someone shot at him.

"Stranger," said the drunken miner, "when you go through this yar town." He paused, "Go as if you hed business and meant to get somewhar." [250]

By the 20th day of September 1860, Horace had prospected $5,000 in gold dust. He gave Augusta one fifth and encouraged her to spend the winter with her parents. Augusta invested the money to purchase 160-acres of land in Kansas. She returned to Maine that fall to stay with relatives for the winter. In the spring of 1861, Augusta headed west, happy to learn Frank and Lilly Pierce, members of her family, were joining them. [251] Horace and Maxcy, who'd joined her in the early spring, bought several pounds of flour in Iowa. Augusta, on the other hand, bought a mule team and a wagon in St. Joseph, Missouri, and they returned to the gold fields. Horace mined and Augusta played the role of waitress to hungry miners and mother to her son. That year, 1861, Horace and Augusta netted around $15,000. When not working, she rode horseback to Denver with their gold hid in her underclothing and deposited it in the express office, carrying a small amount in the open in case of footpads.

Toward the end of 1861, as the War for Southern Independence raged back East, the mine played out. Augusta and Horace went to the other side of Mosquito Range--a camp called Buckskin Joe. The old saying that when something works don't try and fix it was true for them. She'd made several thousand dollars performing her 'womanly' chores at camps, so nothing doing, but she should do the same at Buckskin Joe. Further, she was chosen postmistress and the campsite became their home for the next few years. [252] Horace, on the other hand, had no luck at all. He simply helped with the family business

---

[250]   Willson, p. 143

[251]   Moynihan, p. 47

[252]   Willison states that "Nothing more than this is known of their life here...neither Tabor nor Augusta talk of the day in Buckskin Joe. Nor can anything be learned from the records of the day." p. 146

chores. But the dream remained. Fortune and gold were tangible ideas. So Horace bartered for gold and Augusta frowned upon his dealings. In return for supplies, which he made freely available, the rock miners would trade "any rich finds."

In the year 1868, the Printer Boy mine owners in California Gulch decided to enlarge. This prompted the Tabor's to move back to Oro City. Horace and Augusta built a large four-room log cabin a mile from Leadville, Colorado. As before--so again. They set about their usual chores of operating a mercantile. But lady luck was still frowning at the Tabors. Broke and isolated so far up in the mountains, Horace built a cabin and settled down, "content apparently to live here in comparative poverty for the remainder of their lives." The years passed. Augusta worked and labored at Oro City and Horace cherished his dream. Three years...four...five... Augusta's expressive New England forthrightness grew more caustic. [253] Horace's intolerable ways all those years were becoming more disagreeable. She knew the 'value' of money and felt him careless.

The year 1877 brought great change. The weighty particles of black sand were lead-silver carbonates. A new wave of miners moved into the California Gulch and settled in the lower region. Augusta and Horace decided to move the mercantile down the road. A mile further down to be precise, on the south side of Chestnut Street, next door to the corner of Harrison Avenue. They erected a one and a half story log framed building with upstairs living quarters. In the rear they added a dining and kitchen area. The family business exploded with the growth of the town. Before long he was taking applications for two different clerk positions. These were filled to help with the post office alone. And, because he owned a personal iron safe, Horace was propositioned by the miners to use it for banking services. The cashiers spent their time operating the mercantile and the bank and Horace faced the fact he now had to hire more clerks.

Some seventy tents, shanties and log cabins comprised the new mining area and those miners gathered in January 1878, to elect Horace mayor for the term of one year. The boom-town needed a name. New Oro City was chosen. Then Slabtown. Finally, Leadville. The Tabor's were now worth between $25,000 and $30,000. Horace felt they must expand to live up to their image and way of life. So he built a new home. Upstairs, however, in the two story structure, they added extra rooms where the employees might live. Their new address--310 Harrison Avenue. On the crisp Sunday morning of April 21, 1878, Horace allowed two German miners a grubstake. August Rische and George

---

[253]   Bancroft, p. 10

Theoworth Hook picked out about $17 worth of food and supplies. Rische was "the worst played-out man I ever met. His entire wealth consisting of a pick and a spade and a faithful old dog," Augusta remembered. [254]

"Ve give you a third of our find," they could be heard to agree. Tabor and the two Germans signed an agreement to those terms.

Within a few days they returned. They staked out a claim and needed the working tools to develop the mine. Horace agreed. He still held his belief that one of the dozens of miners he'd supplied would someday strike it really big. And when they did-- BONANZA! The two Germans now owed Horace and Augusta sixty dollars. In May, August Rische came running into the store like his tail feathers were on fire and he needed a bucket of water.

"We've struck it!" He shouted out to Augusta as she descended the stairs. "We've struck it!"

"Rische," Augusta reprimanded him like Mother Superior, "when you bring me money instead of rocks, then I'll believe you."

He reassured her he was correct. And he was. The Little Pittsburgh mine grossed $500,000 over the next fifteen months. All of a sudden, Horace and Augusta and Maxcy were rich beyond their wildest dreams. They had the money to buy practically anything their hearts could possibly want. So Tabor bought another mine--the Chrysolite. Again he struck it rich. Horace sold the store. Within a year, after making nearly a million dollars on his $60 investment, Horace sold his share of the mine for a million dollars in cash to Denver bankers and speculators, Chaffee and Moffat. Horace was Colorado's first great Bonanza King. [255] So it was Leadville became a town that "never sleeps."

Augusta, despite the fact she now had all she could want, continued to practice prudence. Horace, however, spent the money like tomorrow might not come. The November elections voted Horace into the office of Colorado's Lt. Governor. Augusta moved with Horace and their son to Denver. The beginning of the end had come. Life would never be the same for Augusta. Never again. One social fling followed another for Horace and she would find herself at the butt end of his nights out on the town.

---

254   Willison, p. 161
255   Willison, p. 163

Scandal rocked society wherein they walked and talked and lived amid high fashion and finance and politics. The dethroning of Leadville's First Lady was at hand.

Baby Doe Tabor

For several years they would "fight." In January 1883, Horace divorced Augusta and settled in with "that blonde--the former Mrs. Elizabeth McCourt [Baby] Doe." Augusta continued to 'pray' Horace would return. She hoped when he lost all his money, and he eventually did, Baby Doe would leave him. But Baby Doe never. Augusta's lawyer,

Amos Steck, spoke about the five years of quarreling between Horace and Augusta and summed up this woman's undying love for her man.

Augusta Tabor

"She knows all about his practices with lewd women," Steck said. "I never saw such a woman. She is crazy about Tabor. She loves him and that settles it." [256]

Augusta sold the house in 1892 and moved across the street to the Brown Palace Hotel. Shortly thereafter she left and went to California for her health. She died in Pasadena, California on February 1, 1895. She was sixty-two years old. Her social position was intact, her personal fortune amounted to one and a half million dollars. She was still, in the public's eye, Leadville's First Lady. "The nickname [Leadville's First Lady] was spoken in affection and in admiration, and she was interviewed for the Leadville papers under that heading. Yes, she was the First Lady in many ways, courageous and industrious and civic. The tragedy of her life lay in the fact that, although she was beloved of many, she lost the key to the only heart she wanted." [257]

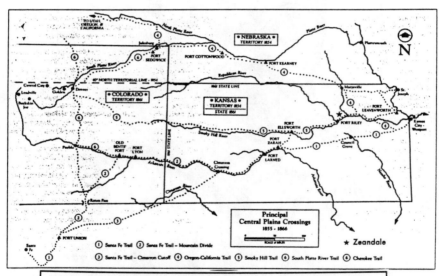

Map showing the area wherein the Tabor's journeyed.

---

256   Bancroft, p. 16

257   Bancroft, p. 16

Augusta L. Pierce Tabor:
Social Profile on Chapter Eight
by
Virginia C. Nelson-L'Aloge, M. A.

Who can rightfully censor anothers' actions? How can we, looking back, say another was right or wrong? Unless we were there to witness what happened, and even then each person acted and reacted based on his or her own perspective, how can we judge? Few of us have learned, unfortunately, the art of looking, feeling or hearing a situation from the other's perspective. At first glance, it appears Horace Tabor was an ungrateful cad taking the support and faithfulness of Augusta during the lean years; and, dumping her when he struck it rich for a younger woman. Leadville and Denver society made that clear to all. Further, Augusta accused Baby Doe of being interested only in Horace's money. Was she indeed a money grabber? Let's look at, feel for a moment, hear the points of view that possibly belonged to this three-person triangle. Let's set personal opinions aside. Join with me now, looking at each from a different perspective.

All evidence proves that Horace Tabor was an unselfish man who never turned away a needy person even when he had little for himself or his family. He was truthful and faithful to his dream. When he married Augusta he was working for her father. He loved her and she was a rich man's daughter. He had something to prove.

At that time in society it was the husband who supported the wife. She was not to earn money but be cared for. He loved her. He wanted to provide her with the things she grew up with. He believed it could only happen if his dream was fulfilled. Each time he was faced with failure he had to work harder at believing in the dream. He would not, could not, take *no* for an answer. Each time the figurative door was closed in his face his ego took on more scars. He was further degraded by his wife's success at her endeavors and they survived because she was successful! Remember society stated he was to be the breadwinner but she made the money for their survival by making the bread!

He remained faithful to the dream until it paid off. He finally could bestow on his faithful wife all the conveniences, jewels and luxuries that he was unable to give her during all those years of hardship. He had the gifts to give his love. But she refused him his triumph. She rejected his richness and all it meant. Imagine for a moment, you have seen your loved one suffer, scrimp and barely get by during hardship for years. Finally you can relieve that and show how much you appreciate their sacrifices and they *refuse your gift!* Imagine that ultimate rejection--that door of all doors--slamming in your face!

Horace, a generous man, could not give to his wife because she refused the gift of success. But he had suffered too during those lean years. It is clear Augusta made sure he knew how much he/they depended upon her success when those years were so rough. In a time when *he* was meant to provide for them. So now, if she would not enjoy the money with him, he would enjoy the money without her. That is where it seems their marriage fell apart. During their life together they had taken on and believed their *roles.* He the unsuccessful dreamer and she the successful doer. When the situation changed he changed the roles. She could/would not give up her former position. It was a power struggle. A clashing of wills!

She had lived so many years on the edge, with her keeping them from dropping off, that she refused to believe they no longer needed to be there. To do so meant she had to give up her position of power and, perhaps, the fear she was no longer needed. Her fear of poverty was so strong she refused to enjoy prosperity.

Horace needed his battered and bruised ego bolstered. Public office and public support gave that to him. He wanted the world to witness his success--to recognize he was not a drifting dreamer anymore. He appeared in flashy jewelry in a time when being conservative was the rule. It told the world he was rich enough to flaunt convention. Augusta became cryptic and critizing. He wanted to enjoy his success. So after years of strife he left her to enjoy life with someone who knew how to enjoy life. Now be honest! If you have a choice to be with someone who points out your faults, is sour on life, believes it must be no fun and hard or someone who is vivacious, fun, full of laughter, willing to let the world know how successful you are--whom would you choose?

But now let's look at, feel for and hear Augusta's point of view as we suppose it to be. We have a rich young girl, rather plain in looks, leaving a life of luxury to be with her love. We suppose she has no idea how life is without the luxuries she is so used to. But she believes her husband will do well by following the conventional route in business and become a solid, steady businessman. Instead he gets a *wild hair* and tears off with her the dutiful wife into some flat, wind-blown, God-forsaken wilderness known as Kansas--with barely enough to keep both of them alive.

But she was a survivor--both enterprising and in love with the man. She found ways of making life not only possible but comfortable where she was. Then here he went, just when things were getting comfortable, off on another *wild goose chase.* And being a wife she must go along. We can only imagine her family wondered what their daughter had gotten into. We can only speculate they encouraged her to stay with them where she was safe--especially after her son was born. Women in those times would hold the secret rather than let their family or friends know how hard it truly was. So the spirit of self-sacrifice was born for her as she returned, motivated by her belief in the loyalty to marriage, forever in love with her husband.

She found now that her business sense really paid off. She, in a time when women were thought and treated as air-heads, was a solid thinker with outstanding managerial skills. However, for her there is some bitterness that she is the success and not Horace because the society of the time would not recognize her intelligence. Society also put Horace down for it. She was in a one 'upmanship' position and, in all indication's, made sure he knew it at every chance she could get!

When Horace struck it rich with the $60 investment--after all those years of dreaming--it was hard for Augusta to accept it. Why? What would keep this hard working woman from enjoying his success?

After many years of hardship people often get into "poor-man's consciousness" combined with a "joyless" script. This is the belief that life is hard and unenjoyable. Sayings like: "don't enjoy or laugh too hard or it will all disappear" support this view. The disbelief that happiness is anything lasting becomes so strong that when faced with giving up the struggle the person does not believe it can be real or that it will last.

The sad thing is that if she had been willing to share in the joy and fruits of their labor her management skills would likely have saved the fortune--or a large portion of it. If these two people had been able to compromise at this point it is very likely that both the marriage and the fortunes could have been saved!

Had she been willing to give up being poor, the one keeping them going, and accepted his gifts, shared in his glory, he very likely would have not found it necessary to look outside his home for "comfort." Had he been willing to accept her financial guidance he likely would not have lost his fortunes. But who knows what truly went on in the privacy of their home during the long, lonely hours of the late night?

Baby Doe proved her loyalty staying with Horace after he lost his fortune. She helped him loose it by joining in extravaganzas beyond belief. They believed the mines and the fortune were bottomless and there was a golden goose who forever would lay the golden egg. So we have the two dreamers and the one practical person. Each was locked into their own righteousness. All ended tragically a victim of their own beliefs about themselves and each other. And therein is the tragedy!

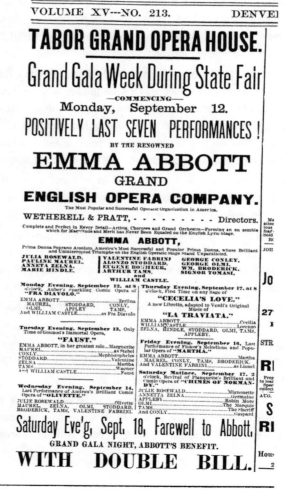

Nancy Kelsey:
Social Profile on Chapter Nine
by
Virginia C. Nelson-L'Aloge, M. A.

It is difficult to even imagine what a pioneer woman felt being the only woman of their nationality in the wilderness. To be among people whose ways and outlook on life was totally different from her own. What would it feel like to give birth in this situation? The courage it took was obviously extraordinary.

Today we have hospitals with all kinds of technology to hopefully insure health and life for both mother and child. Back one hundred and fifty years ago, even in the cities of the day, a new mother faced uncertainty while pregnant and during birth. But in the cities and small towns there were midwives. Lacking that, at least other women were there who knew about or had delivered children of their own. But to be on one's own, no other woman for comfort, particularly on the trail--not even in one's own home--has got to be one of life's greatest challenges. The fortitude Nancy had as she sat atop a mountain alone with her small defenseless child was enormous. She well knew the dangers of the four-footed animals but the greatest danger was from the two-footed animal called man.

We can only imagine the horror of awakening under attack while sleeping, exhausted after traveling, under strenuous conditions. The very real dangers, if not killed by Indians, were the cold, starvation and thirst stalking each step along the way. Mothers and fathers know if there is only a cup of water or a slice of bread we will give it to our child rather than consume it ourselves. Nancy and Ben were no different. Their dream was such all hardships were endured. Today we find the survivors discover "the silver lining" in all life situations. It was no different then. Nancy was such a person.

We see those women who set fire to the wagons or killed their children in order to turn back. It is not those who were the trailblazers. It was the Nancy's who trailblazed. Her love for her husband was strong. She wanted to be with him. She made her home on the trail. She endured and became as strong emotionally as the oxen they drove were strong physically. Even after delivering a baby on the trail she is described as being patient and kind. One can only guess what it was like for Nancy to have protected a daughter and loved her for thirteen years to witness her suffering cruelly at the hands of others. Her worst nightmare realized--she continued on never loosing her heroism, kindness for others, or patience.

Her story is the same as many others left alone with the children's responsibility in the wilderness. We know how hard it is today to be alone and raise small children. We have running water in the house, grocery stores down the street, clothing on the racks, toys for entertainment and television to mesmerize them. There were none of these for Nancy. A child might have one homemade doll or one toy soldier for company.

The women generally had one work dress worn daily and one Sunday dress only for very special occasions. They contrived things like removable collars or lower sleeves so they could be easily washed, ironed and re-worn. A bath was generally a luxury. Water had to be hauled, heated, poured into a tub bucket-by-bucket and then dumped out when finished. So many times one tub full bathed an entire family--each taking his or her turn. We complain if we cannot water our lawns everyday! Cooking was performed over a fireplace in the cold weather and, if fortunate, done outside in hot weather. That is if it was safe outside. Otherwise the women pursued this tedious chore inside no matter how hot the kitchen may have become.

Whole families lived in one room. A loft was often a luxury. But one room was itself a luxury after sleeping on the trail. Our going camping is a treat, a time to get away. But imagine being on the trail long enough to bare *two* children--such was the case for Nancy on the cattle drive. Going through this and so much more we can be sure Nancy was grateful *whenever* she had a roof over her head. Finally, after all the hardships, they had money but then it was lost. She kept her hopes high and bravely withstood a "painful, lingering death." Even during this time gave herself to serve and help others.

Today people complain when they don't have luxuries like their neighbors. They feel upset if there is only one bathroom or no cordless phone in the house. When the electricity goes out whole cities shut down. A car battery won't start and their day is often *ruined.* They sit for hours in front of television being mesmerized into believing they are *living the good life* with owning the newest electronic gadgets, eating prefabricated foods filled with chemicals they cannot even pronounce and using squeezable toilet tissue.

My husband and I stopped our car the other day next to a young driver and could hear the 'rap' music. The repetitious beat lull's a person into a zombie state while opening the brain to the destructive messages issued forth by the negative words. People sit day after day at their jobs bored beyond recognition. They rush from home, to sitters, to work and back--repeating the process day after day after day after day. They stay one payment ahead of losing their home or other *things* they deem important. They don't pay attention to the fact that daily the control from *outside* draws the noose of economic survival tighter and tighter as the breath of their freedoms are extinguished one by one. They hear and see only what is programmed by those in power as to the events around them. They *need* to wake up and open their eyes to revive the spirit that drove people like Nancy and Ben. These pioneers like Ben and Nancy formed this country, they were free to follow what they felt right. They lived the American dream.

The American Dream--to build a life--to do the work--to share one's talents is the goal of all free people. Today we the people are so bogged down in rules, regulations and controls it is like walking on massive sheets of fly-paper to start a business. We are *protected* to such a degree we cannot be the entrepreneurs our fathers and mothers were. We suffocate under burdensome unapproved taxes _beyond_ what England taxed the patriots _before_ the American Revolution. By the time we get home from work there is no energy left to enjoy the "things" we have worked so hard for and programmed to believe we need. Something has gone very wrong in our system.

The government set up to reinforce us is now controlling us to such an extent that soon we will be unable to free ourselves from the strangulation of overpowering restrictions unless we take action *NOW!*

Which life is harder--the ones Nancy and others like her endured, or the one we endure now? Which one of us took or takes the freer breath? Which one of us can live or lived the American Dream? Finally--who really *is* fighting for survival?

Nancy Kelsey

CALIFORNIA'S

FIRST PIONEERING WOMAN?

Often women of the Old West were the *first or last* to have done something in the area they lived or died. Yet, records of names and their existence have often disappeared, been lost, or not recorded in the first place. Many times the women themselves have added to that problem by choosing to "disappear" into history. For example: Who was the *first* white woman to set eyes on the Columbia River in the Northwest?

She was the blue-eyed, yellow-haired, pink cheeked Jane Barnes--formerly a barmaid in Portsmouth, England. [258] A plain-spoken Scotsman approached the fair-haired beauty with "a business proposition." He suggested she go with him to America and he "would outfit her with an unlimited wardrobe of dresses and millinery, and upon their return to England he would assign her an annuity of an undisclosed sum." Thus, Jane became "mistress of an officer on the vessel that made its annual trips to Astoria." That officer was Donald McTavish of the ship called *Isaac Todd*. [259] McTavish was a wealthy, middle-aged Scotsman with "an amorous temperament." [260] He enjoyed "fine wines, rich cheese, roast beef and lively blondes," and not necessarily in that order. He was to become the "Governor of a post for the North West Fur Company, which was hoping to push out the upstart Americans trying for a foothold to secure furs and other booty at

---

[258] The Columbia by Stewart H. Holbrook, p. 58; Rinehart & Co., 1956. Holbrook states her "name *may have been* Jane Barnes...and was such as to make her the heroine...of short stories, longer stories, whole novels, learned essays, and of barroom legends beyond number." Thus, we may conclude, her name may not *"have been."*

[259] Westward the Women by Nancy Wilson Ross, p. 122; Alfred A. Knopf, 1944

[260] The Gentle Tamers by Dee Brown, p. 74-79; Univ. of Nebraska, 1958

Astoria on the Columbia River." Now known as Ft. George, it was formerly John Jacob Astor's trading post. During the War of 1812, prior to Jane's arrival to the Northwest, it had been recaptured by the British and renamed Ft. George.

Ms. Barnes bedecked herself well before leaving England. McTavish gave her money to buy whatever she wanted. On Sunday, April 24, 1814, the ship dropped anchor in the Columbia River outside Fort George. After eight o'clock, a smaller boat called the *Dolly* came alongside. Alexander Henry, "a very proper, almost prudish young man," was among those who, on the *Dolly,* come aboard the *Isaac Todd.*

"McTavish was just up," Alexander wrote in his daily log. "He met me on deck, and we went into the cabin where I was introduced to Jane Barnes." The male population fell in love with Jane. So much so that McTavish insisted she remain aboard the *Isaac Todd* "where he could spend his nights with her in splendid isolation." At one point, however, McTavish invited several, including Henry Alexander, to the ship for a meal. The subject of the local Indian women came up and the way many of them were sexually free for the taking. This promiscuity had its drawbacks, however. Many of the Chinook women, the men argued, contracted venereal disease and were gratefully passing it on. Henry felt Jane Barnes different. [261] A few days after the dinner party, he offered Ms. Barnes the use of his private quarters at the fort. On May 8 she moved in. Jane caught the eye of several at the fort. She dressed in her finest array and paraded herself about the fort, laying claim she was the "greatest curiosity that ever gratified the wondering eyes of the blubber-loving aboriginals of the northwest coast of America. The Indians daily thronged in numbers to the fort for the mere purpose of gazing on, and admiring the fair beauty."

Cassakas, son of the Chinook chief, attempted to capture her affections. He offered "a hundred otter skins to her relatives, and any amount of fat salmon, anchovies, elk, and pipe tobacco for her own consumption, if she would consent to be his wife." [262] But she turned him down. Far from tactful, Jane informed him she didn't desire a husband whose flat head adorned "a half naked body, and copper-colored skin besmeared with whale oil." She even became embroiled with a clerk at the fort. He stated "the many white women he'd known" had no better morals than the Chinook females.

"Oh, I suppose you agree with Shakespeare that 'every woman is at heart a rake'?"

---

[261]   Land of Giants: The Drive to the Pacific Northwest 1750-1950 by David Lavender, p. 107-108; Doubleday & Co., 1958. Lavender refers to Jane as Burns and not Barnes.

[262]   Ross, p. 122-123

"Pope, ma'am, if you please," the clerk replied.

"Pope, Pope!" She exclaimed. "Bless me, sir, you must be wrong, rake is certainly the word. I never heard of but one female Pope." She grabbed the newspaper, pretending to read as though the argument was settled. The clerk stormed out of the room with "a wicked and malicious grin ruffling his sunburnt features."

"What's the matter?" Ross Cox asked. "You seemed annoyed." [263]

"What do you think," the clerk angrily grumbled, "I have just had a conversation with that fine-looking damsel there, who looks down with contempt on our women, and may I be damned if the bitch understands B from buffalo." [264]

Despite Jane's prejudices, McTavish and Alexander remained friends. The Scotsman hired Alexander to care for her in his absence. "My part is mainly to protect her from ill usage," Alexander Henry wrote. "Affection is out of the question...I shall, therefore, make it my duty to render her situation as comfortable as possible; not as a lover, but through humanity." The contract was in vain, however. Crossing the Columbia River in an open boat, him and McTavish "were drowned in an unfortunate accident."

Jane learned she was not welcomed because "officers of the North West Company frowned on a white mistress...when there were so many dusky maidens to be had for a few trinkets." Thus, Jane became aggravated with these white men preferring the "dusky women." She packed her belongings, climbed aboard the vessel which brought her to Astoria and left. She left with "a gallant skipper for Canton, China...Her further adventures in the fabulous country of Cathay have not been recorded." She eventually married a wealthy Englishman in Hongkong. He apparently paid "her way home from China" for he later employed a legal firm in London to "present a bill...to collect." This letter, or bill, also requested information how Jane might obtain "the annuity promised her...by her first protector [McTavish]." [265] It's not known if she got her money for she disappeared into history. It's a tragedy she disappeared, she undoubtedly would have made a fine chapter in the continuing episodes of women in the Old West. [266]

---

263   See also Adventures on the Columbia River by Ross Cox, p. 286; London, 1831

264   The Gentle Tamers: Women of the Old Wild West by Dee Brown, p. 78; Univ. of Nebraska, 1958

265   Ross, p. 123

266   Ka-Mi-Akin: The Last Hero of the Yakimas by A. J. Splawn, p. 436; Caxton Printers, 1980

Even more tragically, many of the female population didn't live to be a major part of the history of the Old West. One example, for which she is solely known, was that of Alice Clarissa Whitman--the *first* white child born in the great Northwest Territory. Alice was Marcus and Narcissa Whitman's daughter, early day missionaries in Oregon Territory--born on March 4, 1837, her mother's twenty-ninth birthday, at Waiilatpu. Mr. Whitman hastily built "the mud-and-log lean-to...to receive her." [267] She was a blonde-haired child who "entranced the Cayuses. One of the chief men, Tiloukaikt...was the most delighted of all and said...that the baby was to be called Cayuse *te-mi,* or Cayuse girl, because she was born on Cayuse land." He even offered her a plot of land. Alice was "a precocious little girl." That is, at the age of one, she was talking considerably. Her extended vocabulary included such words as "Papa, Mama, Sarah, Trim, and Pussy." While the Indian children were taught, toddling Alice Clarissa pointed out her A, B, C's with her own stick. She repeated the church songs taught the Indians at 18-months old.

On June 22nd, the following year, [268] Alice mysteriously drowned in the Walla Walla River. She was playing in and out of the cabin that particular morning. Earlier, she'd thrown a fit when time to take her bath and so, not giving much mind until afterwards, her mother gave it no thought. Her father escorted her to the garden that morning and the two of them examined it together. He'd given her a bite of pieplant. Later, wondering where the blonde-haired child was, her mother sent the "young Indian house-helper" out to locate the child. But the Indian didn't find her. She returned, saying nothing. One person living near the mission dropped by to visit. He reported seeing "two cups floating in the river." Alice Clarissa's mother remembered her playing with two cups earlier. She alerted them and all went looking. Before long, she was found trapped in a root--dead. "I ran to grasp her to my breast," wrote her mother in a letter back East, "but my husband outran me and took her up from the river, and in taking her into his arms and pulling her dress from her face we thought she struggled for breath, but found afterwards that it was only the effect of the atmosphere upon her after being in the water." [269] Not only was she the *first* white child born in the territory, but the *first* white female child to die. [270]

---

[267]   Ross, p. 35

[268]   Ms. Ross, p. 39, says Alice Clarissa drowned on a Sunday. However, a look at the calendar for the year of 1838 shows that June 22 fell on Friday.

[269]   Ross, p. 39-40

[270]   Splawn, p. 437

Another is the first actress to appear in Virginia City theater. [271] Antoinette 'Aunty' Adams, from Boston, [272] debuted at Max Walter's Music Hall. She was six feet tall, long-necked, stooped shouldered with a crooked mouth, light blue eyes and Roman-nosed, topped off with faded blonde hair "that was frizzled with little curls around her forehead." Her most 'conspicuous' quality was her "cracked-voice...a cross between that of a Washoe canary and a squeaky wheelbarrow" causing some to admit she couldn't "sing a lick on the round green earth." At her next performance, however, the miners decided to "put the kibosh on the show until she quit." [273] Earlier that evening, miner Hank Blanchard spread the word for all to congregate before the show. When they showed up, Hank instructed them as to why he'd called the meeting in the first place.

"Look here, fellows," he told them with a twinkle in his eye. "I for one think it's time to retire Aunty from the stage. Let's pension her and let her go!"

"Agreed!" Another husky miner named Mike McClosky said with a shake of his head. No one voiced otherwise and the miners headed for the music hall that night with one thing in mind. Immediately after she'd made her entrance for her nightly performance, a muscular miner stood to his feet.

"Now, boys, three cheers for Aunty!" He shouted. Each miner joined in, paying tribute to the damsel. She sang "Under the Willow." Again the miners cheered her. When the applause subsided, Antoinette sang the song again. Again the miners cheered enthusiastically. "Aunty! Aunty! Give us Aunty!" Each shouted. They continued until she reappeared on the stage to sing again. But this time, her throat was so sore she couldn't get the words out.

"Miss Antoinette begs me to say dot she cannot sing any more tonacht," Max Walker said, coming out on the stage.

"We want to hear Aunty sing," a miner shouted, standing to his feet. "If we can't have what we want, we'll go home." Every miner walked out of the music hall. The following night the same group flooded the music hall and pulled the same identical stunt. Again, not getting Aunty to resign, they stormed out of the hall as though disappointed because she wasn't given an opportunity to sing. On the third night,

---

271 The Gentle Tamers: Women of the Old Wild West by Dee Brown, p. 168; Univ. of Nebraska, 1958

272 An Editor on the Comstock Lode by Wells Drury, p. 41; Univ. of Nevada, 1984

273 Drury, p. 41

however, it was clear nothing short of her resignation would suit them. After her grand entrance and first run through "Under the Willow," one of the miners stood to lead the applause. But this time, concluding their hand-clapping, he suggested they all pitch in money so she could "retire from her profession." Miners threw bags of silver upon the stage. Each cheered and applauded her retirement immediately from show-biz. But Antoinette was slow to take the hint. She cut loose once more with another song. As she opened her mouth to sing, the miners cheered louder. They cheered so loud, as a matter of fact, she could not be heard. They didn't stop throwing her money, either. Antoinette finally got the hint and ordered the curtain be pulled on her performance in Virginia City, Nevada. She collected all the silver the men had thrown upon the stage, stuffed it into two money pouches and caught the stage out of town the very next day. [274]

Another Nevada woman, unnamed to us, was the daughter of Mr. Powell. Powell, a widower, came to Gold Canyon, Nevada in the summer of 1853. Like the others roaming the hillsides that year, he hoped to add his name to the growing list of Bonanza kings. With him were two of his children--one a son and the other a 14-year old daughter. As winter blew across the mountains, Powell decided he'd better find some more suitable lodging for his off-spring. He located a boarding house in Gold Hill and instructed both to "stay clear of confidence men." Apparently, however, Powell failed to instruct his daughter to steer-clear of male suitors casting their affection upon her femininity.

---

[274]   Brown, p. 168. Brown says this was her "first and only performance." However, Wells Drury, an editor of one of the local papers at that time, claims the story went as told here.

It wasn't long before one female-starved miner, a young Missourian named Benjamin Cole, came calling. No sooner had Powell journeyed into Six-Mile Canyon than Cole had persuaded the upright virgin to marry him. Before the moon changed phases the two of them were married in the boarding house parlor. The next day, searching for the elusive Bonanza, Cole left his young bride at the boarding house and headed off to strike it rich.

Before the end of the week, Powell returned, discovering his young maiden married and the ceremony properly consummated. Anger got the best of him and he took his shotgun in search of the Missourian who'd purloined his daughter's virtue. But Cole had "left the diggings." Thus, Powell loaded his two off-spring in the wagon and headed out for greener pastures in California. No sooner had he done this than, lo and behold, who should return to the diggings but Cole. The newly wedded Cole, learning Powell absconded with his bride, rounded up a few friends and went in pursuit. Cole and his makeshift posse caught the Powell family prior to them crossing the Sierra's into California. Words were rapidly exchanged. Eventually, however, at the persuasion of the shotgun Powell wielded, Cole recanted his stand and "reluctantly agreed to give up his young bride." He returned to the diggings without her and was granted a divorce the following month. The Powell's, on the other hand, went on to California, disappearing into the lost annals of history. The young Powell girl, nevertheless, became the first woman married and divorced in Nevada--all within just a few weeks. [275]

Our last *"first"* is our subject--Nancy Roberts Kelsey.

Nancy's claim was as the "first woman to make the perilous emigrant journey westward from the United States across the plains, through the desert, and over the towering Sierras into California." [276] Nancy stated: "I have enjoyed riches and suffered the pangs of poverty. I saw General Grant when he was little known. I baked bread for General Fremont and talked to Kit Carson. I have run from bear and killed all other kinds of game." Baking bread was not an unusual thing to do on the frontier for passers-by. Life was a continuing saga of one precarious chore after another. Many times the women

---

[275] Tales of Nevada by Norm Nielson, 169-171; Tales of Nevada Publications, 1989. I spoke with Mr. Nielson on November 22, 1993, about this story. He stated he conducted a very extensive search for the girls name but was not able to discover such.

[276] Nancy Kelsey by Phillip H. Ault, p. 30-39; True West, December 1989. All facts about Nancy, unless otherwise noted, are from this article.

were without company and, when company came, such as General Fremont, they were often expected to perform certain duties for those visitors.

"I remember many times that cow hunters rode up to my father's house, and telling my mother they were out of bread, asked that she would kindly bake their flour for them. Everything was at once made ready. The sack was lifted from the pack horse and brought in, and in due time the bread wallets were once more filled with freshly cooked biscuits, and the cowboys rode away with graceful appreciation. These acts of consideration on the part of my mother were entirely gratuitous, but the generous-hearted cowboys would always leave either a half sack of flour or a money donation as a freewill offering," Luther Lawhorn commented about women along the frontier, describing this as "an unwritten law, recognized by the good women of the town as well as the country." [277]

A marker at her grave in California states Nancy Roberts Kelsey was born in 1823. Before the spring of 1841, the 15-year old met and married 25-year old Ben Kelsey. She soon gave birth to Martha Ann. A second child, born a few months later, named Samuel, died in early 1841. [278] Ben was a wild-eyed, "footloose man, full of money-making schemes that kept them wandering for forty years." He sported a beard but no mustache, a broad nose and evenly spaced eyes making him appear "a hard-bitten, semi-literate man, quick of temper and crude of tongue, who had his share of scrapes with the law."

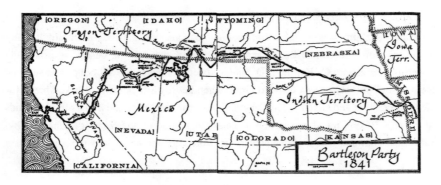

---

[277]   Cowboy Culture: A Saga of Five Centuries by David Dary, p. 147; Avon Books, 1981

[278]   A discrepancy in dates in not an uncommon thing from this time period. Perhaps such is the case herein.

In the middle of May 1841, they joined the thirty men Bidwell-Bartleson wagon train and headed west out of Sapling Grove, Missouri. They journeyed with no maps, no highways and no towns to inquire about the conditions as far as Soda Springs, Idaho before the Bidwell group split from the main body and went on by themselves. "Started early," wrote John Bidwell in his journal, "hoping soon to find fresh water, where we could refresh ourselves and animals, but alas! The sun beamed heavy on our heads as the day advanced and we could see nothing before us but extensive arid plains, glimmering with heat and salt; at length the plains became so impregnated with salt that vegetation entirely ceased; the ground was in many places white as snow with salt and perfectly smooth--the midday sun made us fancy we could see timber upon the plains. We marched forward with unremitted pace till we discovered it was an illusion."

Elements and such forced the group to abandon their wagons and continue on foot. In front rose the eastern slopes of the Sierras. Tall, bewildering and beckoning to all alike. Food supply was dissipating. As a matter of fact, had it not have been for the few oxen, they may not have had any food at all. For that is what they ate. On October 18th, they reached the top of the Sierra Mountains near Sonora Pass--about 9,000 feet. They discovered the first snows of winter. The next day, men cut for sign hoping to locate a path down the western slopes of the mountains. They left Nancy and her 22-month old baby, Martha Ann, amid the hallow wilderness of the vast Sierra Mountains.

"I was left with my babe alone," she later recollected, "and as I sat there on my horse and listened to the sighing and moaning of the wind through the pines, it seemed the loneliest spot in the world."

The men returned, fortunately, and all started down the western side and into California. Along the route, four oxen fell into canyons and, try as they did, the men were unable to save them. "We were then out of provisions, as we had eaten all the cattle [oxen]. I walked barefooted until my feet were blistered. For two days I had nothing to eat but acorns. My husband came very near dying of cramps. We killed a horse and stayed over until the next day, when we were able to go on," she reflected.

Nicholas 'Bear' Dawson, in his memoirs, later had this to say about Nancy. "I looked back and saw Mrs. Kelsey a little behind me, with her child in her arms, barefooted and leading her horse--a sight I shall never forget." "She bore the fatigue of the journey with so much heroism, patience and kindness there still exists a warmth in every heart for the mother and her child...always forming silver linings for every dark cloud that assailed them," recalled Joseph B. Chiles--one of the other pioneers in the small wagon train. Eventually, dirty and debilitated, they stumbled upon the Stanislaus River, followed it out of the mountains and into the valley. November's first days brought good news to the weary travelers. Arriving at the Martinez ranch, they met John Marsh whose letters, sent back to Missouri, had "motivated the Kelsey's to head west." They spent their first Christmas at Sutter's Fort in New Helvetia, California. [279]

The following spring of 1842, Ben, Nancy and their daughter left Sutter's Fort. The Kelsey's established a hunting camp and Ben's gun expertise earned a substantial profit. They purchased cattle, organized a cattle drive, plagued by marauding Indians trying to steal the livestock, and drove them to Oregon, selling the beefs to the arriving settlers. "While they were working with the cattle," Nancy later mentioned, "the Indians came into camp, took all the guns and piled them in a heap. They were entirely nude and I beckoned to the men for help. 'Bear' Dawson came and shot one of the Indians within a few feet of me. Dawson was not to blame for shooting the Indians, as the Indian drew his bow to shoot first." The trail drovers held the Indians hostage, demanding assistance in getting the cattle across the Sacramento River. One Indian, at gun point, was forced to swim the river, towing Nancy and the baby across in a canoe. Yet troubles plagued the journey as a second Indian attack at night killed a group of horses. The following day, drovers, waiting in ambush for returning Indians, shot several gathering up the dead horse meat. But the Indians were not yet ready to quit. A mile up the trail another attack resulted in the killing of several more Indians and horses.

Nancy described the incident: "During the fight, I sat on my horse and watched it all...we had twenty-five horses stolen and a nice mare shot through with an arrow within forty feet of where I was sleeping. The next morning we had a fight with the Indians and counted 12 of them as they went down before our guns." The trail drive, a 600-mile excursion to Fort Vancouver situated on the northern banks of the Columbia River, was where they sold their cattle and bought a hearty supply of goods to take back to California. While at Ft. Vancouver, in early 1843, Nancy gave birth to a daughter called Sara Jane. They stayed until sometime in 1844 before returning to California. "While the arrows were flying into the camp," Nancy recalled one particular incident near Shasta, "I took one babe and hid it in the bush. I returned and took my other child and hid it also. The moon was shining brightly and it seemed to me that every time one of the guns

---

[279]   Sacramento, California.

would fire, I could hear an Indian fall into the river. As I hid the little ones in the brush, I wondered if I would ever see daylight again."

Nancy saw daylight and Ben built a log cabin, situated in the northern portion of Napa Valley, a mile south of where the present town of Calistoga sits. James Clyman, who traveled with them across the Sierras to California, also kept a diary. On July 18, 1845, he recorded about visiting the Kelsey's at the Napa Valley home.

"Left our hospitable hunters camp and proceeded up the valley about 3-miles to another hunters camp found Mrs. Kelsey a fine Looking woman at camp with her two little daughters it appears that they had occupied their present camp only over night Mr. Kelsey being out with his gun soon returned with his horse laden down with the tallow and fat of two large Buck Elk that he had slaughtered during the morning the Kettle was hung over the fire and we soon had a plentiful meal of the fattest kind of Elk meat both roast and stewed In the evening three of us took our Rifles and walked to the hills in about two hours we returned haveing [sic] killed three fin [sic] Black tailed bucks the Evening was spent in telling hunting stories and roasting and packing venison ribs."

The following year, in May 1846, while General John C. Fremont waged war against the Mexicans, Nancy wrote: "I was sent to Fort Sonoma and rode the distance on horseback and carried a one-month-old babe in my arms. I was so weak when I arrived at my destination that I could not stand up." Her next child, Andrew, was born on April 7, 1846. Gold was soon discovered and, as expected, Ben left Nancy and the children behind, heading out for the gold fields. Lady luck smiled broadly upon Ben Kelsey. "He found rich diggings east of Coloma at a sight still known as Kelsey and took out a valuable haul of gold." He returned to Sonoma and his loving family. Ben bought several head of sheep at a dollar a head with the money made in the gold fields, then drove them to the mines and sold them for sixteen dollars a head.

"When he returned," Nancy remembered, "he told me that if I could lift the saddlebags in which was the gold he had received from the sheep, he would give it all to me, but I couldn't move them." Ben went into the savings and loan business lending money at high rates of interest including one loan to Mr. Perkins who borrowed $25,000 at twenty-five percent compound interest. Afterwards, Ben started a trading post on the upper portion of the Sacramento River. Then illness struck. Ben needed a doctor in another town and by the time they returned to the post, Indians had raided. There was nothing left and they lost all they owned. Sometime after that, Kelsey purchased more livestock and herded them to the northwest area of California near Clear Lake. When Andrew, her husband's brother, and another man were killed for mistreating Indians, they trekked another 125-miles to Humbolt County against the Pacific Ocean. They sold the cattle but, unable to collect a large portion of the $13,000, went back to Sonoma.

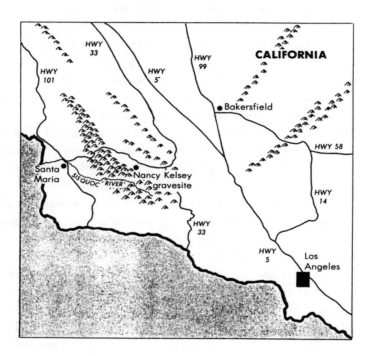

Another daughter, Nancy Rose, was born in 1852. Four years later, Ben built a bridge across the Kearn River and sold the project shortly thereafter. Over the next three years, the wanderlust bug continued to plague the Kelsey's. Nancy was persuaded to take the kids and go on a 1,000-mile journey to Mexico and Texas, buy more cattle and herd them back to California. Along the way, Nancy gave birth to two more children, William, born in Arizona and the other, Samuel Jr., born about 1860 somewhere in Mexico. While on this trip they experienced the most hideous of all disasters. Nancy and another woman stayed to care for the children while Ben and the drovers hunted turkeys. Shortly thereafter the women spotted approaching renegade Comanches.

"I loaded the guns we had and suggested that we hide ourselves," Nancy recalled thirteen years later. "The two oldest girls ran and hid in the brush and the 16-year-old boy, Andrew, looked out for himself by hiding alone. We and the smaller children hid ourselves in a cave in the side of the ravine. I could hear the Indians above, but they did not discover us. I had forgotten to hide the money which we had brought along to buy cattle for the California market, which was all we owned on earth and amounted to $10,000. After they had taken the money, pillaged the camp, and started off, they found the girls. They succeeded in catching one of the girls and the other said she could hear blows that struck her down. Poor girl, she was only thirteen-years-old, and even now I can hear the screams as they caught her." Later the women and other children returned to find the camp in shambles. "We could not find the captured one. She had recovered sufficiently to wander around in search of help. Oh, the anxiety of that night! We found her the next day, and my anguish was horrible when I discovered she had been scalped." Likewise, she suffered greatly from a total of seventeen cuts about her body. That daughter lived another five years before dying in Fresno, California.

By 1870, they lived in Owens Valley, California, amid the Sierra Mountains. In March 1872, a "massive earthquake hit the valley." Three years after, they were in Lompoc--about 160-miles southwest of Owens Valley. The following decade, Nancy and Ben moved another 150-miles further south to live in Puente. Puente was "a little land boom community east of Los Angeles, then a city of about 50,000." On February 17, 1889, Ben Kelsey died at the age of seventy-six. Nancy left Los Angeles and moved to Cottonwood Canyon at the northern edge of Santa Barbara County, nearly 200-miles from Los Angeles. Before her death on August 10, 1896, shortly after her seventy-third birthday, Nancy, "lonely, isolated, and perilously poor,"contracted cancer of the face.

"She faced the verdict of a painful, lingering death with the courage that had maintained her in the hard, uncertain life of the people who had made the 'great trek,'" wrote Minnie Heath in The Grizzly Bear. [280] "Up to within a few weeks of her death, she would mount her pinto pony and ride across the mountains to help bring a baby into the world, bind splints on a broken leg or minister to a fever ridden child." She had two wishes, she told friends and family, before dying. One was to be buried next to Ben. This didn't happen. The second was to be buried in a real coffin. This did. Her body lies

---

[280]   The Grizzly Bear by Minnie Beatrice Heath; Native Sons of California, 1937. This publication is referred to by Philipp H. Ault. I was't able to locate any copy.

buried "on a private ranch, four miles up a narrow road off the Cuyama River two-lane highway, then across a pasture to Cottonwood Creek." The branches of a tree provide shade to the peaceful setting. There, Nancy Kelsey, "the first white woman to cross the plains and over the Sierra Nevada range into California," eternally rests. [281]

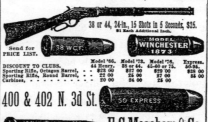
Ad for Winchester Repeating rifles

---

[281] This quote is from a sign at the gravesite placed there by the Boy Scouts, Troop 569, Lomita, California. Ault denies that she was the first white woman.

HOW WEASEL WOMAN CHANGED HER NAME

In the early days of the Old West there roamed a Nomadic tribe called Blackfeet. Much is known about the warriors and the way they lived and died. But little is known about the women and the manner in which they lived and died. One of the best sources for this information is George Bird Grinnell. [282] Grinnell explores their routinely, daily life in his exceptional book--*Blackfoot Lodge Tales: The Story of a Prairie People.*

Every morning while the warriors bathed in nearby waterholes, women prepared and cooked the meals. They served their families, offering the men about "three or four pounds" of boiled meat and the children "as much as they can eat, and the wives take the rest." During the hunt, warriors were "followed by women, on travois or pack horses [who] do most of the butchering, and transport the meat and hides to camp." If the men go off by themselves, the women remained behind to "tan robes, dry meat, sew moccasins and perform a thousand and one other tasks." If the camp members moved, the women packed all the possessions, disassembled the lodges and loaded everything aboard the horses and travois. [283]

The daily routine of the female children around the camp was much the same as their adult mothers. While the boy children played, the young girls would learn about tanning robes and furs, constructing lodges, travois and such. If too young, they were assigned to carry wood or water. Children were never spanked but "instructed." This being true of the boys and the girls. The Blackfeet "like to see women more or less sober and serious-minded, not giggling all the time." A custom was for the father to "get a buffalo's front

---

282   Blackfoot Lodge Tales: The Story of a Prairie People by George Bird Grinnell; Univ. of Nebraska, 1962

283   Grinnell, p. 182

foot and ornament it fantastically with feathers." He would call her to him. "Now I wish you to stand here in front of me and look me straight in the eye without laughing," he would tell his daughter. "No matter what I may do, do not laugh." Then the father would begin to sing funny songs and to get her to laugh. If she laughed, he would stop and wait until she finished. Then he warned her once more not to laugh. He would begin his song. He did this performance to all his daughters. Those who showed the "steadiest characters, he would give good advice." This included "the duties of a woman's life and warn her against the dangers that she might expect to meet." [284]

Blackfeet women were bound by traditional duties even when they died, and were buried "on platforms placed in trees...a few cooking utensils and implements for tanning robes were placed on the scaffolds." Likewise, whether the death of man, child or woman, "the body [was] immediately prepared for burial by the nearest female relative." These women would cut their hair short when a relative died. If the death was a husband or son, the women would "not only cut their hair, but often take off one or more joints of their fingers and always scarify the calves of the legs." Likewise, Blackfeet women went into the hills where they could be alone and they would "cry and lament, calling the name of the deceased over and over again." [285] Another source speaks about Indian women in general concerning death. The woman would strip "off all her finery; her hair was cut short and gouged in the most shocking manner; [and] slash her breasts and body with her knife." She would smear black paint upon her face becoming "a revolting picture of hideousness, painful to the eye and to every feeling of female beauty or taste." She would then "literally grovel in the dirt and cover herself with sack cloth and ashes." [286]

Death is, always has been, and always will be a part of the cycle of life. According to the religion of the Blackfeet, "on account of a foolish woman, we all must die...when Old Man [Blackfoot term for God] made the first people," people were strong and never suffered from any disease. Somehow a small child became sick. Daily the child grew worse. Finally, the mother went to Old Man and "prayed him to do something."

"This will be the first time it has happened to the people," Old Man told her. "You have seen the buffalo fall to the ground when struck with an arrow. Their hearts stop

---

[284] Grinnell, p. 190

[285] Grinnell, p. 193-194

[286] On the Border With Mackenzie by Capt. Robert G. Carter, p. 285-286; Antiquarian Press Ltd. 1961

beating, they do not breathe, and soon their bodies become cold. They are then dead. Now, woman, it shall be for you to decide whether death shall come to the people as well as to the other animals, or whether they shall live forever. Come now with me to the river." She followed. At the edge of the river bank, Old Man reached down to the ground and picked up a dry buffalo chip and a rock. "Now, woman, you will tell me which one of these to throw into the water. If what I throw floats, your child shall live. The people shall live forever. If it sinks, then your child shall die, and all the people shall die, each one when his time comes." The woman thought. She pondered the situation. Dare she choose the stone? Or the buffalo chip? What should she do?

"Throw the stone!" She finally said. The Old Man reared back and hurled the rock into the river. Naturally it sank.

"Woman," Old Man cried to her, "go home; your child is dead." Thus it was and always has been men, women and children must die. [287]

Style was as important to Blackfeet women as any other woman of today. Her apparel was "a shirt of cowskin, with long sleeves tied at the wrist, a skirt reaching half-way from knees to ankles, and leggings tied above the knees, with...a supporting string running from the belt to the leggings." More often than not, these articles were made from "the tanned skins of elk, deer, sheep or antelope." Winter moccasins were "made of buffalo robe" while summer one's were "of tanned buffalo cowskin." The soles of footwear were made "from parfleche...which greatly increased their durability." The toe areas of the moccasin were decorated with such things as porcupine quills or beads. Men and women alike wore necklaces and earrings. These were made from "shells, bone, wood, and the teeth and claws of animals." Women would decorate their dresses with elk tushes--which "were highly prized." Contrary to today's women, the Blackfeet women didn't take "particular care of their hair." [288]

Several legends about Blackfeet tribal women have passed down. Grinnell, in his book, speaks of two. One concerned an unnamed woman who prompted her husband to take her to Backfat Creek. She wanted to pick berries. He warned her about the Crow and the Snake Indians but she paid him no heed. Because he loved her so much, he agreed to take her where she wanted to go. While picking berries, the enemy came. Her

---

[287]   Grinnell, p. 272-273
[288]   Grinnell, p. 196-197

husband alerted her and the others to flee. He mounted aboard his horse and fled with those women upon the fastest horses. Speeding away, he heard a voice call out to him.

"Don't leave me!"

He turned and found it his wife. "There is no life for me here. You are a fine-looking woman. They will not kill you, but there is no life for me."

"Do not leave me," she again beseeched him. "My horse is giving out. Let us both get on one horse and then, if we are caught, we will die together."

This greatly touched his heart. He swung about and grabbed for her. She leapt onto his horse. By this time the enemy had caught them. Arrows struck his horse, wounding the animal. The enemy struck her husband with war clubs. Not wanting to harm her, however, they tried to pull her from the horse. But the woman clutched her husband and they only tore her clothes from her flesh. Her grip prevented her husband from fighting back. She eventually lost her grip and fell from the horse. He sped away. Though he killed several as he sped back toward camp, he didn't manage to save his wife. The following day, several Blackfeet returned to the attack scene. They found it as described the evening before. All the women were dead--except his wife. They could not find her and assumed she had been kidnapped. [289]

Another Blackfeet tale involves a ghost woman. The ghost appeared to the Blackfoot warrior Heavy Collar--whistling and "swinging its legs in time to the tune" one night as the warrior camped near where Ft. McLeod was later to be built.

"Oh ghost, take pity on me! Go away and leave me alone," Heavy Collar told the phantom. "I am tired. I want to rest." But the more he beseeched the poltergeist, the more she whistled and swung her legs to the tune. Finally, Heavy Collar became angry at the spirit woman. "You do not listen to my prayers," he shouted. "I shall have to shoot you to drive you away." He grabbed his gun and shot the ghost. The phantom fell.

"Oh, Heavy Collar, you have shot me, you have killed me! There is no place on this earth where you can go that I will not find you. No place where you can hide that I will not come." Heavy Collar jumped up and ran off into the night. Yet he could still hear her voice. "I have been killed once and now you are trying to kill me again!" She

---

[289] Grinnell, p. 13-23

exclaimed as he kept running. The ghost haunted him for sometime before finally giving up and disappearing. [290]

Many Indian women were prone to change their name. The men, for instance, were "entitled to a new name" whenever they counted "a new coup." [291] No doubt, this held true for the women. Changing the name was also done by marriage. Indian women would often marry a white cowboy, mountain man, rancher or farmer and change their name. This was not an uncommon thing. Montana cattleman Granville Stuart married an Indian woman named Aubony. After their marriage, she was "often called Ellen." She gave birth to nine of his children. He remained loyal toward her. [292]

But most Blackfeet women preferred to marry another Blackfoot. "There was apparently no form of courtship." Unless the young Blackfoot girl was a relative, she found "young men seldom spoke to young girls." Worse, perhaps in the eyes of the girl, "the girls were carefully guarded. They never went out of the lodge after dark and never went out during the day, except with the mother or some other old woman." So the majority had "very little choice in the selection of a husband. If a girl was told she must marry a certain man, she had to obey." The only exception was she could always "watch her chance and go out in the brush and hang herself." If she was fortunate enough, she could be the first wife of a warrior--called his "sits-beside-him wife." This honor came "with authority over all the other wives." The advantage was she could boss the others in their daily chores and "look after the comfort of her husband." [293]

But no woman in Grinnell's book surpasses this unique Blackfoot female known as Weasel Woman. [294] This episode is about Weasel Woman and why she changed her name. Weasel Woman was the older sister of two brothers and two sisters--all orphaned. The Blackfoot custom was to parcel these children off to relatives or others in the tribe. Yet, Weasel Woman, though only fifteen, thought otherwise. The young Blackfeet maiden argued, rightfully so, that her brothers were old enough to hunt while her sisters and she could do the rest. That is: the chores necessary for keeping the family together.

---

[290]   Grinnell, p. 70-77

[291]   Grinnell, p. 194

[292]   Cowboy Culture: A Saga of Five Centuries by David Dary, p. 272; Avon Books, 1981

[293]   Grinnell, p. 216-218

[294]   Female War Chief of the Blackfeet by Grace Roffey Pratt; Frontier Times, Jan. 1971; p. 22-23, 46. All source material about Weasle Woman, unless otherwise noted, is taken from this article.

She would care for the children herself. Her brothers would hunt and trap squirrels, rabbits, pheasants and other small sized game. As they grew older they would undertake larger game such as beaver and deer. The other girls would dry the meat, pick and dry berries and fruit. Weasel Woman would tan the skins and make clothing for them.

"The Indian women," wrote Evard H. Gibby, "were probably the worlds 'masters' at processing animal skins into usable buckskins and furs." They used very few tools to do it with, also. Besides clothing, Weasel Woman would make tipis, bags and other useful items. The brain tanning method, considered ideal, was used more than any other. It required the brains of the dead animal and a few homemade tools. This method was done by scraping out "the excess brains and allow the skin to start drying." While the drying was going on, the woman would "start breaking and softening" the skin...scraping the flesh side with a small piece of hardwood about one half inch by two inches by six inches in length. The working end of that wood, of course, had been rounded to avoid ripping or tearing the skin. With one smooth flowing arm motion, she would push the stick from the middle of the skin to the outer edge. The skin would turn milky white and become velvety as the scraping and stretching continued. Then the skin was ready to soften. When the skin had completely dried, they would brush and fluff the hair or fur and trim any rough edges. Then the women would smoke the skins.

The process of smoking the skins was another stage entirely. They gathered the rotten wood from some fallen log. Cool smoke, it was believed, worked the best "so that the heat does not damage the skins." The women tied the skin in some fashion around a tube or tipi-like structure and hung this from a tripod of sticks. A long trench, maybe two to three feet, was dug and a fire was built in the far edge of the trench. The rest of the trench was covered so the smoke could not escape. The fire was fanned so the smoke would travel through the tunnel to the hide. This smoke would then rise up through the top of the tube or tipi-like structure and smoke the skins. This would be done until the desired color for the skin was obtained. Then they would turn the hide inside out and do it all over again. The time involved was "about 15 to 30 minutes for each side" or up to 15-20 hours--depending on the skin size. [295]

Day after day Weasel Woman fulfilled their needs. The spirit of freedom, creativity and industry lived within her heart and soul "for no lodge was better kept." Likewise,

---

[295]   How To Tan Skins the Indian Way by Evard H. Giddy, p. iv, 1-2, 12-13; Eagle's View Publishing, 1991

Weasel Woman was "beautiful in face and form...according to the standards of her people." She was courted by several young warriors. None, however, gathered her most precious affection. Instead, Weasel Woman wanted to be in on the kill. When warriors came galloping back from a battle or raid, Weasel Woman was first to jump in, preparing the honors with a hearty meal. She lauded their brave acts while they reveled in the joy of victory, glory in battle and the spoils of grand raids committed against other tribes-- like the Flatheads, members of the Salish Indians. Blackfeet seldom traveled to the mountains as they were strictly prairie people. Such ventures were confined to "war with the Kutenais, the Flatheads, or the Snakes." Through the years of their free days, the Blackfeet "had conquered and driven out from the territory that they occupied the tribes who once inhabited it." Then, in warrior fashion, they had "maintained a desultory and successful warfare against all invaders, fighting with the Crees on the North, the Assinaboines on the East, the Crows on the South and the Snakes, Kalispels, and Kutenais on the Southwest and West." [296]

Weasel Woman hailed the conquering heroes. That was all, however, for she never allowed any "romantic gestures" toward her. She was interested in only one thing and one thing alone. Victory! The insatiable desire prompted her, during her twentieth year, to sneak off with a warring party. The group rode west toward the mountains. The following morning, her presence amid them was learned. Immediately she was ordered to return to camp. Only men were allowed on the hunts and raids. Only men had a right to work in the work place. Only men were allowed these things.

"If you do not let me go with you," Weasel Woman affirmed, "I will follow!"

"Let her stay!" The Medicine Man spoke up. Weasel Woman stayed.

How long it took them to reach the Flathead Lake is uncertain. But reach it they did! Weasel Woman didn't falter in her affirmation. She rode proudly by their sides. They respected her bravery and challenging eyes. Custom dictated it such. There, at the lake, the Blackfeet gazed upon a village of Flathead and Pend Oreilles and lots and lots and lots of horses. Weasel Woman was amazed at the amount of horses. It was a *game* in one sort of speaking. A sort of proficiency one developed amid the Blackfeet. A mastery of sagacity to take as many of them as she could drive away from the camp grew within her soul. She could feel the thrill of what it would be like to go charging back into camp with her own herd of quality horse flesh. A quality and commodity the Blackfeet

---

[296]   Grinnell, p. 179

cherished. The raiding chief gave the orders they would stay hidden until the coming night. Then they would allow the darkness that overshadows the sun amid the night to conceal their approach. That night, as footsteps approached the Flathead encampment, Weasel Woman turned to her chief.

"Let me go first. I feel I shall take horses."

Medicine Man agreed. The chief said, "Yes!" Weasel Woman went first. As a whisper finding its way upon the gentle breeze of the night she slipped into the sleeping camp, selected three of the finest, sliced their lead ropes with her knife and walked the animals back to her waiting tribesmen. A second trip and she returned with three more.

"I have plenty!" She offered to stay and let someone else have a turn. Each did just that, too. Each brought back several horses and then allowed another to do the same. Minute by minute passed and still no noise. All remained still. When each had satisfied their desire for horse flesh; they all rode away, East, over the mountains and back to their village. They had championed in their raid. What a party they had upon their return. Feasting, laughing, tales of daring, rejoicing and dancing reigned. The warriors had returned. Victory breathed from between the lips of every man, woman and child in the tribe. None had been killed or wounded.

Weasel Woman counted coup along with the other warriors that night. The chief spoke. He praised her in his words. Good luck sat upon the shoulders of this woman, he announced. It stepped where she stepped. It walked in her moccasin. He suggested she be given a different name. Weasel Woman was to assume the name of Chief Running Eagle--Pitamakan. No longer was she Weasel Woman. She was Pitamakan. Pitamakan dressed, acted and lived as other women in the Blackfeet village. But when it was time for a raid, Pitamakan went along. A warrior! Sioux and Crow felt the sting of her bravery. She was never injured and never ran. Before long, Pitamakan became a war chief. Other warriors sought her out to lead them in attacks and raids. It was a proud thing to ride the breeze with Pitamakan. Upon leading one large raiding party, Pitamakan was approached by Chief Falling Bear and several Bloods--a relative of the Blackfeet.

"Tell your Woman Chief that Falling Bear wishes to marry her," he told the young warrior tending her horses. After some discussion with the young warrior, Falling Bear felt it might be best to speak with the Woman Chief himself. After all, he was a chief, too. Falling Bear approached Pitamakan while they were riding. He told her he'd never thought of marriage before but, after seeing her, he wanted to marry her.

"I will not say yes and I will not say no. After the raid I will give you my answer."

That night they raided the Flathead camp containing several Kootenais, also.

"You go first." Pitamakan told Falling Bear.

Falling Bear returned with a horse. Pitamakan went in and brought back two. Falling Bear again went and returned with two horses. Pitamakan went and came back with four horses. On and on they pitched against each other until her horses outnumbered his fifteen to nine. Pitamakan then announced it was time for the others to have a turn. Returning home Falling Bear again asked for her in marriage.

"You have my answer. You had the first chance to take horses. If you had taken the most, I would have married you. I took the most, so I cannot be your wife."

He rode away dispirited. Speculation wonders why Falling Bear allowed her, if he did indeed allow her, to take the most horses. Why didn't he take the most is unknown. Maybe he didn't consider it a contest to see which of the two *could* take the most. Or, perhaps Pitamakan merely needed a way out of the marriage proposal. After all, she'd already turned down several others during her life. She was a Chief and a Warrior. Why saddle herself with the duties of being a wife? She may have thought. Better to be an early day career woman among the Blackfeet people. A role-model in self-reliance.

Legend came down that Pitamakan was the first woman to own a gun in the tribe. She obtained the weapon from the French trappers of the Hudson Bay Company who called her "the Joan of Arc of the Blackfeet." It was known she'd killed three enemies with the weapon and captured their weapons. Furthermore, amid it all, she remained generous with those in need. She practiced the law of giving and receiving, of offering back to the Earth that which she took and life was merit. Pitamakan's military tactics, while a War Chief, brought her eight major victories over the enemies to the West. On her ninth raid, however, she and five of her warriors were killed.

No one but the Great Spirit knows why this happened. Perhaps...

The following spring the Blackfeet went to war with the Flatheads--a war of revenge for the death of a female Indian of the Blackfeet tribe. A girl originally called Weasel Woman. And this has been the story of how Weasel Woman changed *her* name.

Weasel Woman:
Social Profile on Chapter Ten
by
Virginia C. Nelson-L'Aloge, M. A.

W hen a person is born into a society, be it big or small, they know no other way to live. Generally they accept what their parents, grandparents and elders teach them. When raised as a girl child they learn to cook, clean, make clothes, tan hides and tend to the needs of men. Seldom when grown was it questioned by the woman. In return she could expect to be provided with meat and protected from enemies. The roles of women around the world differed little in this aspect during the 1800's. As the 'bearers of life' they had the responsibility of the hearth.

Each American Indian tribe formed the roles of men and women to best suit the needs of the tribe. What worked for one did not necessarily work for another. One was born into, raised and generally died within the one tribe. Some tribes were related and a woman might marry, at the direction of her father or responsible family male and, in some cases the chief, into another band or to whomever the honor was given. The Indian woman found favor in the eyes of the mountain men for many reasons. As a friend of the tribe the mountain man often received her as a gift to wife. The lifestyle of the mountain man differed little from that of the tribes. The duties that fell to her were the same. The American Indian woman was generally taught to be silent and to rely on a man's decisions. For someone who wanted quite, as did most mountain men, their obedience was appreciated. Many of these marriages were satisfying for both the mountain men and the Indian women. The contrast of what she offered and the traditional White female offered was great. The White females were taught that sex was to be endured while their Red sisters were taught it was natural and enjoyable. The White females were generally riddled with Victorian 'shoulds and oughts' and the Red females were taught to serve. One was *tight* and the other was *free*.

13 Female Trailblazers of the Old West

Once in a great while a trailblazing female would come along and break out of the mold. Weasel Woman was such a one. Perhaps the fact that she took responsibility in keeping her sisters and brothers together after the death of her parents set her apart. She learned early on in her life to be responsible and to use her ingenuity to keep them well and alive. She succeeded admirably. Fortunately the medicine man and her chief supported her independent nature. If they had not her story might have been very different. It has taken far thinking, insightful men, supporting women's rights to make it happen. But again we find a woman who would not take no for an acceptable answer. As with all female trailblazers no matter their ethnic background, color or nationality, she knew her worth, acknowledged her intelligence, and had faith in her skills. These sisters in soul, these women whose destiny was to rise above the average, blaze even today across our vision like the bright comets they truly are. They light the way, beckoning to each female alive today to follow and learn from their examples!

The custom of changing one's name, for anyone, was a right of passage. To become Chief Running Eagle or Pitamakan, was a great honor. We can learn from this tradition. So often we go through life with our childhood nickname/name attached and never grow beyond that point. There is great significance in taking a name that reflects our accomplishment, our power. Sometimes we have to 'grow into' our names given at birth. But we need to be open as to who we really are even at great risk. It was at great risk Pitamakan went on the raiding party. She continued at great risk when she became war chief. We must honor the men who followed her. Theirs was not the 'better than female' mentality. They recognized a great leader no matter what the gender. And they followed her to victory after victory. It takes a man who is self-assured, who knows his own worth and is secure in who and what he is to not be threatened by such a woman as Pitamakan.

The true partners of today in marriages or in business are those who see and know not only their abilities but those of their partners. Being male nor female sets either one below or above the other in ability, intelligence or skills. It takes the sharpening of the mind, the willingness to be taught, to learn and to risk. Life *is* the risk be it in the business world or private world. To risk one must have faith in themselves and others. They must be willing to be different, to speak out, to give up what is comfortable. They must boldly stand for what they believe in. It is no different in Pitamakan's case or time than it is for each one of us today. We stand upon change and opportunity, the risks are great and the rewards are even greater.

So we honor another woman trailblazer, Chief Running Eagle--Pitamakan whose courage and self-reliance are a shining example of woman then and now!

Alvira P. Earp:
Social Profile on Chapter Eleven
by
Virginia C. Nelson-L'Aloge, M. A.

Alvira P. Earp's childhood, upon her parents death, is even today being repeated tragically in every town, village and city within this nation. Children are forced into 'foster programs' because they are orphans or rejected by family. There are certainly loving foster homes but, unfortunately, they often are fewer than the ones who are motivated by less than selfish ends.

Allie wanted her family together again and missed her younger siblings but she was not to have family at that time. When she married into the Earp family she got more family than for which she bargained. But even when respectfully married she felt the sting of rejection from society. Family loyalty was strong in the Earp family. She blamed Wyatt for Virgil's being involved with the gunfighters. The fact is that Virgil was his own man and could have rejected that lifestyle but *he* chose not to.

Why did women stay with men who lived the gunslinger lifestyle when what they wanted was stability and home life that was happy? What kept them there even though they were constantly living in fear that the next bullet would be *the* bullet? Why would Kate stay with a man who physically abused her as Doc did? Women then as women now stay in situations because they love the man. They keep believing things will change. All evidence shows Allie and Virgil had a good marriage but Doc and Kate were in conflict. Kate was physically abused by Doc.

The person caught in physical abuse is caught in a cycle of predictable events. The abuser is generally extremely charming when courting. They get the person to where they believe they are not going to be able to leave. Then they go through a cycle of irritation with that person and then comes the abuse. After which they turn charming again, sometimes giving gifts, making promises and they become extremely loving-- promising never to do it again. Then the cycle starts all over again. Alcohol or drugs may or may not be involved. Such was the case for Doc and Kate. Kate finally left which is the only thing that will stop them from being abused and injured.

In Virgil and Allie's case it was the emotional turmoil of not knowing when one of the gunfights would end their life together. The West was a law unto itself. You had to be tough to survive. A tin star was a target not a protector for the wearer. The streets were not safe day or night. The weak were victims of the stronger or faster reacting ones. Have our city streets really changed all that much, even with all the laws and restrictions? We keep hoping that by making more laws restricting weapons we will be safe but it does not work. We are safe only when each person comes from a place of strength. When each person knows how to defend himself or herself, their homes and their young ones.

The two bullies backed down when Allie challenged them with a show of strength-- even from her petite size. Abusers back down more often than not when the intended victim shows strength of character. The more we take away the rights and privileges of the honest, hard-working citizen, the more we arm the criminal to become the abuser. The more we restrict--the more underground the activity becomes.

In speaking with some of today's honest sheriff's and police officers we find they would rather have a responsibly armed populace who honors the rights of each other than have a helpless unarmed populace who fears each other. The West was a 'who can shoot first and fastest' mentality. We have now gone into a 'Big Brother who will protect you' attitude. Let's return to a strong, self-confident populace that respects each other and the Constitution and unitedly is hard on the criminal. Not his or her weapons of criminality.

There is great question as to whose side the Earp brothers were on. They wielded so much power that at times they used it to their own advantage. The evidence appears to be increasing that particularly Wyatt abused his badge. That still happens today as thousands of today's citizens are abused by the people paid to protect them--particularly various governmental departments. There are honest, hard-working law men and women who daily lay down their lives in the line of duty today. But the ones who soil the badges then and now make the headlines. When will we take a stand and clean up our apathetic communities so the ones wearing badges with honor can do their jobs.

We are so fear ridden today we put bars on our doors and windows. Who is imprisoned now? Who is afraid to go out at night? Whose rights are being protected--the honest citizen or the criminal? What has happened to a system where a thief caught in the act of robbing and is injured in that act and can then sue the person whose property he/she is on at the time they are injured? *And they generally win!* Something is wrong with this picture folks! Something is wrong when the average citizen has no right to defend his/her own property. Something is wrong when I cannot defend myself legally unless I am threatened with a lethal weapon. Something is wrong when I must wait until the thief, rapist, or murderer are *in my house* to defend myself!

The idea of 'the fastest gun in the West' is as repulsive as the idea I can no longer legally defend property, family or myself unless under armed attack within my own home. But there has to be some middle ground where the criminal really pays for the crime without conning out of it with legal loopholes. The citizenry has to have a means of strength and defense that protects their rights. Allie was afraid her husband would be killed because he wore a badge. What about us who can no longer drive to work safely, who live in self-imposed prisons, with bars on the windows and doors that we have placed there to keep the criminal out?

Which was better: a time when citizens took action or a time when we sit horrified as we watch the news and digest the days' murders and crimes with our dinners? Remember when the children could safely roam and explore the countryside? Remember when you could leave your front door unlocked or car windows down on a hot day? Remember when as a citizen we were allowed to be strong and defend ourselves? Remember...?

What have we lost?

This corset ad appeared in the El Paso Daily Times on August 26, 1896. It offered the women of the Old West a certain style in underclothing.

Alvira Sullivan Earp

ALVIRA P. EARP:
"SHE DON'T GIVE A DAMN!"

"Speakin' of epitaphs. I'll tell you one I made up when I was a little girl in Florence. You know there was a General Packingham who went to the Civil War, and there was an old steamboat that come up the Missouri named *Packingham* after him. Father used to sell all the wood he chopped down around our cabin to this boat, so when I was born he named me Alvira Packingham Sullivan after this old steamboat. Maybe that's why I been puffin' around the country all my life. Kind of a third generation. Anyway some of the children when we was playin' used to call me Lady Packingham and put strings of sunflowers around my head. Then we'd make up epitaphs for ourselves when we died. And this one I made up I reckon would be as good as any, even if I did think of it a long spell ago:

"Here lies the body of Alvira Packingham;

"She's dead as hell and she don't give a damn!" [297]

Alvira, lovingly called Aunt Allie, died twenty-one days before her one hundredth birthday in Los Angeles, California. She had depleted away to a skeletal sixty pounds before death. While fog enigmatically drifted into the city on the dreary Monday afternoon of November 17, 1947; they buried the wife of Virgil Earp, famed brother of the notorious Wyatt Earp of Tombstone. History has made a legend of the Earp's. Dozens of books, movies and television shows have portrayed them in a number of ways

---

[297]   The Earp Brothers of Tombstone: The Story of Mrs. Virgil Earp by Frank Waters, p. 231; Bramhall House, 1960. All data about Allie, unless otherwise noted, is from this extraordinary book.

from 'good guys making the Old West a better place to live' to that of 'blood-thirsty killers who used the law to satisfy an insatiable urge.'

But what about their women? This is the story of one of those women. Alvira Packingham Sullivan Earp--wife of Virgil Earp. [298] The Sullivan's immigrated from old Ireland. Her mother's name was Louise and her father was John Sullivan. Upon their arrival, the Sullivan's journeyed to Florence, Nebraska, a few miles from the Ponco Creek--across the Missouri at Trader's Point. John built a log cabin for his ever growing family. Allie spent her childhood in this area. Life was a daily routine of chores and more chores when she wasn't sitting on a nearby hillside and dreaming of the future.

"We could look down to home and see Mother in the cabin and hear Father chopping wood. Seems like that was what he was always doin'. I heard Mother say he was a terrible restless man," she recalled some eighty years later. "Gettin' a piece of land and when it was all cleared of trees and the brush burnt off and had a nice cabin on it and corn and pumpkins planted, he'd sell it, move off and begin all over again." [299] When the War for Southern Independence broke out in 1861, John told his family he was going off to fight. Though Allie doesn't say he enlisted with the Union, the Sullivan's had no slaves nor believed in slavery. Afterwards, Louise Sullivan packed all their belongings.

"Where we goin', Mother?" Allie asked her.

"Omaha," mother said. The town of Omaha, Nebraska sat about seven miles down along the river. Louise died soon after and now the eight children were left alone. The oldest was only sixteen and the youngest was "a pair of twin babies--a boy and a girl." Since it was during the war, and no one knew where John was, the children were made wards of the county and passed out to different families. Allie was 9-years old. She stayed with the McGath family--Southerners driven from their plantation by the ravaging, looting and pillaging Union armies. Allie recalled one harrowing incident. The McGath family had a girl named Betty--the same age as Allie. The old grandmother, who wore a white turban and black dress everywhere, told Allie to "give Betty a foot bath." Allie had no idea what a 'foot bath' was and so she asked the cook.

---

[298]   Waters states in his book that "there are doubts...that Virgil and Allie were ever legally married...No records of their marriage have been found." Yet, for all her adult life, Allie lived with Virgil as his "wife." p. 241

[299]   Waters, p. 17

"Well, you get Betty to put her feet in a bowl of cold spring water and then you pour over them a tea-kettle of boilin' water. That'll be a foot bath she'll remember!"

Allie did. The young girl screamed in agony as the scalding water hit her cold feet. Grandmother ran downstairs to see what was the matter. She found out.

"If you were a black girl down South I'd see you horsewhipped from top to bottom," she screamed at Allie.

"But I ain't black and I ain't goin' to be horsewhipped!" Allie yelled back at the elderly McGath. "Never got along after that," Allie recalled and she didn't stay much longer with the McGath's. As a matter of fact, she deliberately ran away. She went to be with the woman who had taken the twin babies--her younger brother and sister. The family rejected her desire toward her younger siblings and she went to the home of a family named Thomas but didn't stay there long, either. Afterwards, Allie went to live with the Pottersfield family. But after a remark about their dead child, Allie was banished. Nearly sixteen, she went to stay with her older sister.

"I never stayed long in one place or in one family," she recalled. "I could wash dishes and scrub floors in one as well as another and they're both jobs I ain't seen no end to yet. Besides, I had a hankerin' to keep movin'." [300] Allie worked at the Planters House in Council Bluffs when she first met Virgil Earp. She recalled it was early evening when he walked through the door. "He was tall, just over six feet, and had a red mustache," she remembered. "Virge saw me too. He always said I was just gettin' ready to take a bite out of a pickle when he first saw me...But mostly he said I was not much bigger than a pickle but a lot more sweet. It was funny how I remembered him all the time. I can't say I liked him particularly right off. For one thing, he wasn't the looks of a man I'd figured to fall in love with. I'd always fancied somebody my own size. But Virge was handsome, and he always sat straight on a horse. But it was in the cards for me to fall in love with him and I did." [301]

Though no record of her marriage to Virgil exists, Allie maintained "in about a year we got married...Virge was the only man I ever loved or got married to." She expressed common sense, quipping that "for any woman one good man's plenty, and one poor one's too many." There is a Universal Law stating like attracts like and Allie soon learned her "restless, wandering soul" had married into a family of the same. Virgil was eager to

---

300   Waters, p. 23
301   Waters, p. 26

move to new horizons as life in Nebraska wasn't much for a stage driver and a waitress. Worse still, the Earp's were "a clannish family whose close association was never to be broken and a restless one whom Allie was to follow most of her life." Letters from Virgil's father, Nicholas Porter Earp, arrived stating he wanted to return East and settle his properties, then move the entire Earp clan back to the West. Eventually old Nicholas Earp was to get his wish. The Earp's formed their own private wagon train, consisting of eleven wagons and set out for unconquered regions. They crossed down into Kansas, followed up the Arkansas River around the Great Bend, and came over to Dodge City.

"It was already dark," Allie remembered about their arrival. "Blacker than a mule's wet hide, and it had been rainin' all afternoon. We were crowded in our wagon, cold and hungry, and I was waitin' every minute to feel the wagon start slidin' in the mud and fetch up in the bottom of the gulch. We couldn't see but we could hear the water rushin' by...I looked out and saw a patch of light on the prairie. It was Dodge City. We must of got there pretty late, but the lights of the saloons and all were still bright when our wagons went through the main street." [302] She claimed this was the first time she'd met Wyatt Earp--Virgil's brother. He was walking down the street in Dodge with another brother--Morgan. Virgil climbed down and headed to the front of the wagon train to greet his brother. A few minutes later, he returned with Wyatt and Morgan. Each looked like the other. "Three peas in a pod" she'd often say of the fighting Earps.

"My shoes were off, and when Wyatt and Morg reached out to shake hands I stuck out a bare foot. I never did grow up, I reckon. Size or no way else. Wyatt gave me a cold and nasty look, and turned away. But Morg pinched my toes very friendly." Allie and Wyatt never got along too well. Labeling Wyatt "just a show-off," Allie had a few choice words about Wyatt's favorite crony--Doc Holliday.

"I never could stand him," she confessed, remembering the gunfighter, "and he didn't have any use for me neither...Right away I said, 'How would you like to yank out a loose tooth of mine?' He gave me a nasty look and said, 'Keep your baby teeth in your mouth where they belong. I have no use for them.'" [303]

Allie and Virgil camped in the rain that first night near the 'Dead Line,' an imaginary line within the cow town. All respectable townsfolk lived to the North of the line and seldom, if ever, ventured south. Likewise, all the saloons, gambling halls, prostitutes,

---

[302]   Waters, p. 34
[303]   Waters, p. 43

gamblers, cowhands, etc., remained south of this line. Those observing the 'dead line' seldom met with trouble from local lawmen of the boom-town. The second night in town, Allie witnessed a man trying to steal one of their horses. He came walking up and checking out the animals. Virgil and the other Earp brothers were over on the south side playing cards. Allie noticed the "yellow dog, Joe, growling" and poked her head out to see what was disturbing the animal. She saw the man and gave a shout. The cowboy started toward her with a "picket pin in his hand." Allie called for Bill Edwards--a friend of the Earp's. Bill came running to the wagons with a six-shooter in his hand.

"What you doing among those horses?" Edwards inquired.

The man stopped and slowly lowered the picket pin down next to his leg. "I was just hunting for a lost horse like that gray mare of yours," he told Allie and Bill Edwards.

"Well, prowling among another man's horses at night ain't the way to do it." Bill lifted his six-gun and pointed it at the man. The man tipped his hat and walked away.

"Why didn't you shoot him? You know he was tryin' to steal one of our horses," Allie demanded.

Bill threw the chamber of the six-shooter open so Allie could see. "I didn't have time to load it, Allie."

Later that night, Virgil returned to the wagon and scolded Allie severely for sticking her head out of the wagon. She paid him heed, recalling this was about June or July of 1876--the same time news "from the North came that General George A. Custer and 264 men...had been massacred to the last man."

Allie noticed a change in Dodge City. The Earp brothers, including Virgil, became more secretive. This was strongly due to Wyatt and his influence over the others. She wondered about Wyatt's suspicious actions and mysterious deeds in Dodge City--which he nor Virgil never openly discussed in her presence. "Him bein' a gambler, a cardsharp and shady character, and at the same time a gun-totin' police officer braggin' about the men he buffaloed to keep the peace." [304] All of this bothered Allie. "What he'd [Wyatt] been doin' since he beat out Newton in Lamar [Missouri] I didn't know," she recalled years later. "For the first time since I got married to Virge he wouldn't talk. But from a word here and there I had my suspicions. Later on I found out some things about him I won't ever tell to my dying day, so I know I was right." Allie was not one to mince

---

[304]   Waters, p. 41

words with tact when it came to expressing her feelings about the illustrious Wyatt Earp. "All those books makin' him out a big hero are pure gingerbread." [305]

About May 1877, a month after Geronimo and his Apaches were captured at Ojo Caliente, New Mexico, the whole 'Earp gang' packed their wagons and headed west. Down the Cimarron Crossing, through Santa Fe and into Arizona. Allie described one event really impressing her, a hunt in progress along the Cimarron as they sat atop a small hill watching what might have been one of the last buffalo herds on the great plains.

"It was in a little valley between two rollin' hills. The black bunches of buffalo looked like scrub oak," she recalled. "As we came down closer we could see the bunches growin' together, movin' slowly away, then suddenly breakin' into a run. Then we heard shots. We rode down in a hurry and saw what caused the stampede. Three or four buffalo hunters on horses were spread out at the back and alongside the herd, shootin' on the run. At almost every shot one of the big animals would plow into the ground all humped up with his back legs spread out or roll over on his side kickin' a little. The hunters never stopped but went right on chasin' the herd up the valley, leavin' the dead ones strung out for a mile behind them." [306]

WYATT EARP

The Earp's moved on into New Mexico Territory. Allie described Santa Fe, New Mexico. "Everybody was happy and everybody was poor. But most of all everybody was brown and old and wrinkled." She asked a Mexican about what she was witnessing.

"Senora, I please to tell you," the Mexican said. "The happiness is within and the warm sun outside. Because of these, we of Santa Fe never die."

"I reckon you're right. Nobody dies here. They just dry up and blow away." [307]

The Earp's traveled southwest to Albuquerque and turned west. They passed through the petrified forest in Arizona. She was moved by "all them big trees laying down and turned to stone it was so dry they couldn't live or even rot." [308]

305   Waters, p. 37
306   Waters, p. 52
307   Waters, p. 58
308   Waters, p. 63

The Earp's wagon train stopped in Prescott to winter and later moved on to Tucson and then to their new home, Tombstone--the place that made them famous. "We could see it plain," Allie said about their arrival. "It was a hodgepodge of shacks, adobes and tents...Tombstone when we got there was still a big booming camp. Every house was taken and as fast as men could haul in lumber from the Huachucas and build another one, there was people campin' on the spot in wagons or a tent waitin' to move in." [309] It was December 1, 1879.

Virgil moved Allie into a Mexican one-room adobe house on Allen Street. It had hard-packed dirt floors and cost forty dollars a month rent. They parked the two wagons, one on each side of the house, and repaired the roof before moving in. Allie spread the canvas from the wagons across the top between the wagons and the roof providing two additional rooms. The primitiveness was demonstrated by cooking over an open fireplace and using boxes for chairs.

"It was like livin' at the foot of the Tower of Babel," Allie later recalled. She spoke of life in Tombstone. It was a lonely life without friends or other women with whom she might associate. "All of us Earp women--Mattie, Lou, Bessie and young Hattie, and me, hadn't made hardly any friends in town at all. We weren't rich minin' folks and important business people, and we lived across the Dead Line. But there wasn't any reason I could see why we never got invited to afternoon teas, supper parties or socials like other wives." She claimed late one afternoon, when passing a sort of lawn party while walkin' to town, she discovered the reason. The women were all sitting on the porch under a big tree in the front lawn. Each was "dressed up like Thanksgivin' turkeys, jabberin' like magpies, drinkin' tea and eatin' cake," she recalled. Some were women she knew and had spoken to when they would meet. With hurt feelings at not being invited, Allie took a deep breath and casually strolled past the yard as though it didn't matter. One child, playing in the front yard, threw a ball and hit the picket fence, bounced a way and landed at Allie's feet. She picked the round sphere up to toss it back across the fence when she overheard the loud voice of a woman on the porch.

"It's one of those women in the Earp Gang!"

The words disturbed her deeply. The uncanny memory of Morgan, Wyatt, her Virgil, the other two Earp's, Doc Holliday, Bat Masterson and Luke Short as they all sauntered about Dodge City returned. Like the panoramic previews of an upcoming attraction, the

---

[309]   Waters, p. 77, 90

"queer goings-on there" she witnessed and suspected flashed across her mind. It suddenly dawned on her those men were now all gathered in Tombstone. And the same eerie circumstances that happened in Dodge City were reoccurring in Arizona. "It scared me," she recalled years later. "I reckon it stirred up that Irish temper of mine too. Because I turned and pitched that rubber ball away as hard and far as I could throw it. Then I gathered up my skirts real ladylike and strutted off without a look at them." [310]

In October 1880, Tombstone's Marshal Fred White deputized Virgil due to ranch hands from outlying ranches riding into town for a good time. That good time included shooting their pistols a little too much to please the townsfolk. Late one night White and Virgil went after them. As the cowboys made their escape up a dark street, White and Earp cornered one in an alley. He was Curly Bill Brocius. During the arrest, Bill's gun "accidentally went off, killing White." Before White died, he was able to make a statement. He claimed the shooting "was accidental and that Curly Bill had not intentionally tried to kill him." Brocius was taken to Tucson, tried and acquitted. Three days before Halloween, the Tombstone city council appointed Virgil assistant marshal to replace White. The position was a temporary one until a special election could elect a new city marshal. The special election was held on November 13, 1880. Virgil was defeated by Ben Sippy--311 to 259 votes. The following January 1881, Tombstone held its first municipal election. The post of city marshal, which Ben Sippy had won out over Virgil Earp, was now up for general election. Virgil again ran. Again he lost. It was the last time any of the Earp's would run for a public office in Tombstone. The 'Earp gang' would wait their turn to forcibly subdue Tombstone...and their turn was coming.

During the evening of March 15, 1881, the Kinner & Company Stage left Tombstone. There were eight passengers aboard and a gold shipment worth $80,000. Bud Philpot drove and Bob Paul was shotgun man. Peter Roerig rode in the dicky seat atop the stage at the rear. Reaching Contention, they stopped and changed horses. The night air was cold and light snow covered the ground. The moon glossed. Bud and Bob changed places so one could warm his hands while the other drove. A mile from Contention, close to Drew's Station, the stage slowed for a steep grade around ten o'clock. Several masked men came out from behind some mesquite and chaparral.

"Whoa, boys!" They shouted at the driver.

---

[310]   Waters, p. 107-108

Bob Paul dropped the reins and grabbed his shotgun. A bandit fired. Bud Philpot fell forward with a bullet through his heart. The horses bolted. Several more shots were fired and Peter Roerig was mortally wounded. The stage tore down the road lickity-split with the remaining passengers, the gold and Bob Paul grabbing at the reins of the runaway team. He succeeded, driving the stage on to Benson, Arizona. In Tombstone a posse was formed. Sheriff John Behan and his deputy, Billy Breakenridge, deputized Wyatt, Morgan, Virgil, Bat Masterson, 'Buckskin Frank' Leslie and some others. They all rode out to the scene of the attempted hold-up finding several "empty rifle shells, some wigs and fake beards made of unraveled rope sewn on black cloth to serve as masks."

Luther King was later arrested for the robbery and jailed in Tombstone. Shortly before March 19, 1881, King "escaped from the Sheriff's office by quietly stepping out the back door...A confederate on the outside had a horse in readiness for him. It was a well-planned job by outsiders to get him away. He was an important witness against Doc Holliday..." [311] Afterwards, Allie recalled something about the 'disguises'. "All the time I was just itchin' to go over to Mattie's and peek in the closet to see if Wyatt's disguises that Doc had took were still there," she said. [312] What disguises did Wyatt have and when did Allie see them? Allie talked about that, also. It happened one afternoon several weeks before the robbery. All the Earp women were over at Mattie's, Wyatt's second wife, and they were gossiping about Hattie--Bessie Earp's daughter. 'Big Nose Kate' Elder Holliday walked in and the women went right on chattering. Hattie was sneaking off and meeting up with boys courting her.

"If I ever catch her crawlin' out the window I'll switch her pants off," Bessie said about that time. "Still, a little sparkin' at her age..."

"Hell, Bess!" Exclaimed Kate. "At her age you was rustlin' with the best of 'em!"

"What if I was a whore!" Bessie shouted back. [313] "If you'd do a little whorin' yourself maybe your husband would treat you like a wife too!"

---

[311]   Tombstone Nugget, March 19, 1881

[312]   Waters, p. 130

[313]   Bessie, wife of James Earp (brother to Wyatt) was found guilty of prostitution in Wichita, Kansas in May, 1874, and fined eight dollars plus two dollars court costs. Her name appears "regularly in the city's prostitution fine list through March of 1875." Great Gunfighters of the Kansas Cowtowns 1867-1886 by Nyle H. Miller and Joseph W. Snell, p. 78-79; Univ. of Nebraska, 1963

"It's that sneakin' con-man husband of yours what's the trouble!" Kate said, turning toward Mattie, speaking about Wyatt. "He's got an evil power over a poor sick man that..." As Kate turned, Allie recalled, she clasped the closet's doorknob. The door opened and out fell a suitcase. The drop caused the case to fly open and out fell several items. Among them was a variety of "wigs and beards made of unraveled rope and sewn on black cloth masks, some false mustaches, a church deacon's frock coat, a checkered suit like drummers wear, a little bamboo cane..." Mattie, Wyatt's wife, gave a faint cry, dropped to her knees and quickly started shoving the things back into the case.

"Wyatt's disguises!" Kate snorted. "I told him if he didn't get them out of Doc's room I'd throw 'em all out into the street...That two-bit tinhorn's caused enough trouble already. It won't be long until he's got that stupid Virge under his thumb like Morgan!" Kate continued shouting at the women. [314] Allie remembered all this after the stage robbery, the death of Bud Philpot and the escape of Luther King.

A week after the robbery, Allie saw Doc Holliday going into Mattie Earp's. She ran to see what was going to happen. Doc was exiting when she arrived. Holliday snarled several angry words at her and walked on past. Allie went inside and talked with Mattie for a while. Later that afternoon, Mattie, Lou and Allie were standing, talking with one another on the street. Kate Holliday walked up to them, sporting a badly blackened eye. Allie claimed Kate was "bustin' to talk." They all went in the house and sat down. Kate started to drink and "as soon as her tongue was loosened, she lit into Doc for beatin' her up. Then she went after Wyatt," Allie remembered.

"Don't it look mighty peculiar there ain't no respectable, upstandin' citizens in this posse chasin' around from hell to breakfast?" Kate questioned. "Why in hell did no-account...gamblers like Wyatt and Morg and Bat...rush into the posse? I'll tell you why! Wyatt's got them and some others in a gang to rob stages. Marshal Williams tipped them off about the money in this one. Doc did the shootin' all right. [315] He meant to kill Bob

314   Waters, p. 108-109

315   Author Grace McCool, in her book Gunsmoke: The True Story of Old Tombstone, p. 28 (Gateway Publishing Co., 1954), states: "Months later Kate Eiller [Elder], the common-law wife of Doc Holliday, swore out a warrant for him, naming him as one of the robbers. Holliday was arrested July 6th by Sheriff Behan. John Slaughter, later sheriff of Cochise County, had met Holliday on the road the night of the robbery and he emphatically declared he believed him [Doc] guilty. City policeman Virgil Earp, arrested Miss Eiller on July 7th on a charge of drunkenness and she was fined $12 in Justice Spicer's court and Holliday was released. Miss Eiller, being under arrest, could not testify against him [Doc]."

Paul but he got Philpot because they switched places. It was him that fixed it so Luther King could escape and not have to tell on him. Wyatt's conned 'em all into this. Poor sick Doc. Marshall Williams. Naughty boy Bat. Solemn old Jim. Easygoing, laughin' Morg." Kate named them off one by one as Allie sat with her mouth agape, feeling cold and alone and a little dizzy from the realization. "And now that stupid, honest husband of yours, Virgil, who ought to have stayed on his farm!"

A vast sickness engulfed Allie and she put her head on her arms. One of them dashed a pitcher of cold ice water over her. Kate grabbed her by the wrists and Allie gazed up into Kate's face. "Doc's going to kill me for this. Mattie's going to get it next. Then it's your turn, Allie," Kate warned her. "Why don't you take Virgil back to the farm or prospect hole where he belongs? I'll tell you why! For the same God-damned reason Mattie don't leave Wyatt. And I haven't left that one-lung, whiskey-soaked, tooth-pullin' shotgun killer of mine long ago. Because women don't have any sense."

"I raised my head," Allie remembered, "feelin' mighty sick with all Kate had told me. 'I ain't going to listen to no more whiskey talk! Virge wouldn't like it!'" [316]

Kate eventually left Doc Holliday, moved to Globe, Arizona and operated a boarding house. "I didn't tell her good-bye," Allie stated, shaking her head at the memory. "But I watched her stage pull out from the corner. It gave me a funny feelin'. All I could think was that poor Kate hadn't been able to draw against a spade flush." [317]

Things were warming up for Virgil and Allie. There were several more incidents she boldly speaks about before the most famous--the gunfight at the O. K. Corral on October 26, 1881, an experience Allie would never forget because that was the day Virgil was wounded in the gunfight. "I flew up the street," she recalled. "People all over were runnin' toward the O. K. Corral. The butcher's wife as I ran past caught me by the arm and slapped a sunbonnet on my head. One of the McLowery brothers was lyin' dead on the corner of Third Street. Was he the one Hattie had kissed and hugged in the moonlight? I never stopped runnin' past him. All I had a mind for was Virge. Bunches of people were collectin' in front of the corral. One of them was carryin' Billy Clanton across the street. He was a young boy, only nineteen, and he was dyin'. I ran to the next bunch. Just then a man grabbed me. A lawyer named Harry Jones. 'My God, Mrs. Earp, get away! There's been an awful fight!'

---

[316]   Waters, p. 130-132
[317]   Waters, p. 141

199

"'I'm huntin' Virge! You take me to him," she cried out.

"He's all right, Mrs. Earp. He's all right!" Jones kept saying as she continued moving through the throngs of people. She found Virgil off a way from the main crowd. There was a group of people gathered around him.

"When I got up to him," Allie remembered, "a big man pushed aside the crowd and hollered, 'Stand back boys; let his old mother get in!' He meant me! And I was four years younger than Virge! It was the sunbonnet, I guess. I knelt down beside Virge. The doctor was bending over his legs, probing for the bullet. Virge was gettin' madder and madder from the pain." Virgil Earp was loaded aboard a buckboard and taken home. The infamous gunfight at the O. K. Corral made it clear to Allie what kind of family she had involved herself in and what was in store for her future. Nevertheless, as Kate Elder Holliday had predicted, Allie could not leave Virgil Earp--nor the Earp gang.

"Well, the shootin' had come and the city fathers had fired Virge as marshal right off. He was mad and his feelin's was hurt," Allie remembered. "Now was the time for us to get out of Tombstone. But of course I knew we couldn't. Morg was still sufferin' with his shoulder, and Virge couldn't get out of bed with his leg. They kept me and Lou busy. We hardly never left the house, and kept waitin' to hear how Wyatt and Doc Holliday was makin' out at the courthouse. I still kept Morg's six-shooter handy, just in case. It was a bad time for all of us. The weeks kept draggin' on." [318] Then, three days after Christmas 1881, Virgil Earp was gunned down after leaving the Oriental Saloon. The load of buckshot hit him in the left side. "All night I sat there watchin' the blood drip, wonderin' why it had to be Virge again. I said my prayers," Allie remarked several years later. "Then I didn't think or say or do anything. I just sat there. There was no gettin' away from Tombstone. There was no going home to the corner of Fremont and First. We moved into the [Cosmopolitan] hotel to live, and I settled down to another long spell of nursin' Virge again." [319]

Allie spent day and night at the hotel and hardly left. One incident she remembered was how she left to buy Virge something special on Saturday, March 18, 1882. "Virge always liked taffy," she recalled, speaking lovingly, "especially the peppermint-flavored kind that made his mouth cool, and whenever they made some fresh I went and got some for him." Returning, two men stepped in front of her and cockingly spoke.

---

[318]   Waters, p. 168

[319]   Waters, p. 186

"I'd like to take that watch off," he said, referring to a watch worn upon the lapel of her dress. "What do you think about it?"

"Why don't you!" Allie snapped. "But you won't get out of this town." The men stood staring at the feisty, petite Allie Earp. Allie stared right back. Eventually, she spoke again. "Oh, go crawl down in your gopher holes where you belong!" She turned and walked past them. "Aggravatin' things like that comin' on top of all our troubles made me want to leave Tombstone right that minute," she later reflected. [320]

Two days later, on Monday, March 20, 1882, Virgil and Allie left Tombstone. They went to Tucson accompanied by Wyatt and Warren Earp. Holliday, Sherman McMasters and 'Turkey Creek' Johnson also went. "We never went back!" Allie proclaimed. They didn't stop in Tucson. Virgil and Allie continued to Colton, California. There Allie, Virgil, Nicholas Porter Earp and Grandma Earp buried Morgan's body on a hill. "It was sad for all of us," she recalled years later. "I watched the coffin bein' lowered and Virge tryin' to stand up during the last prayer. Morg and Virge. It was always Morg and Virge. The black sheep was too dark to shoot at night, I reckon. But when I looked at Lou whose husband was being buried, at Mattie whose husband [Wyatt] had left her for that strumpet [Josephine Sarah Marcus], [321] and thought of Kate whose husband had never treated her as his wife neither, I quit feelin' sorry for myself. I was the luckiest of all the Earp women. I still had Virge." [322]

Sometime in the spring of 1886, Virgil established a detective agency in Colton, California. He and Allie settled down to a more 'normal' life than they had in Tombstone and Dodge City--especially without the presence of Wyatt. "But after a couple of years we struck out prospectin' again. Two-three years at most was all we could seem to stand in one place, we was that restless," Allie remarked. They moved up to Vanderbilt for three years and on to Goldfield and "a dozen other towns and camps in Nevada and California during the next twenty years." [323] Virgil died in Goldfield, Nevada of pneumonia in 1905. His body was shipped to Portland, Oregon and buried at the Riverview Cemetery. Allie lived another forty-two years before she died. And she probably didn't "give a damn!"

---

[320]   Waters, p. 192
[321]   Alaska Magazine, May 1990
[322]   Waters, p. 207
[323]   Waters, p. 215

THE BLACK WOMAN
WHO SUED HER MASTER

Black women were like the Black cowboys of the frontier, only more so. That is to say, they've been grossly under-rated, stereo-typed or thoroughly ignored in the history of the Old West. Between the years of 1840-1900, these lovely (and otherwise) ebony-skinned beauties, graced the streets of such boom-towns as Deadwood, South Dakota; Dodge City, Kansas; Butte, Montana; Las Vegas, New Mexico; Cheyenne, Wyoming; Roslyn, Washington and dozens of lessor known communities throughout the frontier. "From mining town histories and folklore has emerged the most widely known stereotype of the western black woman: the motherly but single former slave who gets rich doing laundry and investing the profits in mines and real estate. The West's best known black women--Aunt Clara Brown of Colorado, Mammy Pleasant, and Grandmother Mason of California--all fit this stereotype," writes Susan Armitage and Deborah Wilbert. [324] But the stereo-type is not completely accurate. Nor does it really tell us anything about how these mulatto women felt, thought and acted. Like the women of any other race, creed or national origin, these Black women's actions were both good and bad, justified and unjustified, right and wrong.

One example was in 1884, in Denver, when Black prostitute Belle Warden conspired with fellow courtesan Mattie Lemmon to murder a male customer. [325] Belle and Mattie

---

[324] Article titled Black Women In the Pacific Northwest by Susan H. Armitage & Deborah Gallacci Wilbert, p. 139; Women In the Pacific Northwest: An Anthology edited by Karen J. Blair; Univ. of Washington, 1988. See also: "Aunt" Clara Brown by Kathleen Bruyn; Pruettt Publishing Co., Boulder, CO, 1970, p. 61.

[325] Daughters of Joy, Sisters of Misery: Prostitutes in the American West 1865-1890 by Anne M. Butler, p. 62, 110-111, 119; Univ. of Illinois, 1985. See also: Detective Sam Howe Murder

enlisted the aid of two men--Charles Smith and Benny Gates. The murder took place at Miss Belle Warden's brothel. Belle was sentenced to 10-years in the Colorado penitentiary for 1884 murder. Twenty-two-year-old Mattie Lemmon, although sentenced to 10-years for her role in the murder, died at the Colorado penitentiary in 1887. Photos of the two Black women reveal both were engaging, well-figured women with what could have been long lives of prosperity ahead. But their deliberate actions altered their fate.

Black women were often a succor to White women, men and even children. A July 21, 1881, inquest in the town of Laramie, Wyoming, revealed a white prostitute calling herself Sallie Thixton had died and that, before her death, she'd been cared for a Black Madame named Lizzie Palmer. [326] Most, if not all, Black women in the Old West occupied positions of 'lessor' priority. Most were not given places of importance. Yet, through it all, they were up front amid the famous names--like Charley Storms, gunned down by Luke Short in 1890; Marshal White, killed by Curly Bill a year before Billy the Kid was murdered; Red River Tom, shot down by an hombre named Ormsby in the same year Jesse James was assassinated.

Bell Warden

Many of these White cowboys are famous for being buried in Tombstone's Boot Hill. But there is another name amid these famous names on that lonely, rocky hillside outside the 'town too tough to die.' It is the name of Delia William--a Black woman. At one

---

Scrapbook, Record of the City and County of Denver, 1863-1913; Colorado Historical Society, Denver, Colorado.
[326] Butler, p. 7

time Delia was the proprietress of a lodging house on Toughnut Street in the town of Tombstone. [327]

Many of them, both before and after the War for Southern Independence, were 'loyal' or friendly toward their 'slave owners.' "In the early 1840's a Black woman" traveled down the Santa Fe Trail as far as Bent's Fort, Colorado. She was Black Charlotte, the wife of a slave called Dick Green. Both were slaves belonging to Charles Bent. Charlotte was famous for her fine cooking. While journeying, Charlotte proudly announced, in a voice loud and clear, she was the "only lady in [the] whole damned Indian country!" [328] Another example is one Black female loyalist, Amanda Johnson--born in Liberty, Clay County, Missouri, on August 30, 1833. In 1853, her slave owner packed his family from Missouri to Oregon Territory. "A man offered my master $1,200 for me," she told Fred Lockley in an interview at Albany, Oregon. [329] "I was 19-years old then. My owner said, 'Amanda isn't for sale. She is going across the plains to the Willamette Valley with us. She is like one of the family. I don't care to sell her.'"

Amanda came to be with her slave owner through being "given as a wedding present to my owner's daughter." She belonged to Mrs. Nancy Wilhite who married Mr. Corum. She claimed she'd never been "sold or bartered for" by any slave owner. The daughter of Mrs. Wilhite was named Miss Lydia. When she married, Amanda was again given "as a wedding present" to Miss Lydia. "I have known seven generations of the family," Amanda proudly boasted of her heritage. "I had five brothers and six sisters; none of us were sold like common Negroes. We were all given away as the different young folks got married." Amanda walked many a step on that six month's journey from Liberty, Missouri before reaching Oregon City, Oregon on September 13, 1853. So did another young slave named Benjamin Johnson. He traveled with them. At some later point in time and somewhere in Oregon, Mr. Johnson married Amanda. [330]

Rachel Briggs was another Black woman whose place in history has nearly vanished. In 1876, the year the Indians got their revenge on Custer, Rachel traveled toward Laramie, Wyoming with Charles Metz and his wife. An Indian attack caused the death of

---

327   The Adventures of the Negro Cowboys by Phillip Durham and Everett L. Jones, p. 54; Bantam Books, 1965

328   New First Lady of the Santa Fe Trail by Marian Meyer, p. 52; True West, Aug. 1992

329   Oregon Historical Society Quarterly 23 (June 1922) p. 111; Knight Library Special Collections, Univ. of Oregon

330   Oregon Historical Society Quarterly 23 (June 1922) p. 111

the Metz's. Rachel, however, was captured and taken prisoner. She might have lived were it not for the fact she tried to escape. [331] Another of the 'loyal slaves' was named Hannah. Hannah stayed "with the Hickcock family for many years." She later moved to Malden, Illinois, and married. The Hickcock family, the most noted member being Wild Bill, is said to still own a tin-type of her. [332] This is but one story about Black women in the Old West. There are, no doubt, many more. But, perhaps, because of little recorded history, we shall never know the full extent they had upon the settling of the frontier. But if an author or historian is willing to look, they find on occasion something with which to 'judge' these dark-skinned women and the lives they lived.

Despite the terrible cold winters and cool summers, Black women were found as far north as places like Wyoming and Montana after the War for Southern Independence. "Perhaps the most remarkable of these was Stagecoach Mary Fields." Mary was certainly an unusual one at least. She'd probably be billed today as the 'Black Calamity Jane of the Old West.' She was a nurse and a servant for the Ursuline Sisters at St. Peter's Mission. Eventually, however, she discovered this was not the life for her. She became a restaurant owner, then a freighter and a stagecoach driver. By the age of seventy, she'd done practically everything a woman could. She took up the laundry business in the town of Cascade, Montana. Stagecoach Mary was adept at a number of things throughout her long life. She could shoot a six-shooter and knew which side of a shotgun to not get in front of; but, most of all, she wasn't afraid. She'd fought at least one gunfight in her life and had a love for good, hard liquor and strong, black cigars. During the latter part of her life, she stopped into one of the local saloons for a shot of whiskey. While standing at the bar like any other patron, she spied a former customer of her laundry business strolling down the street. He'd been putting her off and refusing to pay his laundry bill. Stagecoach Mary tipped her glass and finished her drink. She ran outside and followed the man down the street. Finally, she caught up with him. She "grabbed him by the collar and knocked him down with her fist." Then Mary brushed herself off and walked back to the saloon--confident in her action.

"His laundry bill is paid," she announced when she came back in the saloon and that settled the matter once and for all. [333]

---

[331]   Durham and Jones, p. 60

[332]   They Called Him Wild Bill: The Life and Adventures of James Butler Hickok by Joseph G. Rosa, p. 14; Univ. of Okla., 1974

[333]   Durham and Jones, p. 64

Though we often associate the deep South and the East with the problem of slavery, such an evil institution existed elsewhere. Places like Kansas and Missouri were noted for having solved it by bloody terrorism. Other places, like Oregon, found a different solution to the problem. Prior to the adoption of the Organic Act of June 26, 1844, the people of Oregon Territory adopted the following act:

"Slavery and involuntary servitude shall be forever prohibited in Oregon. In all cases where slaves have been or shall hereafter be brought into Oregon, the owners of such slaves shall have three years to remove them out of the country. Such slaves shall be free at the end of said three years if the owner does not remove them within three years. If a free Negro and mulatto come to Oregon he or she must leave the country within two years (males) and three years (females) after reaching 18th birthday or if over 18 after entering Oregon. If such free Negro or mulatto shall fail to quit the country within the time stated and if found guilty upon a trial before a justice of the peace he or she shall receive upon his or her bare back not less than 20 or more than 39 stripes, to be inflicted by the county constable." [334]

In December, the Provisional Government Legislative Committee cancelled the last paragraph and substituted the following:

"If such free Negro or mulatto shall fail to quit the Oregon country he or she may be arrested upon warrant issued by a justice of the peace and if found guilty upon trial, the justice shall issue an order to any competent officer directing said officer to publicly hire out such Negro to lowest bidder who will obligate himself to remove such Negro from country within 6 months after such term of service."

Thus was the law in Oregon concerning Black men and women until 1864.

One woman, the subject of this chapter, was Polly Holmes who, in 1852, took action with her husband and filed suit against ex-master, Nathaniel Ford. [335] Polly wanted her children back and, with all her motherly fortitude, was going to have them.

---

[334]   The Polk County Slave Case by Scott McArthur, p. 9; Polk Co. Historical Society, Historically Speaking Vol. 2; August 1970

[335]   Oregon Historical Quarterly 17 (June 1916) 107-115 & 23 (June 1922) p. 111-137 about Polly Holmes both by Fred Lockley. See also: The Polk County Slave Case by Scott McArthur; Historically Speaking 2; Polk County, Oregon Historical Society journal, Aug. 1970. See also: Oregon Statesman newspaper, July 5, 1853. See also: The Negro In Oregon by D. G. Hill, p. 17--a thesis Univ, of Oregon, 1932.

In 1841, Polly and husband, Robbin, who'd been the slaves of Mayor Whitman of Howard County, Missouri, were "sold at public vender...to satisfy certain debts" Whitman owed. They'd been his slaves since the year of 1829. They were purchased that day in 1841 by "a Howard County [merchant]...whose name was [Robbin and Polly] no longer remembered." The following morning, Robbin was ordered to the house of [their new master] to procure a wagon to take his family to their new residence. When Robbin arrived, the wife of his new slave owner stated her husband was away and she knew nothing about the arrangement. Robbin went to Nathaniel Ford's house and told him all that transpired. Ford insisted they stay with him. Nothing was said or confirmed they were to be his slaves. Likewise, no word is known at this date whatever became of the "Howard County merchant" who'd purchased them. Perhaps he died and, since his wife knew nothing of the transaction, there was no other thing to be done. Anyway, from that day forward, they remained with Ford.

Times were hard in Missouri during those days. Money was hard to come by and the crops failed due to drought and what not. Creditors, in creditor fashion, clamped down and demanded their money. Slave owner, Nathaniel Ford, a farmer and, though "an unlettered man," was one of the few community leaders in the tiny Missouri town. [336] Ford left Missouri in 1844. He took his wife, six children and his brothers-in-law--Cary Embree and David Goff. [337] The reason given was he "became very much embarrassed in his pecuniary circumstances." [338] He also took his slaves with him. [339] These included Polly, husband Robbin and their three children--Harriett, Celi Ann and Jenny. [340] Jenny had been born in Missouri. James was later born in Oregon Territory in February 1845, and Roxanna, the youngest, "somewhere about February 1847." Ford promised them if

---

[336]   McArthur, p. 2

[337]   McArthur, p. 2

[338]   Oregon Historical Quarterly 23 (June 1922) p. 132

[339]   Here we find another possible controversy. McArthur reports that, according to Pauline Burch (one of Ford's descendants), "Ford took with him only one Negro, Scott." p. 3

[340]   There is some controversy here. McArthur, in his article titled The Polk County Slave Case, states that the children's names were Harriet, aged 7; Celi Ann, aged 4 and Jenny or Mary Jane, aged 2." The other sources I was able to check don't mention Harriet or Celi Ann. They also imply that Jenny was the oldest. One mentioned that "one of the children" had died along the way but didn't list the name [Oregon Historical Quarterly 23 (June 1922)].

they would go with him and assist him in establishing a farm, he would set them free afterwards. Thus, feeling they were the slaves of no one, Polly and Robbin agreed. [341]

Ford, his family and servants, struggled seven months before arriving in Oregon City on December 7, 1844. Sometime afterwards, Ford sent back to Missouri for "a squatter, 'Billy' Doak, and set out to build his farm near the present town of Rickreall." [342] That first winter, "while the slaves remained with the women folk at Oregon City," Nathaniel constructed a large log cabin for him and his family. He also built a second "smaller one with a fireplace" for Polly and her family and a third one for the slave called Scott. The coming spring, the men folk, with the aid of the women, broke ground and started carving "a farm from the wilderness." In the spring of 1849, at Ford's suggestion, [343] Robbin Holmes journeyed down to the California gold fields. Robbin was to assist Nathaniel's son, Mark Ford, who was then in California. Mark's wife, Amanda Tharp Ford, had been suffering from tuberculosis and died in December the previous year at San Francisco. Nathaniel Ford, who also went on the trip, became ill "shortly after arriving at the mines and convalesced at Sacramento for several months." Ford expected Robbin to give [him] a share of the gold that he might dig in California. [344] Meanwhile, Polly and the two children stayed with their owner until the following spring, but not controlled as slaves.

"About the first of March 1850," Robbin and the others returned from California. Before leaving, however, he paid Mark Ford a sum of "nine hundred dollars in gold dust." It was during that return trip tragedy struck once more. Mark lost his life as he and three others were drowned "in an effort to find the entrance to the Columbia River for the skipper of their fog-bound sailing ship." With him was lost $16,000 worth of gold-- $2,000 belonging to his father. [345] It was never recovered. That night, slave Scott died from "the pestilence which had swept the ship." During the latter half of 1850, Polly and Robbin left the Ford family and moved to Ellendale where Robbin was employed at the Nesmith Mills--owned by Nesmith and Owens. By this time, Celi Ann had died and,

---

[341] McArthur says "the circumstances under which the Holmes family accompanied Ford to Oregon are disputed." p. 2. I've merely used the most widely accepted to my knowledge of the facts.

[342] McArthur, p. 3. A look at an Oregon map as of 1991 doesn't show any "Rickreall, Oregon." Perhaps, it is one of the many ghost towns which have faded into history.

[343] McArthur states it was in the "fall of 1848, Ford, his son, Mark, the servants Scott and Robbin and others from the Rickreall area" all struck out for the gold fields. p. 3

[344] Oregon Historical Quarterly 23 (June 1922) p. 117

[345] McArthur, p. 4

shortly after the beginning of 1851, Harriett also died. Both bodies were buried "on the Ford place in graves marked only by three oak saplings on the banks of the Rickreall." [346] Robbin, finding Polly gave birth to a boy named Lon, [347] made an agreement with Ford that he and Polly and Lon were to be freed. The rest, according to Ford, were to remain with him "...as wards...until they respectfully became of age." Ford further claimed since he had kept the children for his former slaves, while those same children could not care for themselves, he had a right to be compensated for his "heavy expense when they were young and their services of very little or no value."

Since a woman could make no claim at that time, Robbin appeared on behalf of Polly before the Territorial Supreme Court's Justice O. C. Pratt on April 16, 1852, claiming he never made the agreement. Polly charged Ford "had promised them their freedom in return for helping him start a farm" in Oregon. But Ford reneged. Both claimed he had, according the writ dated April 16, 1852, by order of the Court, Territory of Oregon, "unlawfully detained...Jenny or Mary Jane Holmes, Roxanna Holmes and James Holmes." [348]   And that started the incident where a Black woman sued her master-- commonly referred to as the "Polk County Slave Case of 1852." What was worse, in the eyes of Oregon's law, was two of the children had been born in Oregon. The newly formed state was not a slave state. Ford was even told "he would not be permitted" to maintain slaves in Oregon and he should "take Robbin and his wife and the children back to Missouri and there sell them." [349] Ford, on the other hand, insisted the mother and father "had agreed to give him custody [of the children]...until they reached legal age in return for Ford's having supported them during their 'unproductive years.'"

Ford displayed socialist-welfare ideals to inflict them upon Polly and Robbin Holmes. He claimed because the parents were Black "poor and ignorant" adults, they were "unfit to have the care, custody and bringing up of the children" within their rights. [350] A letter addressed to James A. Shirley, dated June 22, 1852, signed by Nathaniel Ford himself, had this to say:

---

[346]   McArthur, p. 4

[347]   McArthur, p. 4

[348]   Oregon Historical Quarterly 23 (June 1922) p. 112

[349]   Oregon Historical Quarterly 23 (June 1922) p. 114

[350]   Oregon Historical Quarterly 23 (June 1922) p. 114

"You know I brought some Negroes with me to this country which has proved a curse to me and my fambly. [sic] Scott died. Robin [sic] and his wife done very well until the spring of '50 when the abolitionists interfered--and the country is full of them--the interference was so great that I had to let them go. They have stopped in some six miles of me with a man who owns a mill and the abolitionists are so much about them that the Negroes are continually harrissing [sic] my fambly [sic] by attempts to slander them. Now my dear friend I wish if you care to befriend me--though I am in a distant land, you know Crigler the sheriff had levied an execution on the Negroes and they were brought off to this country. I am of the opinion that the execution may be renewed as to send it here and take the Negroes back to Missouri under the fugitive slave law. If so if you will have it attended to and appoint an agent here, I will pay all the expenses here and git all the evidence which is in my neighborhood...I can get a lawyer here to attend to the business if you can appoint an agent here and leave his name blank, for me to full in I will arrange the whole matter. Robin and his wife are very likely--they have five likely children if you can make the arrangement you may make some 1500 to 2000$ out of them and do me a great favor. If the Negroes can be taken under the fugitive slave law I will make arrangement to send them to you in short order...if the case of the Negroes can be attended to it will relieve me and my family of much trouble and you may be benefited by it. Whether there can be anything done or not please write to me amediately. [sic] I should like if there can anything be done to have the writ here by the first of October next that is the time of the setting of our District Court..." [351]

At the April 1852 hearing, Justice O. C. Pratt merely set the hearing date for the next session of the court in Polk County. It never met again that year, however. The next court date was April 5, 1853. Robbin filed a habeas corpus to get custody of the children. The *Oregon Statesman* printed news of this habeas corpus.

> This was an application for a precept to issue to the Sheriff of Polk Co., to enforce a previous order of the court (directing the release of Negroes held as slaves in Missouri) in this matter.

---

[351]   McArthur, p. 5

> Judge Williams intimated that on Wednesday week, the parties consenting, he would attend, at Dallas, Polk Co., and hear, and finally disposed of the case, which was agreed to. [352]

M. P. Dady and A. G. P. Wood represented the Holmes' in their rights while Nathaniel Ford was represented by James Malabin and Cyres Olney. Sheriff W. S. Gilliam collected his $2.00 fee and served the writ. On June 26, 1853, the Holmes' again appeared in court and filed "new proceedings that Judge Thomas Nelson had refused to rule on his application for return of the children, and further that he feared that the children would be returned to Missouri and sold into slavery." [353] When the case came to trial, Nathaniel failed to bring the children with him, stating the "sixty miles...would have been a great hardship upon him." Joseph Lane was whom Nathaniel Ford relied upon to substantiate his side of the legal argument. Lane was asked by the defendant's attorney if he knew the Holmes'. He said he did.

"Had you ever any conversation with the said Holmes touching the conditions under which his children were held by the said Ford or under his control?"

"Recollect being at Col. Fords March 1850," Lane answered. "Heard a conversation between Ford and Holmes which left the impression on my mind that Holmes was to go where he pleased, but that the children were to be left with Ford, this however, is only an impression as I do not recollect the words which passed between them."

"Please state the time, place and substance of that conversation."

"The conversation took place at Col. Fords in March 1850. He had a conversation with Holmes about keeping house for me in Oregon City, that is I proposed to employ him and his wife to work, her to cook and him to work about the mills. My proposition to Holmes, brought about the conversation between the parties [Nathaniel and Robbin]." [354]

Robbin Holmes, Polly's husband, denied he was "harsh or that his wife Polly was cruel to their children, but on the contrary...he and his wife's reputation for kindness and

---

352   Oregon Statesman, July 5, 1853
353   McArthur, p. 7
354   Oregon Historical Quarterly 23 (June 1922) p. 130

parental care for their children is such that he can safely...inquire thereof, and that his character for honesty, sobriety and industry is good." [355]

> *This day this case came on to be heard before the said Judge at Dallas Polk Co. by the consent of parties...and said Judge having heard the allegations and evidence...decrees that the said children...are hereby awarded to the care and custody of their parents Robbin Holmes and his wife to be and remain with them as their children as fully in all respects as though they the said children had not been in the custody of the said Ford, and it is ordered and adjudged that the said Ford pay the costs of these proceedings.*
>
> Geo. H. Williams
>
> *Judge*
>
> *July 13, 1853*

The judge's decision in the case was final. Polly and her husband won. Ford brought the family to a state where slavery was illegal. Thus, the children were to be turned over to Polly and Robbin--who'd not seen nor communicated with them for the past two years. Nevertheless, Ford's daughter kept one of the children, 16-year old Mary Jane, who was sold for $700 in 1857 to a man who later married her. His name was Reuben and it wasn't until later he learned Nathaniel's claim to Mary Jane was baseless. Reuben thought all along he needed to buy his bride's freedom. Unfortunately, he spent several years paying off this $700 before he learned the truth. Polly Holmes, the Black woman who sued her master, and her re-united family moved to Salem, Oregon. Robbin founded a nursery business and did rather well over the next few years. Those in the know said that "relations remained close between the Negro family and the Fords and their descendants in the years following, and that no further claim was made...after the court decision in 1853."

---

[355]   Oregon Historical Quarterly 23 (June 1922) p. 134

Polly Holmes:
Social Profile on Chapter Twelve
by
Virginia C. Nelson-L'Aloge, M. A.

It has been stated throughout this book that it took courage to strike out into the wilderness; yet, so many people had very little choice but to do so. So it was for those Black people who found living in the East and South so limiting. Because of prejudice, the wide open spaces of the West beckoned. Other Black people went because they were considered property of some of the settlers who went West and there they eventually gained their freedom.

The Black women who went West were often more limited than the White women as to how to earn a living. They were confined to doing laundry, cooking, working as servants or prostitution--all at lower pay. Marriage was seldom a step up since most of the Black men were also forced by prejudice into working as blacksmiths, drovers, cowboys or sometimes gamblers. So they did not earn much money. Thus both husband and wife had to work to keep the wolf from the door. The history book's elimination of western Black history reflects the great prejudice that faced them. We again find that rare person--the one or ones who defied limitation to rise above society's restrictions within this chapter. We again find the ones who would not take 'no' for an answer.

Upon reading Oregon's act we find dire consequences for Black or mulattos who were free and wanted to live in Oregon prior to 1864. It was within this time period that Polly and Robbin Holmes sued her ex-master--Nathaniel Ford. We also find that until the middle 1900's there was little hope by a Black man to expect justice within the court system throughout the United States. No woman could even make a claim--be she Black, White or any other color in the 1800's! The lawsuit had to be filed by Robbin, her husband. The fact that Polly and Robbin won is remarkable and attests to the fact that George H. Williams was an honest judge, dedicated to the cause of justice!

Polly and Robbin had the opportunity to fight for the children they loved to be with them. So many Black people of that time were separated from their children by force. Many were sold and various family members went to different places never to be heard from again. The long, dark nights were filled with the wailing laments of family's torn apart. One of the deepest tragedies was when used as a 'wet nurse' for the mistress of the house, whose motivation for not feeding her own child was her figure or that she felt it was unladylike, the Black woman's child starved because she could not produce enough milk for both. The following lullaby portrays the agony of such a mother:

All the Pretty Little Horses

Hush a bye, don't you cry.

Go to sleepy, little baby.

When you wake, you shall have cake,

And all the pretty little horses.

Blacks and bays, dapples and grays,

Coach and six-a little horses

Way down yonder in the meadow,

There's a poor little lambie;

The bees and the butterfly's pickin' out his eyes,

The poor little thing cries, "Mammy."

Hush a bye, don't you cry.

Go to sleepy little baby. [356]

There were/are people who thought/think that because someone else is different, in any way, they don't feel things the same way they do. That applies to people who are of

---

[356]   Distinctions in Western Woman's Experience: Ethnicity, Class and Social Change by Rosalinda Mendez Gonzalez, p. 240; The Women's West by Susan Armitage & Elizabeth Jameson; University of Oklahoma, 1987. See also: The Black Book, p. 65; Random House, 1974

different color, ethnic background, nationality, religion and people of their own group who are deaf, disabled in some way, or elderly. These people feel superior and they are totally oblivious as to the pain, physical or emotional, felt by the other person. It is hard for those of us who understand and know that people are people with feelings and dreams no matter what makes them 'different.' A parent is a parent no matter what they look like or who they are. Some parents don't care for or love their children and mistreat them or desert them. More people sincerely love their children, they want the family to be together, to see them grow and prosper.

The strides made over the last few decades have been long over due. The progress must continue forward as we learn about each other. All people's have wonderful contributions to make enriching our world. We need to understand and to accept the fact that we all feel, hurt, laugh and love. We need to understand and accept that no one person is better than another. The world is like a tapestry--each person in his or her unique place making his or her personal contribution in that special way only they can.

We need all people's. We need to balance and honor each other by enjoying each other's uniqueness. We need to learn from each other. We need to respect each other. We applaud Polly and Robbin and the great risk they took at a time when they could have been enslaved again. Their love for the children and the ability to stand up and say: "Enough, no more injustice!" We can learn from them!

maids ars simply awful, the c ti don't agree, the editors wuN'T agree, they can't get a slaughter house, flour mills, railroads and factories, but they've got the whooping cough and measles, and—and—oh, well, we would not hve in Denison for anything.—*Sherman Exchange.*

Oh, villian, thou liest. The women of Denison neglect their domestic duties to think of sweet things to say to each other. The men get up at night to shake hands. There was never but one homely girl in Denison, and she married a Sherman man as the easiest mode of suicide; the cats all coo like doves, and would not know how to howl "Maria" if they wanted to; the editors are all brothers, sir, twin brothers, who send each other presents every day of beautiful boquets and cord wood and bottled b—r b—r; and we "h-a-v-e" a slaughter-house and four flour mills, and factories, and strikers, and seven churches, and thirty-nine saloons—with back-doors and every thing—we mean thirty-nine saloons, and seven churches with back-doors and everything; and then we have A FIRST CLASS SHOE STORE, at Sherburne's, 311 Main street, where goods are being slaughtered for a few days, to make ready for fall. We are in earnest
8-18 2w.

In Denison the women quarrel, the men ditto, the girls are homely, the old

This ad speaks about the women of Denison, Texas

Dora Hand:
Social Profile on Chapter Thirteen
by
Virginia C. Nelson-L'Aloge, M. A.

The Code of the West stated: first, you never shot an unarmed man; second, you never shot a man in the back or from ambush; and third, you never shot a woman or child. This Code is similar to that of King Arthur's knights of the round table. Women were to be honored. The Code also included such courtesies as: When a lady walked into the room men stood up removing their hats. A man always stood up giving his chair to a lady. The man always walked on the street side of the lady to keep her from being splashed by passing vehicles. The man always opened the door for the lady. A man never used foul language in front of a lady. When dining, if a lady stood, the men would all rise until she left the table. A man would assist her when she was being seated at the table. The men always helped her in and out of her wrap [coat or shawl]. Such was the Code regarding women who were ladies. The most important one was that women were to be protected and not harmed in any way. *Save the women and children,* was the Code--unless they were other than White. Then the Army felt free to murder them!

Men were often hung for stealing cattle or horses. Men were often lynched for killing another man unless the other drew first. Sometimes, men were imprisoned, then pardoned for good behavior, if they killed a woman prostitute. The fact is that we find case after case of women who, minority either by color or profession, were beaten or killed! Prostitutes were often physically battered or brutally murdered and seldom were the attackers punished. Most of the time nothing was done if it was an Indian, Black, Asian or Hispanic woman.

Then we have the tragic story of Dora Hand.

It seems through history those with money *can* get away with murder. Family money has freed rapists and murderers of women who were of 'lower class,' meaning poorer than they. This has happened from before the Old West time until today! Nothing has changed in this regard. Some men or women of possession and wealth have *bought* the acquittal for their sons, relatives, friends and themselves--and still do. The land owners, the ones who owned the town in the Old West were no different. Prominent ones often obtain their position of height stepping atop the bones of the weaker and poorer. Men are physically stronger than women generally. Unless the woman knows self-defense techniques taught today she is no match for a man in hand-to-hand battle. Unless trained in the use of a weapon she does not stand a chance at the hands of an attacker.

Whether it was by accident or not, Dora Hand was murdered by James Kennedy. He intended to kill the mayor when the bullets went through the walls and the bullets found an innocent victim instead. Would the law have been so lenient if the mayor had been the one shot? Are things any different today? What is it going to take for people to be treated with equality? Whether someone is educated or not, has or does not have money, no matter of their sex, nationality, ethnic background, religion or color, if they have committed a crime of murder, rape, or thievery--they deserve equal punishment! People are people and the victims of those who do not respect life or the value of another's integrity deserve to be avenged immediately.

This book is about extraordinary people. It has taken outstanding men and women to form the back bone of this country. It is always a history of violence, blood, sweat, tears, laughter, joy, determination and fortitude. The common thread for all the heroines of the West is they would not take 'no' for an answer. They knew their own worth and skills and they valiantly took a stand. They risk all they had to achieve their monumental dreams and fulfill their clandestine destinies.

One summer day about twenty years ago I sat upon my parents porch at a turning point in my life. I was emotionally wounded, fearful of the future, wondering if I could go on alone and make it. I wondered if I dared risk what I had to risk. As I sat there, I focused on the rose bush and this message came to me. I give it to you, the reader.

There are some roses that never go beyond the tight bud stage, they die upon the vine. You never get to see the beauty or smell the fragrance of what they could have been. There are other roses in various stages of opening upon the same bush. The ones who open fully are at great risk. Risk from the bugs that chew their petals, the wind tearing at them, the cold rain that falls upon them. But by opening they allow others to see their beauty, smell their fragrance, feel the velvet of their petals. They give their essence of being and so give the greatest gift they have--themselves.

I realized at that moment I have a choice as we all do. We can die upon the bush-- tight and unopened. Or we can take the greatest risk and open to all that comes our way-- continuing to allow the essence of who we are to be shared by those with whom we come in contact. I have lived my life from that day to this by that lesson and I plan to live by this lesson for my remaining days here on earth. We are at a time in history when we need to be alert, vigilant and active. We must remember what our Constitution and Bill of Rights were meant to do. We must stand tall and speak out for our rights as individuals. We must remember we temporarily still <u>have</u> freedom of speech. We must remember and set forth the fact that government was established by the people to reinforce us, to ensure our state rights and individual rights from outside invaders. Government was not established by the people to control us and tax us to death.

Deganawida speaks: "No man [or woman] should ever be afraid to cut falsehood from his life, even if it is the very thing upon which he is standing. Once he recognizes it, he should not fear to let it fall away. For to remain standing upon a lie, once it is known to be false, is to forswear future peace and joy. And there is no value to living if such as these are your roots." [357]

This is where we must take our stand. We must shake the webs of apathy from our daily lives and re-program ourselves as well as our children with the truth of liberty, justice and freedom for all. We must remember those of all walks of life who went before us forging this great nation--the melting pot of the world! We honor them--men and women alike. The greatest way we can honor them is to hold the torch of true liberty high in our own hands, speak out and effect the necessary change to bring us to the way of life our forefathers and foremothers set into motion so long ago. It is time we *claim* our heritage, women and men with no barriers. We *must* honor and respect each other, the earth and the creatures who live with us--all finned, four-legged and winged!

We salute the many female trailblazers--those who showed us the way! These are the women and men who indeed were willing to 'cut the very limb upon which they stood, if it were a lie.' Are you willing to do the same?

---

[357]   Return of the Bird Tribes by Ken Carey, p. 91; Uni Sun, 1988

"THOU SHALT NOT SHOOT A WOMAN"

Had God written the Ten Commandments during the years of the Old West there would have undoubtedly been an eleventh: 'Thou shalt not shoot a woman.' Leastwise, most sources point to that being the consensus of those who lived during the period. One example is told of Ed Tewksbury who attempted to kill a woman of the opposite faction one day in Holbrook, [Arizona]. Tewksbury, involved in the memorable Pleasant Valley War, "according to this old tale," writes Earle R. Forrest, was with "some friends in a saloon...one day when the clan leader saw a Graham girl pass the door. Like a flash he drew his gun, but was seized by friends before he could fire." [358]

"In the Code of the West," B. Johnny Rube begins his article, "was an unwritten law that no man should kill a woman, regardless of circumstances or provocation. A woman, even one with a loaded rifle and an apparent willingness to use it, was to be treated with proper respect." [359] Yet, shooting and killing women did take place in the Old West. "Violence, in particular violence against women, has not been considered and *needs* to be," Susan Armitage adds. "It is important to reconsider the issue of violence precisely because it has been so celebrated [in the Old West]," she stresses. [360] Tombstone, Arizona's famous soiled dove Irish Nellie "was wounded by a bullet fired at the shoot-out of the OK Corral." Nellie apparently "wanted a grandstand seat" and got a bullet for her

---

[358] Arizona's Dark and Bloody Ground by Earle R. Forrest, p. 166; Univ. of Arizona, 1950

[359] A Yuma Tragedy by B. Johnny Rube; True West, Oct. 1982; p. 24-27

[360] Armitage & Jameson, p. 17

enthusiasm. [361] Nothing is said about whatever became of her nor if anything was ever done to the person who shot her.

A second obscure incident concerns the killing of Nigger Liza in Pioche, Nevada. No particular year is given of the murder but it had to be sometime after 1860. [362] Nielson devotes merely one paragraph to the entire murder. A bartender named Faddiman recently opened a saloon in the mining Nevada boom-town. Within two weeks, a miner came in, down on his luck and desperate. He ordered a drink of whiskey and Faddiman poured it for him. The drunk moved away from the bar, drew his six-shooter, aimed it at the bartender and squeezed off a round. The bullet hit Faddiman directly in the chest and he fell dead to the sawdust floor. The murdering scalawag ran out of the saloon and into the neighboring butcher shop. Realizing his guilt, he beseeched the owner, Nigger Liza, to hide him from the law. She refused. He threatened her and she pulled a butcher knife. She forcefully wielded the weapon and demanded he leave. But the blood-crazed killer attacked her, instead. The two wrestled, the drunk gaining control of the knife. He grabbed her by the hair of her head, yanked her head back, exposing her naked flesh, and "savagely slit her throat." Meanwhile, news spread of the killing in the saloon and the local deputy came running. Learning the killer escaped into the building next door, he waited outside for the brute to exit. As the debauched murderer exited the butcher shop, the deputy aimed his weapon and emptied all six chambers. The maniacal miner instantly fell dead. A just ending for the drunk to say the least!

Another case, wherein we know what became of the man who shot a woman, concerns an incident in Yuma, Arizona Territory on the morning of February 7, 1901, and was heralded by territorial newspapers as "The Yuma Tragedy." [363] It was the day a young Somerton, Arizona lawman, Marian T. Alexander, ushered Mary King Burns into eternity by means of a shotgun blast. Mary King Burns lived on the ranch owned by John Powell of Tucson, Arizona for the past seven years. Further still, Mary was a sister of Powell's wife, Annie, and was married to Joseph Burns. Frank B. Miller, on the other hand, claimed he owned the ranch "by right of purchase from Powell." He even moved onto the ranch and made several efforts to evict the Burns.' After several unsuccessful

---

361   Gunsmoke: The True Story of Old Tombstone by Grace McCool, p. 116; Gateway Publishing Co., 1954

362   Tales of Nevada Vol. 1 by Norm Nielson, p. 77-78; Tales of Nevada Publications, 1989

363   Rube, p. 25

tries, Miller went to the law demanding the removal of Mary, Joseph and all their livestock. Newspapers stated lawman Alexander had already gone out at least once to serve eviction papers on Joseph and Mary Burns. On that occasion he'd been met by Mary, armed with a rifle, who had ordered him off "her property."

In the early hours of February 7, Alexander rode back to attempt once again to get the Burns' to vacate accompanied by William B. Fain and Frank B. Miller. Author and historian B. J. Rube states these two "apparently had no official reason for joining the group." As before, however, so again! Armed with a rifle, Mary stood awaiting the approaching three riders. Lawman Alexander instructed his two cohorts to remain mounted and he would deal with this insolent woman. He climbed down from his horse, cradled the shotgun he often carried and approached Mary who stood some several yards away. Miller and Fain did as they were told. Thus, neither heard the words between the belligerent lawman and the supercilious woman. But fervent words were exchanged!

Alexander later stated Mary Burns threatened to "kill him if he attempted to remove [her] horses from" the property. Alexander obviously believed her, "for as his stunned companions watched, he raised his shotgun and fired both barrels into her body." The impact hurtled the woman's bloody body backwards as though lassoed to the end of a runaway horse. There was no doubt about the fact she was dead. Miller, Fain and Alexander returned to Yuma and surrendered to the authorities. Deputy Sheriff Henry H. McPhaul filed criminal charges against the three men. All were charged with "having maliciously, willfully and with malice aforethought, killed Mary Burns." The coroner's jury met on February 8 and concluded her death was "under circumstances not entirely excusable but under mitigating circumstances." A warrant was immediately issued and the prisoners were taken before Justice of the Peace George H. Miles. They were commanded to appear to be arraigned on February 13, 1901. They were incarcerated at Yuma Territorial Prison for protection. That day, February 8, mourners watched as the earthly remains of Mary Burns were lowered into the cold Arizona sands. The editor of the *Phoenix Arizona Republican* commented by saying "few men of normal disposition would even in a position of deadliest peril kill a woman to save themselves." [364]

In early April, a jury convicted Alexander of "murder in the first degree." He was sentenced to the Arizona Territorial Prison in Yuma. Sheriff Livingston, Deputy Robert Hatch and Avran Molina were to escort him to the nearby prison. Along Third Street,

---

[364]   Rube, p. 25

near the railroad tracks and just opposite the north end of the caboose shed, Sheriff Livingston sent Hatch running back to ask Judge Street something. As Hatch returned, Livingston and Molina chatted nonchalantly with Alexander beside the street. A shot ripped through the Arizona silence. Alexander fell mortally wounded to the ground. Even those in the courthouse heard the shot. At ten o'clock that night, Alexander passed into eternity where he probably came face-to-face with Mary Burns--the woman he'd shot. It was never proven who fired the bullet that killed him. But his passing was applauded by the King family who made it perfectly clear that anything less than the death sentence was unacceptable in the Old West. Alexander's right to shoot her was, in their opinion, "in no way diminished by the fact that the deceased...threatened to commit a crime with a deadly weapon."

The words of Col. K. B. Brown describe best Mary Burns and, no doubt, the one who revenged her death. "I love to think that such as [she] represents the true American character--gently disposed to [her] friends, honest in [her] pride of birth, honoring [her] ancestry by maintaining the glory of [her] family name, and going to [her] final reward with the satisfaction of one who has always performed [her] duty under all circumstances...There [she] stands...proud of [her] past and confident of [her] future. [She] was bred a warrior and [she] does not shrink from the steel. [She] looks you in the eye as if to say, 'What would you with me? If you come in peace I am your friend; if you seek battle, draw and defend yourself.'" [365] After all, the Code is the code and you just don't shoot women.

Another episode where a man shot a woman, Kitty LeRoy, is told about in the *Black Hills Daily Times*. [366] Kitty was a 28-year old jig dancer shot to death in Deadwood, South Dakota, by Samuel Curley--her fifth husband.

Kitty left her first husband in Michigan so she could become a performer in an Old West saloon. She went to Texas, acquired a lover and deserted her child--a boy born to her while married in Michigan. After that, she and her new lover went to California. From there they moved up to Deadwood in 1870. Sometime later, the two had an argument, broke up their relationship and he left. Kitty became involved with Curley. "A questionable marriage" was performed and the two set up house. Curley was "a man of solid reputation, well known and well liked in the territory." Curley was about thirty-

---

[365]   An Editor on the Comstock Lode by Wells Drury, p. 92-93; Univ. of Nevada, 1984
[366]   Black Hills Daily Times, December 9, 1877

five years old and had the reputation of a peaceful individual. [367] Still, Kitty pursued her career at the Lone Star Saloon [368] and Samuel R. Curley didn't interfere. That is, except for "some of her conduct." Kitty apparently used the saloon to attract herself various 'lovers.' One of these suitors was a German prospector who'd struck it rich. The story goes that "Kitty married him, took him for eight thousand dollars in gold, and then crowned him with a bottle." [369]

Sometime afterwards, in the fall 1877, [370] Curley made a business trip to Denver. While in the mile high city, he got word "a reconciliation between his wife and the Texas traveling companion" had taken place. Well, he was as mad as hell and he wasn't going to put up with it anymore. So on December 5, 1877, he immediately went back to Deadwood. Curley sneaked into town and "attempted to arrange a showdown with his rival."

MURDER AND SUICIDE.

The Texan, however, didn't show up. Curley was even more furious. He informed a Black saloon employee it was time for Kitty to meet her maker. On December 6, Kitty, in her upstairs saloon room, had no idea Curley had returned to Deadwood. The infuriated husband crashed in the door around seven o'clock in the evening and the two

---

[367] Kitty Leroy: The Cause of the Tragedy--Jealousy by Larry D. Underwood; Old West, Summer 1989, p. 56-57

[368] Ronald D. Miller says "Kitty's gambling hall in Deadwood was called the Mint." Shady Ladies of the West by Ronald Dean Miller, p. 18; Westernlore Press; 1985

[369] Miller, p. 18

[370] Underwood, p. 56-57

argued. It lasted but a few minutes. Curley murdered her and committed suicide. [371] On December 8th, the two were prepared for burial, displayed in the front room of the Lone Star Saloon for the crowds to view and were buried.

An admiring editor of a newspaper wrote of Kitty:

"[She] was what a real man would call a starry beauty. Her brown hair was thick and curling; she had five husbands, seven revolvers, a dozen bowie-knives, and always went armed to the teeth, which latter were like pearls set in coral. She was a terrific gambler, and wore in her ears immense diamonds, which shone almost like her glorious eyes. The magnetism about her marvelous beauty was such as to drive her lovers crazy; more men have been killed about her than all the other women in the hills combined, and it was only a question whether her lovers or herself had killed the most. She married her first husband because he was the only man of all her lovers who had the nerve to let her shoot an apple off his head while she rode by at full speed. On one occasion she disguised herself in male attire to fight a man who refused to combat a woman. He fell, and she then cried, and married him in time to be his widow." [372]

"The old superstition that thirteen is an unlucky number hasn't worked out in my case. I killed thirteen men and never once saw the inside of a prison," Buckskin Frank Leslie told J. H. Macia in a Tucson hotel room one night after Leslie had been pardoned from prison. "It was my fourteenth that caused all my trouble. But my fourteenth was a woman." [373] Leslie's murder of Mollie Williams, alias Diamond Annie, is best told by the editor of the *Tombstone Epitaph*. [374]

On July 11, 1889, William Reynolds rode into Tombstone and told of the ghastly murder committed by Buckskin Frank Leslie, "well known in Tombstone as a hard character." Leslie and Mollie spent the previous evening drinking and carousing together at his ranch. Like all drunks, the two argued first about one thing and then another. Leslie even "slapped her and knocked her down several times during" their drunken

---

[371] Daughters of Joy, Sisters of Misery: Prostitutes in the American West 1865-1890 by Anne M. Butler, p. 25; Univ. of Illinois, 1985

[372] Miller, p. 18-19

[373] Tombstone: An Iliad of the Southwest by Walter Noble Burns, p. 196; Penguin Books, 1927

[374] Tombstone Epitaph, July 11, 1889. The newspaper article doesn't refer to Mollie by any alias. Rather, the alias is given only in Burns' book. There is also a discrepancy about who else was shot at the scene of the murder. The newspaper reports it was a man named James Neal. However, Burns states it was Jim Hughes.

debauchery. Details are a bit sketchy as to what happened next. One source says they ran out of whiskey and Leslie went to get some more--leaving Mollie and Hughes behind. The *Epitaph,* however, says that Leslie went to pick a fight with a neighbor and returned. Upon his return, he found Mollie and Neal "sitting outside the house." Leslie took another drink, shouted, "I'll put a stop to all this," and rushed into the house. He returned with "a Colt's pistol, took deliberate aim at the woman and fired." Leslie shot the other man who ran off into a field before collapsing. The other man, whether named Hughes or Neal, eventually crawled a mile or two to a neighbor's house. He alerted the neighbor, William Reynolds, and Reynolds went to tell the law. Leslie was arrested and, like all drunks, claimed he could "remember nothing of the affair." The well-known gunman/murderer was placed on trial, convicted and sentenced to 25-years in the Yuma Territorial Prison, serving only four before pardoned. [375]

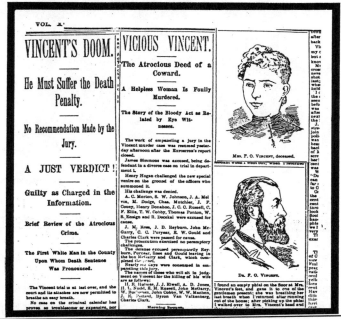

This news clipping reveals the headlines of Dr. F. O. Vincent, who killed a woman and was sentenced to be executed.

---

[375]   Burns, p. 195-196

Dodge City Peace Commission
Top row, L-R: W. H. Harris; Luke Short; Bat Masterson; W. F. Petillon
Bottom row, L-R: **Wyatt Earp**; M. F. McLean; Neal Brown

Our most notable case, the one this chapter focuses upon in depth, was the shooting of an actress in Dodge City, Kansas. It involved such famous names as Wyatt Earp and Bat Masterson in the year of 1878. [376] Sometime during the summer 1878, the proprietor of the Alhambra Saloon and Gambling House, Mayor James H. "Dog" Kelley expelled a

---

[376] Dodge City--Queen of Cowtowns: The Wickedest Little City In America 1872-1886 by Stanley Vestal, p. 138; Bantam Books, 1952

drunken cowboy from his saloon. [377] That Texas cowpuncher was James W. "Spike" Kennedy--a fellow Irishman and son of Capt. M. Kennedy, the wealthy "famous South Texas cattleman of the firm, Kennedy and King."

A year earlier, Charlie Siringo reported James had "brought in a herd of steers and turned them loose above Tascosa, Texas." [378] Likewise, in the summer of 1878, driving the herd belonging to Kennedy and King, James was among the thirty-seven other Texas herds brought in to Dodge City and delivering approximately 15,000 head of cattle. One other company, Littlefield and Houston, also brought in 15,000 and, the biggest, Snyder and Company, topped them by delivering 25,000 head of cattle. [379] So James was familiar with the manners of the trail drives and cowtowns such as Newton, Wichita and Dodge. Likewise, his attitude promoted involvement in several troublesome episodes, caring less who might be hurt. The only positive thing said was that James knew how to carry a grudge and acted impulsively upon those grudges. Two of these grudge skirmishes were reported in the docket of police records for Dodge City alone. On July 29, 1878, James was arrested by Wyatt Earp for "carrying a pistol." James plead guilty and, as the irresponsible rich kid always does, donned a smirk and paid his fine. Nineteen days later, August 17, Marshal Charles "Senator" Bassett arrested James Kennedy on the charge of "disorderly conduct." Once more his vast amount of money rescued him from a long term in jail. One of these instances may have involved Mayor Kelley. [380]

Several days later, James Kennedy left Dodge by train and went to Kansas City, Missouri. The moneyed son of an opulent rancher bought the fastest horse in the city and headed back across the prairies of Kansas to the cowtown of Dodge. Meanwhile, back in Dodge, Mayor Kelley, known to sleep in a small two-room house behind the Comique Theater, the Green Front Saloon and the Western Hotel, located east of Bridge Street and south of the railroad tracks, had recently fallen ill and been taken to the hospital at Fort Dodge. Because of Kelley's illness, he had rented his house to two actresses appearing in town. These two actresses were Fannie Garrettson and Dora Hand. [381]

---

[377]   Vestal, p. 139-140

[378]   Maverick Town: The Story of Old Tascosa by John L. McCarty, p. 46; Univ. of Okla., 1988

[379]   Vestel, p. 113

[380]   Ronald D. Miller, in his book Shady Ladies of the West (Westernlore Press, 1985), p. 137, states that "in the summer of 1878, Mayor James H. Kelley and James Kennedy got into a fight over Dora. The cowboy was run out of town before further trouble developed."

[381]   Vestal, p. 140

The *Ford County Globe* is the first place we see Dora's name mentioned in the Dodge City press.

> ## COMIQUE
>
> This favorite place of resort is at present giving to its patrons the best show or entertainment ever given in Dodge. They have Billy and Nola Forrest, Dick Brown and Fannie Garrettson, May Gaylor, Belle Lamont, Fannie Keenan, Jennie Morton, and that unequaled and splendidly matched team [Eddie] Foye and [Jimmie] Thompson. All the members of this troupe are up in their parts and considerable above the average in ability. [382]

Each night, at closing time, Fannie and Dora meandered to this small cottage belonging to Mayor Kelley and slept the remaining night and early morning hours away before returning later that following afternoon. One of them, however, was to go to sleep and never again wake up. During the late night hours of October 3 or early October 4, Dora and Fannie, tired as a Kansas cyclone after a full day on the open prairie, ambled back to the cottage and went to bed as usual. Both longingly sought to snuggle into their warm beds where the oncoming chill of the autumn night may not reach them.

Having arrived back in Dodge this identical night, James Kennedy was one of the "few persons up at this unseasonable hour, though all night walkers and loungers [were] not uncommon in Dodge." Kennedy and another cowhand were "gyrating in the dim shadows of the flickering light of the solitary opened saloon." [383] At approximately 4:30 a.m., Kennedy rode up in front of the small house wherein the two unsuspecting women reclined upon their appropriate beds nurtured by the sanctity of dreamland. He withdrew the metallic weapon from the leather holster strapped to his waist. His sinewy finger wrapped itself about the cold trigger, squeezing death from its bowels. The iron instrument recoiled with every triggered assault as death and hell belched out. He fired four shots aboard his nervous horse. The animal wanted to escape the explosive sound as the fiery missiles rushed forward from out of the barrel and made a spattering sound

---

[382]   Ford County Globe, July 30, 1878
[383]   Dodge City Times, October 12, 1878

228

when it hit the wall of the building. In the front room, awakened by the sudden noise, Fannie Garrettson [384] heard the shots and leapt from under her covers to see what was the matter. Someone, she realized, was shooting into the house. Someone! But who?

From the rear bedroom, Dora Hand never heard any shots. Nor did she get up. She was dead! The beautiful woman known to history as Dora Hand, alias Fannie Keenan, was said "to have been raised in a genteel Boston home. She studied voice abroad and had made a successful career in opera." [385] The local newspapers on August 10 of that year read: "Hattie Smith and Fannie Keenan take a benefit at Ham Bell's Varieties next Wednesday night [August 14]. They are general favorites and will be sure to draw a crowded house." [386] The next time her name appeared, she was dead.

Dora was "as handsome, generous, and talented as she was versatile...a kindly, resourceful, and energetic person, always ready to help anyone in trouble." She could be counted on when a person needed assistance and she required "no security or even the names of the men she helped." She bounced from late night dance hall girl to day time concerned civic citizen. For surprisingly, on Sundays, Dora dressed herself in simple black and strolled across "the deadline to the little church on the North Side to lead the hymns and anthems in a voice at which those who heard her forever marveled. [387] The only thing anyone could hold against her was her after-dark profession, and by Godfrey, I allow she elevated that considerably," one of Dodge's senior citizens once remarked. [388]

She was referred to as the "Queen of the Fairy Belles--the most popular of the dance hall women." [389] Rumors spread about how this grand vocalist was once "a singer in grand opera...[as]...she charmed her listeners singing sentimental ballads in Dodge City theaters." It was a fact Dora arrived in Dodge City earlier that summer from St. Louis, Missouri where she had been employed at Esher's Varieties, located on Fifth Street. Just prior to leaving St. Louis, Dora played to an audience at the Tivoli varieties. She had gone to Dodge City "for the purpose of making arrangements for her approaching

---

[384]   Vestal spells the name "Garretson" but N. H. Miller and J. W. Snell have used the spelling most accepted--"Garrettson." Great Gunfighters of the Kansas Cowtowns 1867-1886 by Nyle H. Miller and Joseph W. Snell, p. 232; Univ. of Nebraska, 1963

[385]   R. D. Miller, p. 137

[386]   Dodge City Times, August 10, 1878

[387]   R. D. Miller, p. 136

[388]   Wyatt Earp: Frontier Marshal by Stuart N. Lake, p. 217; Houghton Mifflin, 1931

[389]   Vestal, p. 139

marriage." [390] It was her second marriage, at least. An earlier husband, Theodore Hand, a musician, Dora had divorced in Indiana. Prior to her two year stint in St. Louis, Dora had been in Memphis, Tennessee, and "appeared in every variety theater in the south" before that time. Her ever widening audience made her "universally popular among her associates." She was so loved and liked by her public one acquaintance remarked Dora "had not an enemy in the world." [391]

After the shots were fired and the gun smoke cleared from the air, James Kennedy "and his companion were seen in the opened saloon. The arrival of the officers and the movements of the two morning loungers threw suspicions in their direction. Kennedy mounted his horse [and] was soon galloping down the road in the direction of the Fort [Dodge]." The other person, name withheld, knew "something of the firing though he had no connection with it. He was arrested and placed in jail." [392] Assistant Marshal Wyatt Earp and lawman Jim Masterson, Bat's brother, questioned the prisoner and learned it was Kennedy who fired the four fatal shots that "awakened the echoes in that dull misty morning and aroused the police force and others." A coroner's inquest was held and issued the following report:

The State of Kansas, Ford County, S. S.

An inquisition holden at Dodge City in said county on the fourth day of October A. D. 1878 before me a Justice of the Peace for Dodge township, said county, acting as coroner on the body of Fannie Keenan, there lying dead, by the jurors whose names are hereunto subscribed. Said jurors on their oath do say that Fannie Keenan came to her death by gunshot wound and that in their opinion the said gunshot wound was produced by a bullet discharged from a gun in the hands of one James Kennedy, in testimony whereof the said jurors hereunto set their hands, the day and year aforesaid.

It was signed by P. L. Beatty--foreman. The other names upon the coroner's verdict were John B. Means, J. H. Cornell, W. Straiter, Thomas McIntire, John Lougheed and R. G. Cook--the same who would later try and acquit James Kennedy for the death of Dora

---

390   St. Louis Daily Journal, Oct. 11, 1878
391   St. Louis Daily Journal, Oct. 11, 1878
392   Dodge City Times, October 12, 1878

Hand. [393] Mayor Kelley told Wyatt Earp to bring Kennedy back alive. "Dodge'll want to deal with him as a community." [394]

Friday afternoon, nearly ten hours later, the posse pursued James Kennedy, journeyed down the river road, stopping at one of the ranches below the fort--traveling nearly 75 miles. Making camp that night, October 4, a heavy rain storm moved into the area and slowed them down considerably. They turned and headed toward Meade City, Kansas and stopped off at a ranch there--a full hour ahead of the murdering Kennedy also delayed by the storm. Kennedy had gone a circular route, fording the Cimarron near Wagon Bed Springs and turning south, headed back to his father's ranch at Tascosa, Texas. The posse, however, took the "direct route of the Jones and Plummer Trail...taking the short cut." At about 4 p.m., a lone rider neared the ranch where the posse hid. He approached cautiously, having already made inquiries along his route about any posse. He stopped his horse a few hundred yards away from the main building and scrutinized the area as an uncertain wolf does.

Posse members jumped from concealment and demanded he throw up his hands. Kennedy struck his horse with a quirt. The silent Kansas prairies were shattered with the firing of several shots by the posse. A metal missile hit Kennedy in the left shoulder and his clothing was quick to absorb the blood. The woman killer was badly wounded but he would live. That was more than could be said for Dora Hand or the horse Kennedy rode for three bullets struck the animal during the shooting scrape, killing it instantly. Falling, it pinned Kennedy to the ground. Bat and the others pulled him from under the dead animal. Kennedy quizzed Masterson why they had ambushed him. Masterson informed Kennedy of the killing of actress Dora Hand. Realizing he'd made a terrible mistake, Kennedy feared the citizens of Dodge might lynch him and he "cursed [Bat Masterson] for not making a better shot."

Fannie Garrettson, Dora's roommate that fateful night, wrote a letter to J. E. Esher on October 5, 1878. Esher, their former employer was a good friend as seen in the familiarity expressed throughout the letter--best explaining how Fannie felt about the death of another actress in the Old West. It offers a tremendous amount of insight into the life of these two women--the loss, the hardship, the injustice and the fears.

---

[393]   Vestal, p. 143

[394]   Vestal, p. 143. Vestal is quoting Earp biographer Stuart N. Lake. Today, many historians do not feel Lake's book to be completely accurate.

Messrs. Eshers:

No doubt ere this you have heard of the very sad and fatal end [of Fannie Keenan, one of the most] fiendish assassinations on record. Although the bullet was not intended for poor Fannie, yet she was the innocent victim, and so it is invariably. Any one gets it but the one for whom it is intended, and particularly in this wretched city. This is now the third or fourth instance and still nothing is done. But the man who perpetrated this deed will never exist for a judge or a jury, as the officers have sworn never to take him alive. They were offered a big reward to get him but they declined to accept it, for they were only too well pleased to get the order to start after him. He is either a half breed or half Mexican; but let him be what he may I know him to be a fiend in human form or some one else who will go at such an hour, and attempt to take the life [of] any individual, and knowing at the same time there were other occupants in the same house and occupying the same bed. It shows what a fiend he must be and that he regarded no one's life. The party he was after is the mayor of Dodge City I have written to you about. My room was the front one and Fannie occupied the one back of me. Both our beds stood in the same positions, mine being a higher bedstand than hers. They were four shots fired, two in the air and two penetrating through the door leading into my room. One was fired very low, hitting the floor and cutting two places in the carpet. It then glanced up striking the inside side piece of the bedstead, the one I occupied. It penetrated through these and through the plastering and lath and part of the bullet was found on the floor. They said it was a forty-five caliber. The one that did the horrible work was fired directly lining for my bed and had the one whom they were after been there, the probability is there would have been three or four assassinated. Certain there would have been two, probably Fannie and myself. But I was alone. The mayor has been very sick for two or three weeks, and last Monday he was obliged to go to the hospital to the post where he could be under the best of treatment.

"There is no very good doctor in town and consequently people who have any means go to the post, as the doctor there [W. S. Tremaine] is considered the best. But these parties who were in search of the mayor were not aware of that, as they had been away from town, and only came in that evening. Of course he did not dare to make any inquiries, as they all knew he held a grudge towards the mayor. But you can rest assured his aim was a good one. The death-dealing messenger penetrated through the bed clothes that covered me, and so close to me that it went through the spread, then the heavy comforter that covered me, and the sheet that was next to me, cutting a hole through all, and again passing through the clothes the same way only nearer to the wall, and then penetrating through the wall and passed between Fannie's fifth and sixth ribs. I suppose tearing her heart into atoms."

"Poor Fannie she never realized what was the matter with her. She never spoke but died unconscious. She was so when she was struck and so she died. [395] *She closed her eyes as though she was going to sleep. The only indication of any pain were the moving of the head once or twice on the pillow, a few gasps and her sufferings were over in this world. Peace to her soul. I think she died happy, as her look was such; but what a horrible death! To go to one's bed well and hearty and not dream of anything and be cut down in such a manner, without a chance to breathe a word. She was killed between the hours of 4 and 5 and was*

---

[395] The bullet struck Dora in the right side under the arm, killing her instantly. Vestal, p. 143

*buried yesterday between the same hours, everything being
done that could be, and every respect and honor shown her
to the last, the leading gentlemen of the city officiating at
her funeral and following to her lonely grave. They have
gone in search of the fellows who committed the deed and
yesterday evening were within five or six miles of them, but
I am afraid the trouble has not ended, as some twenty of the
Texas men went out after the officers and there were only
six of them. This man has been allowed more privileges
than the rest of them because he has plenty of money, and
now he has repaid their liberality. Well, I want to leave
here now, while my life is safe; I think I have had enough of
Dodge City."* [396]

She signed it "Fannie Garrettson." [397]

The posse brought the rich kid back to Dodge on Sunday, October 6, 1878. He was thrown into the calaboose and three doctors attended his wound. They were Dr. T. L. McCarty, W. S. Tremaine and E. B. Fryer of Kansas City. [398]   The physicians reported him being "in a low and critical condition." [399] James' wealthy father, Capt. Kennedy, was sent for before the murderer could stand trial. While the no account murdering son of a rich Texas rancher recuperated in his jail cell, Fannie's dear friend, lovely Dora Hand, was buried north of town in the Prairie Grove Cemetery. [400] The funeral given by the citizens of Dodge was "the biggest and finest in Dodge's history." Dance hall girls, gunslingers, gamblers, saloon-keepers, cattlemen, and even an entourage of "the town's most respectable ladies" attended as the minister spoke on the words of Jesus: "He that is without sin among you, let him first cast a stone at her." [401]

---

[396]   A person can't help but wonder what Fannie meant by such lines as "this is now the third or fourth instance and still nothing is done" and the fact that there may "have been three or four assassinated." Nor can it be dismissed that she continued to refer to more than one assassin.

[397]   St. Louis Daily Journal, Oct. 11, 1878

[398]   Vestal, p. 144

[399]   Dodge City Times, October 12, 1878

[400]   Vestal, p. 145

[401]   R. D. Miller, p. 139

The *Dodge City Times* carried a detailed report of the posse's pursuit and capture of James Kennedy. The posse consisted of "Sheriff Bat Masterson, Marshal Charles E. Bassett, Assistant Marshal Wyatt Earp, Deputy Sheriff William Duffy and William Tilghman--as intrepid a posse as ever pulled a trigger." [402] During the week of October 20, 1878, James Kennedy was brought before Judge R. G. Cook in an unannounced, unpublicized trial held within the *'secrecy'* of the sheriff's office, which was too small to admit spectators. "James Kennedy, charged with the murder of Fannie Keenan," reported the *Times* on October 26, 1878, "had a preliminary examination Tuesday before Justice Cook. The evidence being insufficient the prisoner was acquitted." [403] "We do not know what the evidence was," reported the editor of the *Ford County Globe*, "or upon what grounds he was acquitted. But he is free to go on his way rejoicing whenever he gets ready." [404] "The grounds were unusual in terms of jurisprudence but made some sense in terms of Western practicality," wrote John M. Myers on the killing of Dora Hand. "Miss Hand had not been shot on purpose, so it was ridiculous to talk about assaulting with intent to kill." [405]

Nevertheless, a woman was dead and all the legal jargon in the world would not bring her back to life. Vestal states "Kennedy was acquitted on the ground that the evidence was not sufficient to convict." [406] The fact men got away with murdering women in the Old West was not uncommon as seen in other cases like Severo Gomez, Charles "Scotty" McNeal and Tomas Licon. [407] He was most assuredly guilty of murder through deliberate negligence and carelessness. "Whereupon everyone went about clucking their tongues and reminding each other that young *Kennedy's father was one of the richest men* in Texas," states Jahns in his assessment. [408] The irresponsible son of a wealthy Texas rancher named Kennedy had successfully killed a woman in the Old West without reprisal from a law that would do nothing!

---

[402]   Dodge City Times, October 12, 1878

[403]   The Frontier World of Doc Holliday by Pat Jahns, p. 120-121; Indian Head Books, 1957

[404]   Ford County Globe, October 29, 1878

[405]   Doc Holliday by John Myers Myers, p. 90-91; Univ. of Nebraska, 1955

[406]   Vestal, p. 144

[407]   Riders Along the Rio Grande: A Collection of Outlaws, Prostitutes & Vigilantes by Bob L'Aloge, p. 155-168; RCS Press, 1992

[408]   Jahns, p. 121; italics added for emphasis

Let us again affirm, as was done in the beginning of this historiography, the women of the Old West were more than "the angel of man's home, the wife of his heart, the mother of his children, the sharer of his joys, and the soother of his sorrows." [409] They *were* the Old West and they are the New West. Absorbing both the intellect and creative emotion of pioneer life itself. But the women, whether White, Black, Yellow or Red skinned, are still the brunt of men's vulgar, chauvinistic frauds since those thrilling days of yesteryear. They are still lied to, cheated, deceived and degraded. They are still used and abused. They are still seduced by words of charm and raped by passions of anger and hatred. They continue to be attacked, murdered and undergo abasement on every level.

Doesn't history ever change?

---

[409] Ordeal of the Union: Fruits of Manifest Destiny 1847-1852 by Allan Nevins, p. 136; Charles Schribners Son's, 1947

Appendix

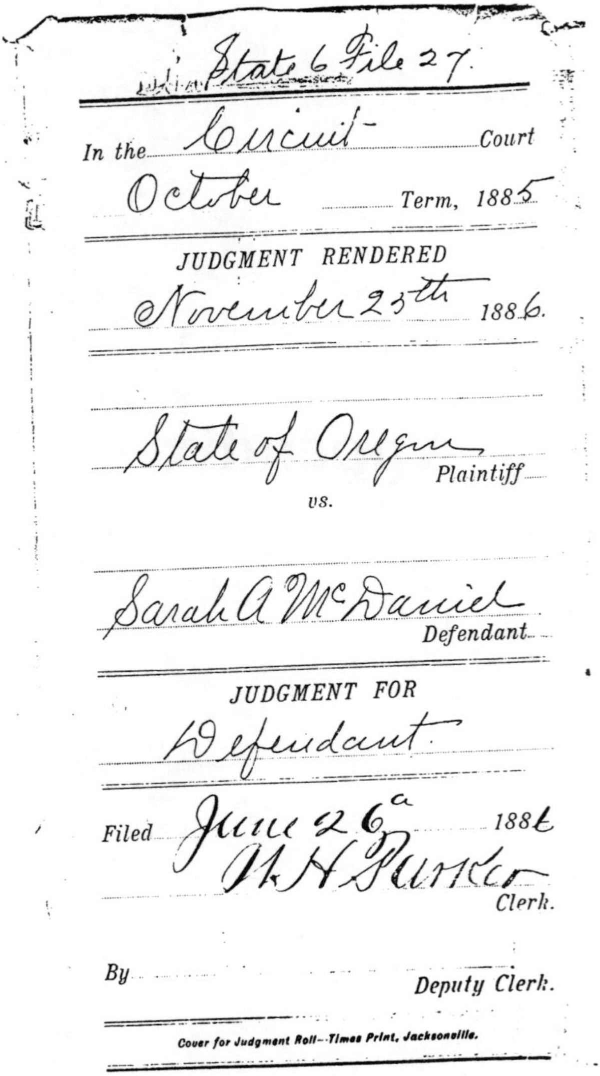

In the _Circuit_ Court

October Term, 188_5_

JUDGMENT RENDERED

November 25th 188_6_.

State of Oregon
Plaintiff

_vs._

Sarah A. McDaniel
Defendant

JUDGMENT FOR

Defendant.

Filed _June 26a_ 188_6_

M. H. Parker
Clerk.

By _____ Deputy Clerk.

Cover for Judgment Roll—Times Print, Jacksonville.

This document, dated November 25, 1886, reveals the judgment to be
rendered was in favor of Sarah Amanda McDaniel.

Dated October 20, 1885, this is the indictment of Amanda McDaniel,
"accused by the Grand Jury...of the crime of murder."
It is signed T. B. Kent--District Attorney.

Record of Thursday November 19th AD 1885 Hon L R Webster Judge presiding present the same officers of the Court as heretofore. When among other the following proceedings were had to wit;

State of Oregon Plaintiff

—vs—

Sarah A. McDaniel Defendant

Indictment for murder in the first degree

Now comes the State in the above entitled cause and by H K Hanna Associate Counsel with Dist Atty and the Deft comes in her own proper person and by J R Neil J T Bowditch and C W Kahler her attorneys and come the Jury heretofore empanneled to try this cause and the said Jury having sat and heard a portion of the evidence on the part of the State said cause is adjourned until the coming in of the Court tomorrow morning and said Jurors under the charge of the Court are given in the charge of the Bailiffs to be kept together in the mean time

(Record Signed) L R Webster
Judge

Dated Thursday, November 19, 1885, "the following proceedings were had to" record the highlights of the Sarah A. McDaniel's hearing that date. It is signed by Judge L. R. Webster.

> In the Circuit Court for
> Jackson County Oregon at the
> October term 1885 Thereof
> The State of Oregon
>   against
> Amanda McDaniel
>   Indictment for murder
> in the first degree
> ———— Verdict of the jury ————
> WE, the jury in the above entitled
> action, find the defendant
> Amanda Mc Daniel not guilty
> as charged in the indictment.
>
>   Geo S D Walton Foreman

This document, signed by Geo. S. Walton--Foreman, is the verdict of the jury in the case against Amanda McDaniel for the murder of her husband.

In the Circuit Court of Oregon for Jackson County

State of Oregon
vs
Lewis O'Neal

Indictment for murder in the first degree

I. L. R. Webster Judge before whom the above named defendant was tried and convicted of murder in the first degree on March 12th 1885 and who was by me sentenced to be hanged on May 21st 1885, do hereby certify that in my opinion there is probable cause for the appeal of said action to the Supreme Court of Oregon; Witness my hand at Chambers this May 15th 1885

L. R. Webster,
Judge.

This document, signed by Judge L. R. Webster and dated May 15, 1885, states "that in my opinion there is probable cause for the appeal of said action [against Lewis O'Neal] to the Supreme Court of Oregon."

This document, signed by Judge L. R. Webster and dated February 23, 1886, is the *Death Warrant* for "the death penalty, by hanging...the said Lewis O'Neal by the neck until he be dead." It was read to O'Neal within a few minutes of his hanging.

Bibliography...

Archives:

Arizona Historical Society, Tucson, AZ
Colorado State Archives, Denver, CO
Kansas State Historical Society, Topeka, KS
New Mexico State University, Las Cruces, NM
Territorial Archives of New Mexico, Santa Fe, NM
University of Montana, Missoula, MT

Articles:

_____ ; Gender-Bending in the Wild West; *Parade Magazine*, August 22, 1993

Agonito: Rosemary & Joseph; She Fought to Save Cheyenne Way of Life; *True West*, November 1983

Ault: Phillip H.; Nancy Kelsey; *True West*, December 1989

Boyer: Glenn G.; Wyatt Earp: Legendary American--Part 4: Family Amnesia; *True West*, November 1993

Coleman: Jane; Gamblin' Man; *Alaska Magazine*, May 1990

Corless: Hank; The Saga of Peg-Leg Annie; *Old West*, Winter 1990

Dunlap: Patricia Riley; Abigail Scott Duniway: Pioneer Woman; *Old West*, Winter 1991

Everett: Donald; Too Many Husbands; *Frontier Times*, Jan. 1971

Farley: Alan W.; An Indian Captivity & Its Legal Aftermath; *Kansas Historical Quarterly*, Winter 1954

Hardy: Harvey; A Long Ride With Matt Warner; *Frontier Times*, November 1964

Holden: Jan; Lillie No. 5: San Francisco's First Firewoman; *Old West*, Spring, 1991; Dr. Louisa Wright: Medicine Comes to Clark County; *Old West*, Spring, 1994

Mabry: Charles; Silver King; *Frontier Times*; Spring, 1962

Mayeux: Lucie; Saints & Sinners Alike Touched by Sister Blandina; *New Mexico Magazine*, October 1992

McArthur: Scott; The Polk County Slave Case; *Historically Speaking Vol. 2*; August 1970; Polk Co. Historical Society

McBryde: Carolyn Bullion; The Thorny Rose; *True West*, Apr. 1992

McDearmon: Kay; Silver Queen; *Frontier Times*; Spring, 1962

Meier: Gary; Bizarre Case of the Church Street Murder; *Old West*, Summer 1991

Meketa: Jacqueline Dorgan; Sadie's Mountain Pride; *Old West*, Spring, 1993

Meyer: Marian; New First Lady of the Santa Fe Trail; *True West*, Aug. 1992

Moynihan: Betty; Pioneer Pathways; *True West*, January 1993

Oregon Historical Quarterly 17, June 1916, Knight Library Special Collections, Univ. of Oregon

Oregon Historical Society Quarterly 23, June 1922, Knight Library Special Collections, Univ. of Oregon

Pharo: Agnes M.; Silver Princess; *Frontier Times*, Spring, 1962

Pratt: Grace Roffey; Female War Chief of the Blackfeet; *Frontier Times*, Jan. 1971

Rube: B. Johnny; A Yuma Tragedy; *True West*, Oct. 1982

Schoenberger: Dale T.; The Tall Texan; *True West*, Apr. 1992

Traywick: Ben T.; Martyr by Intent; *Old West*, Fall 1993

Underwood: Larry D.; Kitty Leroy: The Cause of the Tragedy--Jealousy; *Old West*, Summer 1989; Real Woman: The Fanny Kelly Story; *Old West*, Summer 1987

Zachry: Juanita Daniel; They Called It Content; *Frontier Times*, March 1971

Books:

A Dictionary of the Old West by Peter Watts, Promontory Press, 1977

Adventures on the Columbia River by Ross Cox, London, 1831

An Editor on the Comstock Lode by Wells Drury, Univ. of Nevada, 1984

Arizona's Dark and Bloody Ground by Earle R. Forrest, Univ. of Arizona, 1950

Augusta Tabor: Her Side of the Scandal by Caroline Bancroft, Bancroft Books, 1983

Aunt Clara Brown by Kathleen Bruyn; Pruettt Publishing Co., Boulder, CO, 1970

Bandit to Lawman by Roscoe Sheller; Franklin Press Inc., 1966

Ben Snipes and the Great Roslyn Bank Robbery of 1892 by Bob L'Aloge; BJS Brand Books, 1993

Best of the Old Northwest by Marge Davenport, Paddlewheel Press, 1980

Blackfoot Lodge Tales: The Story of a Prairie People by George Bird Grinnell; Univ. of Nebraska, 1962

Calamity Jane and the Lady Wildcats by Duncan Aikman; Ballantine Books, 1927

Captured By Indians by Howard H. Peckham, 1954

Cheyenne Memories by John Stands In Timber and Margot Liberty, Univ. of Nebraska, 1967

Conquest of the Southern Plains by Charles J. Brill, Oklahoma City, 1938

Cowboy Culture: A Saga of Five Centuries by David Dary, Avon Books, 1981

Daughters of Joy, Sisters of Misery: Prostitutes in the American West 1865-1890 by Anne M. Butler, Univ. of Illinois, 1985

Death Song: The Last of the Indian Wars by John Edward Weems, Indian Head Books, 1976

Doc Holliday by John Myers Myers, Univ. of Nebraska, 1955

Dodge City--Queen of Cowtowns: The Wickedest Little City In America 1872-1886 by Stanley Vestal, Bantam Books, 1952

Down the Santa Fe Trail and Into Mexico: The Diary of Susan Shelby Magoffin, 1846-1847 edited by Stella M. Drumm, University of Nebraska, 1962

Emancipation & Henderson: The Man Behind the Reality by Bob L'Aloge, Freedom Press, 1990

Fighting Cheyenne by John Grinnell, Univ. of Okla., 1956

Following the Guidon by Elizabeth B. Custer, New York, 1890

Frontier Regulars: The United States Army and the Indian 1866-1891 by Robert M. Utley, Indiana Univ. Press, 1973

Frontier Women: The Trans-Mississippi West 1840-1880 by Julie Roy Jeffrey; Hill & Wang, 1979

General History of Oregon by Charles H. Carey, Binfords and Mort, 1971

Ghost Towns of Wyoming by Mary Lou Pence & Lola M. Homsher, 1956

Great Gunfighters of the Kansas Cowtowns 1867-1886 by Nyle H. Miller and Joseph W. Snell, Univ. of Nebraska, 1963

Gunsmoke: The True Story of Old Tombstone by Grace McCool, Gateway Publishing Co., 1954

How To Tan Skins the Indian Way by Evard H. Giddy, Eagle's View Publishing, 1991

I Fought With Custer: The Story of Sergeant Windolph, Last Survivor of the Battle of the Little Bighorn as told to Frazier & Robert Hunt, Univ. of Nebraska, 1947

Jacksonville: Biography of a Gold Camp by Francis D. Haines Jr, Gandee Printing Center, Inc., 1967

Ka-Mi-Akin: The Last Hero of the Yakimas by A. J. Splawn, Caxton Printers, 1980

Land of Giants: The Drive to the Pacific Northwest 1750-1950 by David Lavender; Doubleday & Co., 1958

Maverick Town: The Story of Old Tascosa by John L. McCarty, Univ. of Okla., 1988

Narrative of My Captivity Among the Sioux Indians by Fanny Kelly, Gassette & Loyd, 1880

Notable American Women 1607-1950 Vol. 2 by Howard H. Peckham, 1971

Notorious Ladies of the Frontier by Harry Sinclair Drago, Dodd, Mead & Company, 1969

Ordeal of the Union: A House Dividing 1852-1857 by Allan Nevins, Charles Scribners' Sons, 1947.

Old Deadwood Days by Estelline Bennett, Univ. of Nebraska, 1982.

On the Border With Mackenzie by Robert G. Carter, Antiquarian Press Ltd., 1935

Path Breaking: An Autobiographical History of the Equal Suffrage Movement in Pacific Coast States by Abigail Scott Duniway, Schocken Books, 1971

Pioneer Women: Voices from the Kansas Frontier by Joanna Stratton; Simon & Schuster, 1981

Riders Along the Rio Grande: A Collection of Outlaws, Prostitutes & Vigilantes by Bob L'Aloge, RCS Press, 1992

Shady Ladies of the West by Ronald Dean Miller; Westernlore Press, 1985

She Watched Custer's Last Battle by Thomas Marquis, Hardin, 1933

Silver Hillside: The Life & Times of Virginia City by Barbara Richnak, Comstock-Nevada Publishing Co., 1984

Silver Queen: The Fabulous Story of Baby Doe Tabor by Caroline Bancroft, Johnson Publishing Company, 1983

Sitting Bull: Champion of the Sioux by Stanley Vestal, 1932

Six Months in Kansas by A Lady, H. A. R.; 1856

Tales of Nevada Vol. 1 by Norm Nielson, Tales of Nevada Publications, 1989

Tales of the Colorado Pioneers by Alice Polk Hill

The Adventures of the Negro Cowboys by Phillip Durham and Everett L. Jones, Bantam Books, 1965

The Battle of the Little Bighorn by Mari Sandoz; Univ. of Nebraska, 1966

The California Trail by George R. Stewart; McGraw-Hill, 1962

The Called Him Wild Bill: The Life & Adventures of James Butler Hickok by Joseph G. Rosa, Univ. of OK Press, 1974

The Colonel's Lady on the Western Frontier: The Correspondence of Alice Kirk Grierson edited by Shirley A. Leckie, Univ. of Nebraska, 1989

The Columbia by Stewart H. Holbrook, Rinehart & Co., 1956

The Earp Brothers of Tombstone: The Story of Mrs. Virgil Earp by Frank Waters, Bramhall House, 1960

The Earps' Last Frontier: Wyatt & Virgil Earp in the Nevada Mining Camps--1902-1905 by Jeffrey M. Kintop & Guy Louis Rocha, Great Basin Press, 1989

The Frontier World of Doc Holliday by Pat Jahns, Indian Head Books, 1957

The Gentle Tamers:Women of the Old Wild West by Dee Brown, Univ. of Nebraska, 1958

The Gold Rush: The Search for Treasure In the American West by George F. Willison, Indian Head Books, 1992

The Grizzly Bear by Minnie Beatrice Heath; Native Sons of California, 1937

The Maiden Waved A Snowy Scarf: The Story of Springfield, Missouri During the Civil War by Bob L'Aloge, BJS Brand Books, 1993

The Spectacular San Franciscans by Julia Cooley Altrocchi, Dutton & Co., 1949

The Story of Cole Younger by Himself, Triton Press, 1988

The Women's West edited by Susan Armitage and Elizabeth Jameson; "Beyond Baby Doe: Child Rearing on the Mining Frontier" by Elliott West, Univ. of Okla. 1987

The Women Who Made the West by The Western Writers of America, Doubleday & Co., 1980

They Called Him Wild Bill: The Life and Adventures of James Butler Hickok by Joseph G. Rosa, Univ. of Okla. 1974

Tombstone: An Iliad of the Southwest by Walter Noble Burns; Penguin Books, 1927

Tombstone's Epitaph: The Truth About the Town Too Tough to Die by Douglas D. Martin; Univ. of New Mexico, 1951

Two Thousand Miles On Horseback by James F. Meline, New York, 1867

Westward the Women by Nancy Wilson Ross, Alfred A. Knopf, 1944

Wildest of the Wild West by Harold Bryan, Clear Light Publishers, 1988

Women and Indians on the Frontier 1825-1915 by Glenda Riley, Univ. of New Mexico, 1984

Women In the Pacific Northwest: An Anthology edited by Karen J. Blair; "Black Women In the Pacific Northwest" by Susan H. Armitage & Deborah Gallacci Wilbert, Univ. of Washington, 1988

Women In the Pacific Northwest: An Anthology edited by Karen J. Blair; "Of Women's Rights and Freedom: Abigail Scott Duniway" by Ruth Barnes Moynihan, Univ. of Washington, 1988

Women of the Sierra by Anne Seagraves, Wesanne Publications, 1990

Women's Diaries of the Westward Journey by Lillian Schlissel; Schocken Books, 1982

Wyatt Earp: Frontier Marshal by Stuart N. Lake, Houghton Mifflin, 1931

Calendars, Journals, Scrapbooks, etc.

At the End of the Santa Fe Trail by Sister Blandina, 1932 (journal)

Detective Sam Howe Murder Scrapbook, Record of the City and County of Denver, 1863-1913; Colorado Historical Society, Denver, Colorado (scrapbook)

Painted Ladies & Bordellos of the Old West 1993; Published by Frontier
  Calendars, Missoula, Montana, 1992 (calendar)

Government Records:

Jacksonville [OR] Cemetery Records
Jackson County [OR] Courthouse

Interviews:

Jeanine Jenkins, Jackson County, Oregon, courthouse (interview July 6-7, 1993)
Norm Nielson, Reno, Nevada, historian/author (interview November 22, 1993)

Newspapers:

Ashland [OR] *Tidings*
Black Hills [SD] *Daily Times*
Dodge City [KS] *Times*
Ford County [KS] *Globe*
Jacksonville [OR] *Democratic Times*
Las Vegas [NM] *Daily Optic*
Portland *Oregon Statesman*
Portland [OR] *New Northwest*
Santa Fe [NM] *Weekly Gazette*
Silver City[NM] *Enterprise*
St. Louis [MO] *Daily Journal*
Tombstone [AZ] *Nugget*
Yakima [WA] *Herald Republic*

Thesis:

On Trial For Murder by Larry Derry, term paper presented to Dr. Frank Haines,
  December 1961
The Negro In Oregon by D. G. Hill, thesis Univ. of Oregon, 1932

Index...

Virginia C. Nelson-L'Aloge M. A.

Ms. Virginia Nelson-L'Aloge, M. A. earned her Master's in Psychology with specialization in Counseling Psychology in 1977. Her twenty years of experience has formerly centered on abuse issues, crisis counseling and assessment and management of psychiatric programs throughout Texas and Nevada hospitals. She was formerly a field instructor for Texas Christian University, University of Texas in Arlington and University of North Texas.

Her career includes the changing roles of women and men, abuse issues, grief recovery along with chronic illness and injury. Her broad media exposure in radio and television was seen nationally for three and one half years on the COPE Show--dealing with physical, mental and abuse issues.

Ms. Nelson-L'Aloge has written for various newspapers back east and in New Mexico. She authored and published the Centennial publication for Charlotte Hall Military School in Maryland and is currently working on her own book titled From the Ashes of Dreams: Growth and Reality.

Ms. Nelson-L'Aloge currently lives in central New Mexico with her husband and son--Bob and Joshua. She has married children, Dorothy and husband Dennis, living in El Paso, Texas; and David and wife Kathy, living in Maryland. She has seven grandchildren. She is also an artist, Mediator and Reiki Master Teacher. She has successfully created and conducted self-help workshops, lectured nationally and presently is the public relations agent and publisher of Flying Eagle-Thunderhawk Enterprises in New Mexico. The company specializes in non-fiction books and other works of literary value. She is currently available for public speaking to various organizations and non-profit groups.

Historical Journalist Bob L'Aloge

Historical Journalist Bob L'Aloge

Bob L'Aloge's writing has been described as *"time capsules taking the reader back to New Mexico's colorful and often violent history"* and *"a breezy and colorful journalistic style."* Book reviewers have favorably compared him to Louis L'Amour and Mark Twain. "It's no wonder the West sticks to Bob L'Aloge like a good cow pony sticks to a maverick steer," recently wrote book reviewer Ollie Reed Jr. of *The Albuquerque* [New Mexico] *Tribune*.

L'Aloge describes himself as "a real Westerner," born and raised in southwestern Missouri--the home of Belle Starr, Jesse James and other Old West legends. He drafts his articles, stories and books with a flair, talent and devotion for Old West detail and accuracy. He has earned his 'real Old West reputation' in many ways from bronc busting (where he once broke seven ribs) to herding cattle to "making his get away out the back door" when confronted by lawmen after refusing to surrender his six-shooter to a security guard at a book signing in Farmington, New Mexico in June 1992.

Of French-Irish descent, L'Aloge is proud of his blue-blooded Confederate heritage and the fact his ancestors fought for Old Glory as well. He gallantly volunteered and served in the United States Marine Corps during the Viet Nam war.

L'Aloge has lectured widely where his travels and research have taken him to 40 of the 50 states. His articles and short stories have appeared in dozens of newspapers and magazines in the United States as well as around the globe. He is adamant about his writings and strongly upholds the Constitutional issues of freedom of the press, speech and no censorship.

He first came to the Southwest, moving to Tucson, in 1980. Eight years later, he and his son moved to Las Cruces, New Mexico. In 1993, they toured the far Northwest for eleven months and then went to Reno, Nevada, where they again toured briefly before returning to New Mexico in 1994.

Presently, his wife and son, Virginia and Joshua, live with him in New Mexico.

Miss Mollie Monroe...

Mollie Monroe was arrested for wearing men's clothes and put in jail on January 7, 1877. Mollie was one of the most fascinating women to enliven the Arizona frontier. She first came to the territory in 1864 as the 18-year-old bride of a young army officer stationed at Ft. Whipple near Prescott. Despite her cultured New England upbringing, Mollie soon left her husband and took up with a rough prospector named George Monroe. She used his last thereafter, although she had numerous other consorts. Over the years, Mollie become a singular figure in the territory--prospecting, fighting Indians, and drinking and gambling in the saloons with the boys. She always dressed in men's clothes (but did not impersonate a man) and was as tough as any male frontiersman. However, in the late 1800's many communities had ordinances prohibiting the wearing of clothes typical of the opposite sex. In many places it was until the early 20th century that laws were amended to allow women to wear pants or overalls in public. Of course, the wearing of women's clothes by men remained against the law until recently, the practice universally being regarded as perverse.

Apparently Mollie was released on bond or some other means for on January 8th, the following day, she visited with George O. Hand, bartender at Foster's Saloon, twice during the day. On the 9th, George and Mollie made several calls about the town of Tucson, Arizona.

George Hand recorded that Mollie was "very crazy today" when he was entering notes in his diary on January 17, 1877. Later in the year of 1877, the 31-year-old Mollie was declared insane and sent to the Langdon and Clark Asylum in Stockton, California. She was the first Arizona woman confined because of insanity. Upon completio of the territorial insane asylum in Phoenix in 1887, she was transfered there. Mollie was never released and died in Phoenix in 1902.